Kolyma Diaries

A Journey into Russia's Haunted Hinterland

JACEK HUGO–BADER

*Translated from the Polish
by Antonia Lloyd-Jones*

Portobello

Published by Portobello Books 2014

Portobello Books
12 Addison Avenue
London W11 4QR

First published in Polish in 2011 as *Dzienniki kołymskie* by Wydawnictwo Czarne, Sękowa, Poland.

This book has been selected to receive financial assistance from English PEN's 'PEN translates!'
programme, supported by Arts Council England. English PEN exists to promote literature and
its understanding, uphold writers' freedoms around the world, campaign against the persecution
and imprisonment of writers for stating their views, and promote the friendly co-operation
of writers and free exchange of ideas. www.englishpen.org

A CIP catalogue record for this book is available
from the British Library

9 8 7 6 5 4 3 2 1

ISBN 978 1 84627 502 9
eISBN 978 1 84627 503 6

www.portobellobooks.com

Typeset by M Rules
Printed in the UK by Page Bros Norwich Ltd

For Anna and Tomek

Contents

PART I: THE SYNDROME OF SILENCE

PART II: BATTLEFIELD SYNDROME

PART III: TRAVELLING-COMPANION SYNDROME

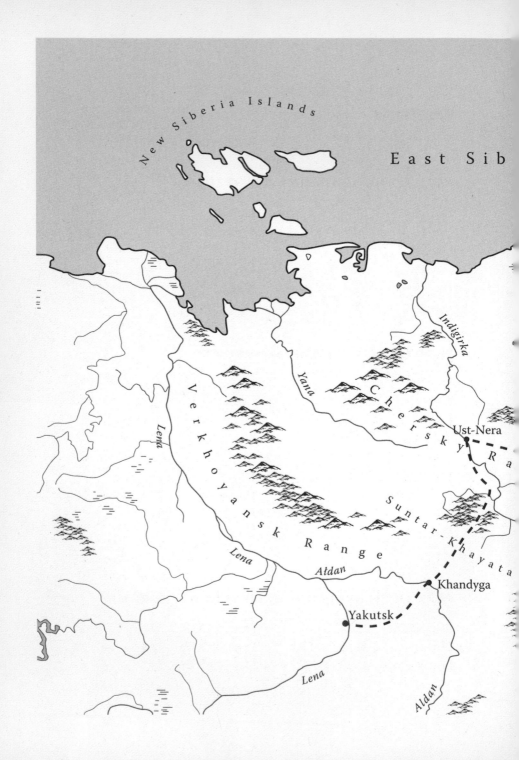

Hawking at great length, she brings up some phlegm. What's she going to do with it? I wonder. Will she spit it into the ashtray, the rubber plant or the waste bin? Or maybe she'll swallow it?

Ediiy Dora stands up and looks around, says something in sign language, so our interpreter (who is there because the spirits only allow Dora to speak in Yakut) obligingly hands her a small piece of paper. The Teacher makes a cone into which she spits green mucus, which hangs from her lip for a long time, like a melting icicle.

This is a good moment to make my excuses concerning the structure and cover of this book — to explain why it is in three parts, and why dark green with gold lettering. It's because Ediiy Dora saw all this in her mind's eye a year ago.

According to her identity card, her name is Fiodora Innokentyevna Kabyakova. An *ediiy* ('older sister') is a shamaness, teacher and healer. It is a highly honourable, almost religious title, bestowed on an individual by the community. When she was only twenty Dora was already called that in Yakutia.

I have only reached the fifth paragraph of this book, but I have already discussed the matter of the green and gold cover with the publishers. They hesitated, saying it would look like the Koran, but they let themselves be persuaded that Ediiy Dora knows best. She knows everything. Even how and when I shall die, what sort of tree grows outside my house, what I think, and when my book will be ready. Exactly twelve months after our meeting, in December 2011. And if the work isn't going well, I am to go outside and feed that tree of

1

mine. Her spirit will be in it. Or even better, I am to go to the *matushka* – little mother – river that flows through my city, and feed it too. Leave a small piece of bread or meat, or some butter and milk, as an offering on the riverbank, and it'll be easy to write.

'But I advise you to write as simply as possible,' says Dora. 'About me too. And not much. Because you don't understand much.'

After an hour, the Teacher's cone is full of green gunk.

'I know you're wondering if I'm ill,' says Dora, reading my mind. 'What I am holding here is the stuff I have gathered from you. Here are all your bad experiences from the journey you have just finished, all the bad memories and people, the impotence, illnesses, vodka, fear and tiredness. I have cleansed you. And all the people who will read your book, and who won't like it. Look how much of it I've collected.'

Finally, some practical advice from me. You don't have to read this book from cover to cover. It's enough to read just the diary entries. But the best things I encountered along the way – the people and the contents of the cone full of snot – are described in the other sections.

PART ONE

The Syndrome of Silence

Hammer and sickle, sickle and hammer
Both feature on our Soviet banner,
So reap or forge, if in the mood,
Whichever way, you will get screwed.

'Were you afraid?' I ask.

'Not in the least. After all, I'm dying.'

I burst out laughing like an idiot, but he's not offended, because lots of people react to stress that way. In my defence I will add that I had just remembered the old Czech joke about Pepik Vondráček who, when there was talk of the communists, would say: 'I'm not afraid – I've got cancer.'

But Ivan Ivanovich is seriously ill with heart disease and the end is near, meaning that he has a few weeks, perhaps months, to live. So say the doctors. He is dying, so he was the only one who wasn't afraid and, like me, he failed to get drunk as our fellow passengers did. I had no idea the seven most terrifying minutes of my life were just ahead of me, or that I would be more scared than on the day the Russians took the town of Shali during the first Chechen war, and I failed to escape with the civilians in time.

How do I know it was only seven minutes? Because as I boarded our tiny boat I switched on my Dictaphone, which measures the length of the recording, and I switched it off when we reached the other side of the river. Now I can hear that everyone else was as silent as the grave as great hunks of ice swept along by the current crashed into the boat with a horrifying clatter, and at full throttle the engine howled as if possessed, while I was laughing my head off.

That's what our journey across Siberia's mighty Aldan river was like in the last few days of October 2010.

But why am I telling this story? Well, because I reckon you have to have cancer or serious heart disease, or be sick in the head, to live here.

You must have nothing to lose, or no alternative, in order to settle at the cruellest extremity on earth. That's what people say and write about Kolyma. They also talk about one of the worst nightmares of the twentieth century, the most terrible and most remote island in the Gulag Archipelago, its glacial extreme, the Russian Golgotha, a snow-white crematorium, an arctic hell, an industrial machine for grinding meat and crushing bones.

And did you know that human flesh tastes just like reindeer meat – subtle, lean and slightly sweet? I don't know how the locals know this. My guess is that it's an opinion that has been handed down from generation to generation. They say half the present inhabitants of Kolyma are the descendants of zeks, in other words former prisoners of the camps – the second or third generation. 'Zek' is short for the word *zaklyuchonny* (written in the Soviet documents as *z/k*), meaning 'locked up', or simply a prisoner. When they escaped from the camps they sometimes took a weaker pal into the taiga with them. This was called 'escaping with a sandwich' or 'with a cow', willingly trotting after somebody who would eventually eat it.

It must be because of the similarity in taste that the local bears are so devilishly dangerous. Reindeer are their favourite delicacy, and to them a human is a reindeer that can't run, a victim without antlers, a creature on its last legs, easy prey. Once one of these cuddly teddies has tried human flesh he gets a taste for it. He won't feel like running about the mountains in pursuit of reindeer and elk any more, he won't pick blueberries or rowanberries, or go in quest of mushrooms or rubbish tips. He'll stick to the Kolyma Highway, the human settlements, or gold prospectors' campsites.

How many stories I've heard about them! There was the one about the miner from a town called Susuman who stopped on the road with a burst tyre, and when he saw a bear he locked himself in the car. The crazed beast ripped open the metal roof and extracted its victim like

Spam out of a can. This sort of bear is known as a *shatun*, which in Russian means a vagrant, but in Kolyma the word is reserved only for insane, man-eating bears.

In the past decade the most talked-about *shatun* was the one that spent many years prowling along the Kolyma Highway in the Verkhoyansk Range. A male the size of an army tank, it was a real monster, a living, breathing machine, known by the steel noose around its neck.

In Kolyma they set snare traps for bears, and some years earlier our creature had fallen into one. A few days later the hunters arrived, a father and his two sons. The bear was hanging by the noose in a pit which it had dug out with its claws as it struggled desperately for its freedom. It was still alive. The hunters sat down and had a smoke. They watched the animal's convulsions, taking pleasure in its torment. Then they lit a bonfire, set a can of water on it to make tea, and ate some dried fish. Finally the older man told one of his sons to hand him a rifle.

From only a few paces away he aimed at the back of the giant bear's neck and fired.

He hit the steel noose, and broke the wire that had trapped the animal. The bear ripped him to shreds, then attacked the lad who had handed his father the rifle. And so it became a *shatun*.

For many years the Verkhoyansk *shatun* hunted people, and people hunted it, even with helicopters.

'I ran into him at Shaman's Brook,' Yura tells me. 'I got out of the cab to get some water from the spring for my tea, but on the way I climbed onto the tank to make sure the lids were properly shut. I was just about to jump down, when I saw him there, waiting for me. He appeared as suddenly and as silently as a ghost. I recognized him at once.'

I'm riding with Yura in his Kamaz tanker lorry from Ust-Nera to Khandyga. This is the toughest and least-frequented stretch of the

Kolyma Highway. As usual, my driver stops for the night at Shaman's Brook at Kilometre 1459 of the Highway in the Verkhoyansk Range.

'In late April,' Yura continues, pouring vodka into our mugs, 'at night the temperature falls to around fifteen degrees below zero, and I was just in my sweater, with no gloves or hat, because I had only got out for a moment to get the water. I moved onto the cab and tried to reach the door handle from the roof, to slip inside from on top, but he was just waiting for that, standing on his hind legs and trying to catch me. He was huge – he could easily reach the edge of the roof. He knew very well that sooner or later I'd have to come down.'

Yura found a lighter in his pocket and set the plastic water bottle ablaze, but the bear wasn't even afraid of fire. It was a devil, not an animal! It had only just awoken from its winter sleep, so it was ferociously hungry. All night it circled the lorry, waiting for the man to freeze to death and fall into its paws. It had plenty of time, because on this stretch of the Highway only a few cars ever appear, and none drive through the night.

For ten hours Yura hopped about the roof of his Kamaz truck, doing squats and press-ups and shadow-boxing, until finally he ran out of strength and fell asleep in the cold. His life was saved by the piercing blare of a horn. He saw a great big KrAZ lorry, whose driver was trying to run over the bear, but the bear dodged the bumper, so Yura's saviour lined up the lorries side by side, allowing him to scramble across the roof into his warm cab. The vehicle had been standing there all night with its engine on.

'But my hands were frostbitten,' he says, passing me the empty bottle. 'They always start to hurt in the cold. If you think I'm going to get the water, you're mistaken.'

'Calm down! Apparently they shot it two years ago. They say it had thirteen people on its conscience.'

★

Every evening of my journey I write up my Kolyma diary, which each day I try to dispatch in an abbreviated version to the website of *Gazeta Wyborcza* (the newspaper for which I work), along with some photographs. So let's do things properly and go back four weeks to the start of my journey, on Saturday 18 September 2010.

Magadan. Mid-September. There is already snow on the hills surrounding the city.

Day I

Magadan on the Sea of Okhotsk

This is the capital of Kolyma, the city which appears in the very first paragraph of Alexander Solzhenitsyn's fundamental work, *The Gulag Archipelago*. But my book isn't going to be about the Gulag, the camps, prisons, starvation, death and torture.

From Magadan I'm going to set off along the Kolyma Route, also known as the Kolyma Highway, and in the Russian motoring atlas, the Kolyma federal road. But the locals usually just call it *Trassa* (meaning 'the Route'). It is the only road in this vast territory, equal in size to one-third of Europe, with only 2025 kilometres of road linking Magadan and the city of Yakutsk in the part of Russia known as Yakutia.

I want to travel this road. The land is completely inaccessible and wild, or rather it has reverted to wilderness (a bit like Poland's Bieszczady region after the Second World War), with fewer and fewer human settlements.

The mountains. They worry me the most, because they're completely white. From the window of the plane in which I'm flying from Moscow, I can see that in the depths of Kolyma, far from the coast, it is full-scale winter. It's coming early this year. I could have major problems at the passes and the rivers, because lots of them have to be forded or crossed by ferry. Once the water starts to freeze, the ice floes pile up, the ferries stop running, and you have to wait until almost December to travel by winter road, across the ice.

The only way to cover this route is by hitchhiking, travelling on solid Russian-made trucks: Kamaz, Ural and KrAZ lorries, known colloquially as *bolotokhody* – 'mudmobiles'. The Belarusian LiAz trucks perform well here too.

The old people say that this road is the world's longest graveyard. I calculated that if all the victims of the Kolyma camps in the Stalin era were laid head to foot, they wouldn't all fit on it. The fact is no one knows how many people died there. If we were to count all the seaborne shipments of prisoners from spring 1932 to summer 1956, we would find that more than two million people were transported to Kolyma.

Through the window of his office on Proletaryatskaya Street, diagonally across the junction with Lenin Prospect, Professor David Semionovich Raizman, head of the humanities faculty at the Magadan Institute of Economics, points out the old NKVD prison which has been changed into a secret-police archive. The prisoners' files are still lying there as before – in the cells, on the zeks' wooden bunk beds. The professor points his finger further north and shows me a large roundabout beyond the Magadanka river, where there's a bus stop marked 31 – the part of town where from 1940 there was a transit camp for three thousand Polish soldiers taken captive by the Soviets a year earlier. From there they were sent off in groups to various destination camps, mainly attached to gold mines all over Kolyma.

How many victims were there? In her book *Gulag* (GULag is short for *Glavnoye Upravlyenie Ispravitelno-Trudovykh Lagerei i Kolonii* – Chief Administration of Corrective Labour Camps and Colonies), for which she won a Pulitzer Prize in 2004, the *Washington Post* journalist Anne Applebaum writes about 28.7 million forced labourers in the Soviet Union, of whom, according to the archive records available today but which in her view are incomplete, 2,749,163 lost their lives. From this it would emerge that the 'mortality coefficient' in the camps was ten per cent.

The so-called capacity of the 160 Kolyma camps was two hundred thousand people (that many could be held in them at any one time). They were people exiled to the Far North, to their destruction. They were supposed to perish there. One in five camp prisoners survived the first winter of 1932–3. Anyone whose sentence came to an end was given another one, and went back to the *zaboy* – meaning the pit-face – back to his gold mine; or became a 'sitter-out', in other words a prisoner who after serving his sentence was not released from the camp until the end of the war, for instance, although there wasn't a single economic reason for him to be there. Any job done by prisoners could be done better by *volniashki* – meaning free people as opposed to prisoners – and at lower cost. It is peculiar that in Russian the word *zaboy* also means 'slaughter' (in the sense of cattle or pigs). Thus the NKVD tried to combine two contradictory aims: to mine as much gold as possible, while exterminating as fast as possible people whom the Bolsheviks regarded as enemies.

In his book *An Army in Exile: The Story of the Second Polish Corps*, the Polish General Władysław Anders wrote that according to his findings, in the years 1940–1 more than ten thousand Polish citizens ended up in Kolyma. Among them were those three thousand prisoners of war mentioned by Professor Raizman of Magadan. When the USSR joined the Allies and freed Polish prisoners from its labour camps, allowing them to join the Polish army which Anders then formed at Buzuluk (near Samara in southern Russia), only 583 were released from the Kolyma camps. That was how many Poles had survived for two years, through the two terrible winters of 1941 and 1942. One of them was Ryszard Kaczorowski, the last president of the Polish Republic in Exile.

In my view, the most reliable indicator of the mortality rate in Kolyma is the single 171-man group of former camp prisoners to have made their way from there to Buzuluk. They were the surviving Polish soldiers from the September 1939 campaign. Almost all of them had had fingers and toes amputated because of frostbite. This has to be the most reliable indicator of mortality – 171 survivors out of three thousand people over two years. That's an annual mortality rate of 88.6 per cent.

But there will be almost nothing about those times in my account. If I do go and see those last few people who are still alive, I'll be doing it because this is the final opportunity to record what they were fated to experience and to endure. They are exceptional people – they have seen the lowest depths of human existence; in the camps they crossed the border beyond which every soul falls apart. But most of all I'll want to hear what happened to them later on, how they managed to live with this experience. What have their lives been like?

I'm going to Kolyma to see how people live in such a place, in such a graveyard – the longest one of all. Is it possible to love here, to laugh, or shout with joy? And how do you weep here, how do you bring up children, earn a living, drink vodka, and die? That's what I want to write about. And about what they eat here, how they pan gold, bake bread, pray, heal, daydream, fight, or beat each other up . . .

On landing at the airport in Magadan I see a large sign saying: WELCOME TO KOLYMA – THE GOLDEN HEART OF RUSSIA.

A wedding party driving around the city makes a stop at the roundabout where there was a camp for three thousand Polish prisoners of war. One hundred and seventy-one of them survived.

SASHA THE MOUNTAINEER – A DOOR
INTO THE FOREST

Sasha Shafranov lives on Komsomolsky Square, with its defunct television tower. This is the starting point for calculating distances along the Kolyma Highway. This is the very centre of Magadan. The first few kilometres of the Route are called Lenin Prospect, the city's grand main street which runs down from the square. Across the small Magadanka river it changes its name to the Kolymskoye Shosse, and beyond the city limits it becomes the Kolymsky Trakt – the Kolyma Highway.

For the past fifteen years Sasha, a local photographer, painter and mountaineer, has been living with his wife, two grown-up daughters and three Scottish terriers at Kilometre Zero of this road. Before that he lived deep inside Kolyma, at Kilometre 626, in Susuman in the Chersky Range.

'There's a big lake there, called Malik, shaped like a boomerang,' Sasha tells me. 'As long as I can remember, Dyedushka [meaning "Grandpa"] Naumov lived on its shore. He was an *otshelnik* [a hermit], one of those people who choose to lead a solitary life far away from others. A particularly large number of them appeared from 1953 onwards, when they started to liberate the camps. Lots of zeks never went home, because after all those years there was no one left waiting for them. Others holed up in the taiga out of shame, despair or fear. In the zone (the camp) they had made enemies, and they were afraid for their lives. Dyedushka Naumov was one of them. He lived on that lake for more than fifty years, and never left the place. Not even to go

16

to the doctor's. He said he'd been the camp scribe and had condemned himself to solitude. He wanted to atone for his wrongdoings – everyone knew he was a grass, a nark. He informed on his fellow prisoners. And he did beautiful calligraphy.'

'What's that got to do with it?' I ask.

'Nothing. I just want to tell you that he was over eighty, and even if there were no lines printed on the paper, he wrote line after line perfectly straight, verse after verse, and without wearing glasses either. He wrote poems. Ordinary, rhyming ones about his tough, solitary life in the taiga. Whenever I went into the mountains I used to drop in on him. I'd bring him buckwheat, salt, matches and cartridges, and he'd make us tea.'

Naumov had a dozen dogs, including a three-legged one. This dog had lost a paw in one of the snares his owner set for hares and foxes. All his dogs were laikas, very clever creatures. Laikas live throughout Siberia, but they vary somewhat in appearance. The laikas belonging to the Evenks (one of the Siberian indigenous peoples) are big and very strong, the ones bred by the Yakuts are smaller but aggressive, snappy and resilient. They spend the entire Yakutsk winter – and thus at temperatures of minus fifty, sixty or seventy degrees – in the open air, and the Yakuts make the best gloves out of their fur.

The last time Sasha saw Naumov was in autumn 2009. There was a board nailed to the wall of his cottage with a message saying not to bury him in the earth when he died, but to cremate him and all his property inside the hut. Naumov told Sasha his final winter was approaching.

'I went back in the spring,' says Sasha, 'and his hut was gone. Burned down. All that was left was a charred door, still in its frame. It was like a door into the forest, into the taiga, into the mountains. Some itinerant hunters had got there before me. They'd found the old man dead in bed, the board with his last wish and the three-legged dog lying on his chest. They tried chasing it out, but it wouldn't move. They laid the fire, but the dog still didn't move, so they tried dragging it out to save its life, but it went for them with its teeth … So there it lay on Dyedushka Naumov's chest as they went up in flames together.'

'I always thought those tales of boundless fidelity and dying together were myths,' I say.

'So did I. But I was at the site just after the hut burned down. It was still smoking. I found an old iron pot, gathered up the remains in it and buried them. On the board I wrote: "Here lies Dyedushka Naumov and his dog." Because the dog's bones and the man's were together.'

'What was the dog called?'

'*Shary* [meaning "Grey"]. Or maybe *Vierny* – ["Loyal"]. I don't remember. But everyone started walking through that door which had survived the fire, as if they were passing through the gates of a temple. Hunters, geologists, gold prospectors and my friends and I whenever we go climbing – we take the long way round just to go through it for good luck.'

After his funeral Naumov's surviving laikas ran off into the mountains. The hunters had been firing at them for years, because they stole the animals out of their snares, and in winter they gathered in a pack and prowled about like wolves. Worse – they would attack people, because they weren't afraid of them.

A similar situation, but on a much bigger scale, occurred in the 1990s. People started leaving Kolyma in droves, but they left their dogs behind, after driving them out into the taiga. The mountains became even less hospitable than ever.

'Would you believe, there are still unconquered peaks out there?' says Sasha happily. 'Even two-thousand-metre-high ones. My team has seven of them to its name. Do you know what it feels like? You reach a peak where no man has ever set foot before, and inside you can hear your soul singing to you. As their conquerors we had the right to name them. Our highest mountain was Challenger – it's two thousand three hundred and forty-seven metres above sea level, and the last seven hundred metres looks like a vast, stunningly beautiful space rocket ready for take-off. We conquered it in 1987, soon after the American space shuttle of that name crashed. Fifteen years later we made a second ascent to the peak, and to this day no one has achieved a third. In the north, in the Arctic mountains, it's hellishly difficult to climb. The height is the same as your Carpathians, but the lack of vegetation and oxygen is like in the Himalayas at five thousand metres, and there are enormous glaciers and avalanches even in summer. Fifty metres below the peak of Challenger we were hit by a *purga*, a horrific blizzard. For four days it held us against a wall of ice, although it was late June. We couldn't go forwards or backwards. They say a mountaineer from the north has to have enough enthusiasm to spare for three blizzards on that scale.'

'How long can they last?' I ask.

'A week.'

Sasha usually goes into the mountains alone, even on climbing trips. Once he set off for a peak called Mardzhot, which is 2027 metres high, but to his despair his beloved laika Yakut never left him for a single step of the way.

'That day I go off to climb,' says Sasha, 'and he comes trailing after me and won't let himself be chased away. He disappears, but in a short while he turns up again, and he keeps playing with me like that for about twenty kilometres, the whole length of the valley to the foot of the mountain. Next day I sit facing him, I look him in the eye and very solemnly say: "Stay down here at the bottom, don't come any further," and he wags his tail and is highly amused. He follows me up an almost perpendicular gulley, and once we're on the ridge, he falls seven or eight metres off a small shelf and gets wedged in a crevice between two slabs of rock. I go down to him on a rope and spend several hours trying to haul him out. All for nothing. There's no alternative—'

'What?'

'I've got to drop him. Tip him over the precipice. After all, he'd spend days and days dying of hunger and thirst out there! So I unwedge him and give him a push, to the north side. I'm going down from the ridge to the south. An awful descent. Twelve, thirteen hours battling against a wall of ice. In the valley I make an igloo for the night, lie down to sleep, and a few hours later I hear my Yakut barking. Would you believe it? He survived a fall from several hundred metres! By some miracle he climbed back onto the ridge again, came down the other side and found me. I loved him, though he was moody.'

Sasha goes into the taiga without a gun, which isn't very wise, so when he's there to take photos, he brings along a dog to defend him against bears. Laikas cope with them very well. They can catch the scent of them from many kilometres away, sooner than the bear scents the man, they're faster and more nimble than bears and they're fiendishly malicious as well as noisy, which bears can't stand.

'Once we went into the mountains to take autumn photos, and we came upon a bear's den. I had eighteen of them within sight – I'd never seen so many all at once before. They'd gathered by a stream, and were peacefully catching fish together, and we calmly walked past them, with our rucksacks above our heads and our hearts in our mouths.'

'You did what with your rucksacks?'

'You have to carry them as high as possible to look very big. Luckily they didn't take any notice of us. And all day we roamed the glaciers and scree, until we came to a lovely green pasture. I set up my tripod, took out my camera, chose a little yellow flower to be in the fore-ground, and was just about to press the shutter . . . when into the frame sloped the dog and lay down on the flower. He simply flopped on his side and lay there, staring at the camera. "Get away, you scumbag!" I screamed at him. So he gets up and goes, heading for home.'

'He was offended.'

'And the night's coming, and I've still got to walk through that bear territory. Without a dog that's certain death. So I hotfoot it after the dog, and start apologizing, promising I'll never bawl him out again, saying he's a good dog, clever boy, come back, don't leave me ... Finally he stops, but he doesn't even look at me, so I run up to him, get out some rusks and try to bribe him. We had a snack together, sat there for a while, said sorry to each other, and he escorted me home. That's what a dog means in Kolyma.'

'What became of him?'

'He drowned in a flood. In a single night the Berelokh stream broke its banks and flooded the whole of Susuman, where we were living at the time. Miraculously I managed to save the family on a tiny fishing dinghy. But he as usual wasn't there.'

'Maybe there wasn't enough room in the dinghy?' I wonder.

'We'd have carried him in our arms. He'd wandered off somewhere.'

'But maybe he managed to survive.'

'Impossible. Otherwise he'd have come back.'

Day II

Arman, 52 kilometres west of Magadan

This place is a dying fishing village. I'm staying on the stony shore of the Sea of Okhotsk in the fisheries inspector's cabin. I wasn't planning to come here at all, but the first driver to pick me up on the road was Andrei, a sub-officer at EMERCOM, or Ministerstvo Chrezvychaynikh Situatsii (the Ministry of Emergency Situations). This is the rescue service that brings help in the event of various disasters, and its employees are people in uniforms, organized in military fashion. As soon as I get in his car I regret it, because Andryusha is well oiled. His car goes reeling down the road, and he tries overtaking too, because this guy is from the Caucasus, from South Ossetia, so he's hot-blooded, he's not going to drag along behind anyone like a slowcoach, he's on the attack. Of course he is in uniform. He always puts it on when he gets in the car after drinking, in case he's stopped by the police, because – as we all know – people in uniforms have a sort of understanding. Andrei encourages me to change my plans and come fishing with him. The salmon-fishing season is just ending, and he and his friends are going to celebrate.

By the road into the village there is an unusual sight: a woman in crimson lipstick, large earrings down to her shoulders and high-heeled shoes is sweeping up dry cowpats on the bridge. She moves gracefully, as if she were floating. And she's full of joy.

It's Sunday.

Arman is a typical Kolyma village. It has a fragile social structure based around only five or six families, married couples with several children and a handful of relatives. They alone set up all the businesses, wheel and deal, amass capital and create jobs. They almost all start with little shops, then set up big arable farms, fishing companies, forest-produce wholesalers, refrigeration units and so on. People like these can gather as many as fifteen hundred to two thousand people around them, which is the number that were living in Arman in the early 1990s.

But if one couple leaves, followed by their children, and then a second family, the exodus begins. It's a domino effect; one by one the local firms, which had been living in symbiosis, go under, and it all starts to crumble. People lose their jobs and life loses its meaning. Only the drunks, the paupers and people with no energy or initiative stay behind in the village. Such is the fate that has befallen Arman. It lies on one of the most resource-rich seas in the world, but it is dying. Of the two thousand inhabitants, five hundred are left, and dozens of abandoned houses are falling into ruin as the local vagrants rip the scrap metal and timber out of them for firewood, although there is taiga all around them and wood in abundance.

There are dozens of these villages in Kolyma. Of the five hundred thousand-plus inhabitants who were living here when the Soviet Union fell apart in 1991, only about a hundred and fifty thousand are left, in fifty settlements.

So we're at the fisheries inspector's cabin, celebrating the end of the season. We're drinking vodka and devouring heaps of red caviar, which an hour ago was still swimming, and *ukho*, a cold fish soup. They make it in buckets. The best is yesterday's, and the most highly prized ingredient is the heads. Once every sixty to ninety minutes we go down to the beach and pull in the net, in which there are always a few enormous fish more than half a metre long. They are coho salmon, the largest of the local species, ugly-looking fish with predatory curved jaws, which in August

23

and September migrate along the sea coast to the river mouths, then swim upstream to spawn and die in the upper reaches. There are always pairs in the net, and the females are full of eggs. They weigh about 4 kilos each, of which 800 grams is delicious red caviar. My companions don't know what to do with it any more, or with the fish. Today they caught thirty-eight of them. The record ones are more than a metre long and weigh 20 kilos. Inspector Nikolai Nikolayevich Dyemchenko, who has been posted here to maintain the law, does a roaring trade in them – for kopecks. In my presence he sells four fish (weighing over 15 kilos, including 1.5 kilos of caviar) for 200 roubles. For 20 zlotys! (£4.) At the market in Magadan a shopkeeper would get 2000 roubles (£40) for the caviar alone.

Apart from the coho salmon, in June the pink salmon swim up the Kolyma rivers, whose caviar is regarded as the best, followed in July by the chum salmon and two other species in small numbers. Every other year the migrations are more abundant, and every four years there are so many fish that there is hardly room for them in the rivers, to a point where you could almost walk across their backs to the opposite bank. A unique sight.

Anyone can cast his nets here. You only have to buy a day licence from the inspector for 100 roubles (£2). Then you have to pay 60 roubles for every fish you catch. Victims of Stalinist oppression and war veterans are given a free licence for twenty fish, and indigenous inhabitants of Kolyma – Evens, Evenks, Chukchis, Yakuts, Koryaks, Yukaghirs, Itelmens, Kamchadals and Chuvans, of whom in total there are only four thousand in the entire oblast (an administrative region roughly equivalent to a province, its sub-division is called a *raion*) – can catch as many as they want. This may be why they have been the most desirable matrimonial commodity in recent years. Spouses also gain the rights to an unlimited catch and to trade in fish.

Preparing the caviar seems very simple. You have to gut the fish, extract the caviar from the membrane surrounding it, toss it for nine

Dima the Chekist and Vanya the blatnik *playing* durak.

minutes into a water-and-salt solution, and then strain it. Your nine-minute caviar is ready. The firm grains will pop luxuriously against your palate, as your hand reaches for a shot glass. Eight-minute caviar is viscous and too soft, while the ten-minute variety is too salty. The secret of its preparation lies in the liquid. It has to be almost saturated with salt. The word 'almost' is of major significance here. The solution has to be of a consistency where raw eggs will only just float in it.

Years ago I met a man in St Petersburg who in 1986 had taken part in the clean-up at Chernobyl. The rescue team were fed mainly on red caviar from the Sea of Okhotsk, which was brought to them by the tonne, and were given red wine from Georgia and Moldova to drink. My friend was convinced that this diet had saved his life.

'Come on,' says Dima, immediately addressing me informally as *ty*, although he's seventeen years my junior, 'I've got a gun for you.'

'What am I supposed to shoot?' I ask.

'Anything on legs or with wings.'

'I don't want to,' I say, and look around for an empty beer can. I have no trouble finding one — there are dozens of them lying about, as well as old tins, vodka bottles, gherkin jars, fish heads, fish guts, decayed ropes, nets, crab shells, human shit, seagulls and ducks at various stages of decay — a dreadful mess produced by the combined forces of people and the sea.

I shoot, and miss. Dima shoots, and another great big bird falls to the beach. It's a grey seagull, in other words it's still young, hatched this year.

'Don't you feel sorry for it?' I ask.

'That's its fate,' he says, scowling.

Some of the ducks are ready for cooking — gutted and featherless. The people of Kolyma don't pluck poultry, but very deftly skin it. A few cuts, one tug, and that's it. And that's all my hosts have the energy for. The bald mummies of birds have been drying out in the sun for days on end, and these guys are celebrating.

Dima is a guest here, as I am, but he fills the fisheries inspector's cabin with his presence. He talks the loudest, swears the most coarsely and belches the most often. He does everything more repulsively and more abominably than anyone else. He's big, fat, and hung over. To the despair of Kolya Dyemchenko, the fisheries inspector, Dima is spending his leave at Kolya's cabin, which involves acting the boss, demanding to be fed, sending for vodka, and in completely un-Russian style addressing the rest of us informally, even though he's the youngest man here.

He's thirty-six and holds the rank of colonel in the Federal Security Service, the Russian secret police. We've only just met when he calls his work and asks if there's a foreign journalist in Magadan right now. They call back five minutes later. There's one Pole, staying at the Central Hotel. Dima tells them to inform the hotel that the Pole won't be back for the night.

So we're celebrating the end of the salmon-fishing season. Also with us are Dima's driver, known as *Zhaba* (meaning 'Frog') because he looks like one, and Kolya's assistant, Vanya Katlar. And once we are very tipsy, the world's most unusual game of cards begins, a truly sacred ritual bordering on the fantastical.

The Russian secret-police colonel sits down to play with an *avtorytet* (literally, an 'authority'), a prince among *blatniye* ten years his senior, an aristocrat among professional *urki*, convicted *ugolovniki*, the *krutoy baron* ('tough baron') of recidivists, a worthy old lag among numerous *kriminalisty*. All the incomprehensible words cluttering up the previous sentence denote 'criminals' in the underworld slang known as *fenya* or *fenka*. To put it plainly, Dima and Vanya are playing the simple game involving twenty-four cards known to us Poles as *durak*, meaning fool. In Russia it is called *kozyol*, meaning 'goat'. The stake is 1000 roubles (£20) per deal.

Suddenly, for these two men the whole world ceases to exist. They are only here for each other, only talk to each other, and only pour vodka for each other, drinking steadily. They're off on a cards-and-alcohol binge, a real bender. And as they play they let fly with the *mat*, in other words they swear so monstrously it's as if the game depended on it, like in what the Russians call a multi-storey insult-hurling competition. They shower each other with abuse, run each other down mercilessly, sneer at the enemy and triumph over every point they win like small boys, but there's nothing personal about any of it – quite the opposite. Contempt? Nothing of the kind! They save their contempt for suckers – for me, for Frog, for Kolya, and the entire rest of the world. Only *blatniye* and secret policemen aren't suckers.

So I can see a liking between these two characters growing right before my eyes, a thread of understanding, a form of respect, in principle 'Respect' with a capital R, meaning admiration, even though they belong to two separate, theoretically hostile worlds, set against each other. These two giants have ended up in the same place, so they've teamed up and joined forces.

Here in this cabin on the Sea of Okhotsk they're reviving the old Stalinist alliance between the *blatniye* – or *blatniki*, the caste of professional criminals – and the secret police, the entire apparatus of repression. For who are these vagabonds, these criminals and bandits? They're 'our boys', the salt of the earth, they're the proletariat, they've just come a cropper, things have gone wrong for them in life. The *blatniye* never got the longest sentences, meaning twenty-five years or the death penalty, not even for murder. Those sentences were for political prisoners, and in the camps the *blatniye* were the only ones who didn't have to work.

It was a terrifying alliance. It was brought into being in the 1930s to torment 'enemies of the people', intellectuals and opponents of the Soviet regime – all the political prisoners in the camps and prisons of the entire Gulag Archipelago. In their stories Varlam Shalamov and Alexander Solzhenitsyn, who survived the Gulag, write about the *kriminalisty* as the worst nightmare afflicting their fellow political prisoners. They beat, murdered, raped, and stole food and clothing.

Meanwhile our card-playing allies are into the sixth hour of their game by now. They only get up from the table to step across the threshold and piss right there.

Vanya's having luck. He's won 27,000 roubles (£540). They've drunk a litre of vodka and have stopped eating, except for the occasional snack. The table is like our entire modus vivendi in miniature. It may be covered in newspaper, but the mess on it is unbelievable. There are fish bones, crumbs, bits of paper, plastic cups scorched by cigarette butts, broken glasses, bits of sausage, tomato and caviar lying around at random, which they keep tracking down with their fingers and stuffing into their mouths. There's barely enough space to put down the cards.

Vanya is supposed to be the assistant here, but Kolya, the inspector, waits on everyone, serving the soup and making the sandwiches. Once again they send him out for vodka. So I'm going with him.

VANYA THE *BLATNIK* — THE
MILLION-DOLLAR METEORITE

'Where did you come by a guy like Vanya?' I ask on the way. (It's incredibly odd, because *blatniye* never work. It's against a bandit's honour to work.)

'He volunteered for the job himself,' says Kolya. 'But it's a blessing, because they were stealing everything I had. A Yamaha six-kilowatt generator, nets, shovel, two buckets . . . Even the wood I'd chopped for kindling. But since Vanya came along, I can leave a can of petrol outside and it won't get nicked. There'll be an axe lying around, and no one will touch it. Everybody around here is afraid of him. He's made it known that if anything goes missing, he'll tear the culprits' heads off. But don't tell him I told you: he's an *av-to-ry-tet*.'

'You don't say! That's the second-highest rank in the bandit hierarchy, right after the *vory* in their caste.'

'Yeah,' says Kolya, switching to a whisper. 'His tag, his nickname, is "Marchela", he's the nephew of "Jam" from Komsomolsk, who ruled the far east, until he was shot dead in Moscow. He was one of the most powerful bandits in the entire country. And that Vanya of mine isn't scared of anything. He doesn't give a damn. Yesterday the police came here to drink vodka off duty, because it was Sunday, and he sent them packing! Can you imagine? He drove away the policemen!'

'Why did he do that?' I ask.

'Because this is an official site, for fishing, not picnicking. And how well he knows people! He sees right through everyone. As soon as a man comes in he instantly knows all about him. He's sure to know all about you by now too, and me. It only takes him a quick look.'

Before we go back to the terrible Dima, Kolya tells me about his connections with the sea. In 1996 he signed on at a huge floating fishing base called Felix Kon, but the day before going out to sea his ship sank in Nagayev Bay at the entrance to Magadan.

'You'll never believe what happened!' he exclaims.

'Oh yes I will. I've been travelling to Russia for twenty years now, and I can believe anything.'

'They scuttled it. They opened all the hatches and sent the ship to the bottom, just so it wouldn't emerge that someone had stolen three hundred tonnes of fuel oil. A stupid three hundred tonnes for such a fabulous ship, from the Gdańsk shipyard! It was the doing of the *blatniye*, who at that point somehow started being called the mafia. And those shitty democrats were in power in Russia, who said now there was freedom and everything was allowed, so the mafia did whatever they wanted, too. They shot, murdered, and sank ships, because they needed money urgently. There was privatization going on, so they were buying whatever they could.'

We get the vodka and go back to our *blatnik* and his card partner. Vanya is 57,000 roubles up on Dima (£1140). The card game is entering its tenth hour, and in comes Dima's wonderful, masterful strategy based on psychology. He wants to put everything on a single card and play just once more for the entire stake. Vanya refuses, because he thinks that sort of win is a waste, but they raise the stake to 5000 roubles (£100) per deal.

But Dima keeps putting on the pressure, constantly wanting to raise the stake. It sounds like drunken, friendly banter, but Vanya is thrown off balance, starts making mistakes, and stops noticing his opponent's cheating (obviously, they're both trying it on). He even makes a stupid error in his accounts, by missing out a zero in the columns of figures he writes down (thus losing 10,000 roubles). I'm just about to correct him, when Dima gives me a hefty kick under the table.

The tide is definitely turning, and Dima is pushing Vanya to the limits of psychological endurance. It's like an interrogation! And he seems to have the stronger head. Now he's arguing about the deadline for repaying a card debt – sacred to all bandits, as Dima well knows. He says he'll hand over the cash in seven months.

'Seven what?' screams Vanya, shaking all over. 'By twelve on Monday! Card debts get paid by noon the next day.'

'Screw your bandit rules,' replies Dima. 'Seven months, and there's fuck all you can do to me.'

'I'll send people!'

'I'll shoot the lot.'

They spend a good hour arguing about it, maybe longer. I don't know because I'm out of it; at dawn I doze off with a tablespoon full of caviar in my fist. When I wake up, the card players are talking about meteorites. They're polishing off their second litre of vodka.

'Do you know what the Seymchan meteorite is?' Vanya asks me.

'No, I've never heard of it before.'

'It's a great big rock like this,' he says, manually demonstrating something the size of a grown man's head. 'It fell from the sky, and now I've got it. And there's a million dollars right there.'

'Oh screw you, you fucking cunt!' They normally swear at each other like that all the time, but this time on Dima's lips it sounds oddly threatening. 'I did not hear that!'

The secret policeman jumps to his feet, and suddenly he's stone-cold sober.

'So how the fuck are you going to get it out, you arsehole?' he roars straight into Vanya's face. 'You just did not say that! And never say it again to the day you die! I've known where it is for years and who brought it to you! Don't you ever say another fucking word about it again in your fucking bastard life!'

Vanya instantly sobers up too and starts to apologize, then looks me hard in the eyes.

'Nobody here said that,' he drawls. 'You never heard a thing.'

I never heard a thing, and I go back to sleep again. I dream that now I understand what Varlam Shalamov meant when he called the Soviet legal system an organized mess. When I wake up, the sun is high in the sky. The game has been going on for eighteen hours now.

By the time I leave the cabin Vanya has only won 7000 roubles. I walk to the road and catch a ride to Magadan.

The misfortune of this country is that here everything is agreed upon in advance. The state makes an agreement with its citizens whereby they aren't allowed to drive while drunk, but they all do. There's an agreement that they have to do up their safety belts, but no one, including the president and prime minister, ever bothers. They have to pay for the fish they catch, but nobody does – they just pay bribes instead. The state agrees with its citizens that they're not allowed to trade in caviar, but anyone who can, does it; they're not allowed to poach, but they all do . . .

Here they've even made an agreement that the authorities, the security agencies, are to pursue criminals. But nothing of the kind

33

happens! The authorities have known for ages where the priceless meteorite has gone, but it seems they're just pretending to be looking for it. Why is that? I can take a guess. For what would Dima gain from returning the meteorite to the museum? Or from taking it off Vanya? He'd never be able to flog it on his own – how on earth, where, to whom? It's very dangerous, but the criminal world will find a buyer. Once Vanya manages to sell the meteorite, Dima will come forward for his share. For his million dollars.

Day III

Magadan

Today feels like an Indian summer, which means the beautiful weather will last another two weeks, and straight after that comes a hard winter. In Russian, as in Polish, an Indian summer is called an 'old wives' summer'. In Poland the same phrase refers to the gossamer threads made by tiny late-summer spiders, but here in Kolyma it's too cold for them, and instead it's the name for the seeds of forest flowers carried on the wind, similar to dandelion clocks. This is the loveliest time of year in Kolyma. The larch trees are completely yellow by now, but they haven't dropped their needles yet, so the hills surrounding the city look as if they're on fire.

The radiators in this part of the world have been on since mid-September. That's actually nice; what's not so nice is that the Internet in my hotel is possibly the most expensive on earth. Three hundred roubles (£6). No, not per month – per hour! And it's the slowest on earth too. To send this report, I have to open my mailbox, which takes me one hour and twenty minutes. There used to be a 'Point for collective access to the Internet' at the main post office, but they've closed it down, so I'm doomed to the hotel. On top of that, hordes of venomous Russki spam and viruses have attacked my mailbox, the sort of bastards that are impossible to delete.

Everything here is expensive. Potatoes and onions cost 40 roubles (80p) per kilo at the vegetable stall, beef tomatoes are 280, apples

260, grapes 160, and lemons 160 roubles per kilo. Almost everything has come in by ship from China. Even fresh dill costs 600 roubles per kilo.

But I'm not complaining, not even when the wind is blowing from the east, from the site of Magadan's biggest cemetery. There's a cloud of oily black smoke coming from that direction – the gravediggers are burning old tyres, warming the ground for digging graves. That's their 'ecological' way of dealing with the permafrost which in summer starts a metre below the ground surface.

Radiy Netslov is twenty-three. He's helping me with the technical preparations for my expedition – maps, equipment, the addresses of acquaintances along the Kolyma Highway … He and his friends have founded a club for fans of off-road vehicles and an Internet site called M49 (which designates Magadan on registration plates). Radiy's club organized a campaign among the youth to boycott the most expensive petrol stations in the city. He was summonsed by the prosecutor's office, where they made threats and tried to frighten him. Then some young people banded together on the M49 site and organized a protest against increasing the prices of used cars imported from Japan. Radiy wasn't worried, because nobody in the city could possibly have hard feelings about this campaign. They drove about the streets in a column of cars without sounding their horns. But even so the police nicked him, issuing more threats and frighteners, some pushing and shoving, and a 'final warning'.

Now Radiy sits quietly without making the slightest complaint. But his mother is worried that they've ruined his enjoyment of life.

'And on top of that there are financial difficulties,' she says sadly. 'Under Russian democracy you just want to curl up and die.'

Babushka Tanya asks God for death.

Babushka, babula, babulichka, babulenka – how many ways are there to say 'granny' in Russian? When it comes to terms of endearment, this language is unrivalled.

Here we have Babushka Tanya, born in 1917, in Kolyma since 1942. Ten years in a labour camp for Article 136 of the penal code (in other words, murder), and when she protested because she didn't agree with the verdict, she got another eight years for anti-Soviet agitation, 'ASA' for short. That's number 10 of the fourteen terrible paragraphs of Article 58 of the Soviet penal code. Anyone caught telling political jokes was penalized under this paragraph. Esperanto-speakers got paragraph 6, for spying. Article 58 of the penal code, the so-called political one, was written by Vladimir Lenin in person. Half the prisoners in Kolyma were 'enemies of the people' sentenced under this article. The other half were criminals, but a criminal could mean a man who had stolen three bottles of paraffin, a woman who had gathered some leftover grain from a collective-farm field after the harvest, or a young person who'd been caught riding the train without a ticket.

Babushka Tanya is exceptional, because hers is the only case I know of where the prisoner requested to be sent to Kolyma. Somewhere she had heard that each year here counted as two, so she thought she would serve her eighteen years in nine, be released and seek out her seven-month-old son, whom, after her arrest, she had delivered to a children's home in person. Her husband had disappeared on the Front without a trace.

Babushka Tanya was one of the last people to be released from the camp, in 1956. She had served fourteen years.

'I went to the children's home, but he wasn't there. He died. Died! That's what they told me. He lived a year, that's all. They showed me the documents.'

During the war years, according to the official data, fifty-five out of every hundred children born in the USSR did not survive. The highest mortality rate was in the orphanages. After the war there were nineteen million orphans in the Soviet Union, including five million homeless 'street children'.

'So I went to the militia,' says Babushka Tanya, 'and asked where the chief was who took the child away from me. He's gone, they said. No one knew where. That man had wanted to take my child for himself, because he had none of his own. That's why he had me locked up. So I was left alone, and went back to Kolyma. I married Bobkov, my guard, with whom I'd already been living for four years at the women's camp in Elgyen. He died of cancer that same year. And then I married Gavrilov, my Kolya, with whom I lived for fifty-five years. He was a militiaman, but later on we worked together at the boiler house. He was a stoker, and I shifted coal in a wheelbarrow.'

They didn't have any children. Early in 2010 Babushka Tanya was widowed for the third time.

'I was born in the tsar's day, then there was Lenin, and Stalin, and I survived them all. And God won't take me away. I keep begging Him for death, but He does nothing. Everyone says: "You'd better ask Him to send you an easy death," but why should I ask for an easy death? Send me whatever death you've got, I say! I've buried one husband, then a second, and a third, but I'm still alive. What for? God is unfair. I used to have a little cross and a gold chain I bought myself for my christening. It was this thick. Seven thousand I paid for it. The social worker stole it from me. She was washing my hair over the bath and broke it, as if accidentally. Then she put a chain on me, but it wasn't made of gold. My God, what a snake! I give her money, but she doesn't buy anything. She doesn't bring me medicine. For years we put a little aside out of our pensions, so the one who died first could put up a fence and an iron cross on the other one's grave. I gave the money to the social workers to get a fence and an iron cross for Kolya when he died, but the lady next door tells me it's wooden. What a sin they've taken upon their souls. A wooden cross costs three thousand, but an iron one is fifteen thousand, and I can't walk, so I'm not going there to check. O God, send me death, whatever kind You've got.'

Day IV

Magadan

Today I'm performing my first operation ever. On a broken thighbone. It's an open break, very complicated, with severe bleeding, because the bone has cut the femoral artery. The patient is losing a lot of blood, but thirty-seven-year-old Vlad – chief surgeon at the Magadan oblast hospital – and I are drinking beer laced with brandy at the Magnolia restaurant by the bus station. Vlad's junior colleagues keep phoning and begging him to come to the hospital, but he can hardly stand upright. Apart from that, we're having a nice chat.

First he asks whether there's anyone there who's seriously sloshed, because he'd sure be revived by this operation. Then, over the phone, he guides his colleagues' hands, telling them what to do and how – what incisions to make, how to apply the clamps and drill holes for the screws – while I run to the nearest kiosk to buy Vlad a phone top-up and some cigarettes, because he hasn't a kopeck on him. The operation continues for five hours, and it's a success.

The Magnolia is the worst shack in which I have ever drunk beer laced with brandy. The only thing to eat is pork chops with cheese and chips, but customers are obliged to read the entire menu, where the longest section is about fines. Damaging the TV screen – 20,000 roubles (£400), damaging a dining table – 3000, and a soft chair – 2500. The fine for a beer mug is 300, and for a plate or a glass it's 200 each.

You get the best value out of smashing an ashtray – only 100 roubles.

Vlad insists on showing me around town. It's supposed to be a tour of the historic sites, but somehow we keep coming across bars. First an Uzbek one on what used to be Lenin Square, where four years ago there was still a statue of the revolutionary leader. Behind him in 1987 they started building a vast House of Soviets, the local parliament, but a few years later when the Soviet Union collapsed, the construction work came to a halt. Four years ago they began converting the building into a large Orthodox cathedral, and the statue was moved to a small square outside the new headquarters of the FSB (Federal Security Service, successor to the NKVD and the KGB). The city fathers renamed Lenin Square Soborovy [Cathedral] Square, although work on the cathedral has stalled.

So the local parliament, now called the Magadan Oblast Duma, situated in what is known as Vashkov's House, has remained there to this day. It is a former Stalinist prison, so named after the chief administrator, though nowadays nobody can remember who Vashkov was. There are still dozens of narrow little cells in the basement.

The main street is still called Lenin Prospect. President Medvyedev features on almost every blank wall, flashing a Hollywood smile. Sometimes he's accompanied by Prime Minister Putin. And at the local theatre there are noticeboards showing portraits of Magadan's honorary citizens. In first place is a Chekist, one of the heads of the NKVD in the 1930s and 1940s.

So where's the portrait of Sergei Korolyov, father of Soviet space exploration? Or those of the writer Varlam Shalamov, actor Georgiy Zhzhonov and singer Vadim Kozin, the great Soviet artistes who spent years rotting in the local camps?

Vlad tells me the answer from the bushes into which he has tumbled while going to take a leak. He says I'm looking at Russia from my own small, wobbly European seat, and that if the Russians condemn their

Dr Vlad in front of the bust of Eduard Berzin, absolute ruler of Kolyma.

past they'll have nothing left. Their history isn't easy. It's easy to piss on your own fingers, says Vlad philosophically, and turns to face the bushes again.

Vlad's father was a high-ranking KGB officer in Magadan.

'How did you already manage to get plastered?' I ask Vlad two days later when we meet for morning coffee.

'What do you mean? I've just come off shift! I look bad because I haven't slept for twenty-four hours.'

'You stink of vodka—'

'It's not alcohol,' he replies. 'It's disinfectant. The day before yesterday I was hammered, but . . . Hey, that's a point, where was I after that?'

'I have no idea. We parted after midnight outside my hotel.'

'I got home at eight in the morning. Where was I?'

'What's the word for that in Russian?' I ask him.

'*Vykluchilo mnye* – I was switched off.'

'That's it. You lost the plot.'

'For eight hours, apparently. I switched off at my mother's house. Because that's where I'm living. I can remember going up the stairs. But where was I before that? I've called everyone, but nobody knows where I was.'

'Have you eaten today?'

'Just wheels,' he says.

'Wheels?'

'Pills. Drugs.'

By now I know that Vlad hasn't been working at the hospital for several months. He just goes there to help his colleagues with operations. He works at the customs office as an escort for a drug-sniffing dog. He insists he resigned from the hospital because the customs people gave him 50,000 roubles straight up (£1000), instead of the 20,000 per month he was earning at the hospital, but I know he was sacked for drinking and screwing up on the job. His wife ran off, taking their fifteen-year-old son with her, three years ago for the same reason.

Vlad brought her back to his family home from a holiday when he was still a student. She was pregnant, so his father decided to put the relationship to the test. Until the year 2000 the graduates of all the medical schools in Russia were bound by a two-year obligatory work assignment. Vlad's father could have fixed it for his son to work at the best possible place, but he sent him to one of the worst instead, to the icy tundra at the mouth of the Indigirka river, where it flows into the Arctic Ocean.

'But this is the worst place, the neuropsychology emergency ward. A delirious madman at a workers' hotel carved up my face and tongue with a razor. I had two paramedics with me, massive brutes, not humans, but I went down the corridor first, and it was dark in there, the usual thing, because of course the light-bulbs had been stolen. Then he showed up, and swish-swish, it was all over. I felt a burning sensation, as if my tongue was coming out through my cheek. My colleagues spent three hours stitching me up. Another time a guy pinned me to the wall with a big spike. He stabbed me a few centimetres from the liver. That thing was sixty centimetres long. He had it hidden up his sleeve. I don't know how he did it, because it was at the airport and he'd just got off a plane.'

Vlad pulls up his shirt and shows me a scar on his belly. Then he offers me his hand, as if to be kissed.

'And here I got hit by an axe in the admissions ward,' he says. 'This man was a quiet type, politely answering my questions, I was filling in the sheet, and then whack! he almost hacked off my hand.'

'And what was the spike made of?'

'Sharpened reinforcing wire. A very dangerous tool. There's almost no wound or bleeding, and you don't feel any pain, but if it hits an artery, that's it. I wondered whether to pull it out, but if I'd moved it, the blood might have flowed into my liver, and they wouldn't have got me to hospital in time. So I travelled fifty kilometres from the airport to Magadan with that sword in my stomach.'

'Is there a lot of crime around here?' I ask.

'It's police territory. They took control of everything because this is the golden heart of Russia – strategic raw materials.'

That means gold, and the world's biggest deposits of silver, as well as platinum, uranium, cobalt, mercury, tin, lead, nickel, iron, copper, molybdenum, wolfram, coal, oil, gas and whatever you fancy. So there's bound to be mafia too, gold dealers and big-time bandits, but not much common street crime, partly because it's not easy to get away from here.

This needs explaining.

It's not easy to get away because every inhabitant of Kolyma, including the prisoners, came here by sea. And to this day that's still the only way to get out of the place – by showing your identity card and buying a ship or plane ticket. Kolyma is like an island. For two hundred years it's been described as an island so remote it's like another planet, and so that's what they call it too, Planet Kolyma, and everything that's beyond it is *materik* – the 'mainland', or the 'continent'.

Kolyma is the name of a river and also a mountain range. There is no geographical region or administrative unit which bears that name, but in common parlance today's Magadan oblast is referred to as Kolyma, and so in the past was the entire vast territory of Dalstroi, which occupied one tenth of the USSR from the lines marked by the Aldan and lower Lena rivers to the Bering Strait in the east.

This needs explaining too.

47

Dalstroi is the name of the Kolyma trust established on 14 November 1931 by decree of the Central Committee of the All-Union Communist Party (Bolsheviks), as the Communist Party of the Soviet Union was then called. The Soviet authorities only wanted one thing from the new enterprise: gold.

That very same month (because in December the Sea of Okhotsk freezes and navigation comes to a halt) the steamship *Sakhalin* sailed into the port at Magadan carrying a thirty-seven-year-old Lithuanian Chekist with the rank of general called Eduard Berzin, a graduate of the Academy of Fine Arts in Berlin. He was the first manager, director, absolute ruler, and tsar of Kolyma. The next spring a ship sailed to shore carrying the first transport of prisoners, and in the autumn Berzin sent the first half-tonne of gold to Moscow. In 1935 he sent fourteen tonnes, and the next year thirty-three tonnes of gold. As a reward for 'exceeding the extraction plan' Dalstroi got thirty tonnes of standard-issue barbed wire, and Berzin got the Order of Lenin. Maria Ulyanova, Vladimir Ilyich's sister, took the opportunity to give Berzin Nadyezhda Krupskaya's Rolls-Royce as a gift. After returning from Moscow, where he received his medal, Berzin gave an order for outdoor labour only to be interrupted when the temperature fell below minus fifty-five degrees Centigrade.

After nine years of existence, in the terrible, hungry year of 1941, Dalstroi gave the Land of the Soviets, at war with the Nazis, seventy-five tonnes of gold. That was one-third of all the gold extracted worldwide, roughly the same amount as is mined annually in this region today, but now it is done by powerful machines. In those days picks, shovels and wheelbarrows had to suffice.

And two hundred thousand slaves dying of hunger, cold and hard labour.

Day V

Magadan

It's my fifth day here, and to my horror I realize that I haven't laughed once since arriving. That never happens to me. But I really haven't come across anything nice or pleasant here yet. The people are the biggest disappointment. They're good, they'd even be willing to help, but for four days nobody has smiled at me or responded to my smile, although the weather is fine and sunny, close to zero. It's that strange Soviet moroseness, as though they've been put into hibernation by the murderous Kolyma climate, a mood I remember from the early 1990s, and which hardly exists in Russia any more. The people are pissed off, brusque, sullen and sad, and do little more than growl at your every question. And try asking for anything. How dreadfully unhappy they are. Even the young people have got it. Even my friend Radiy, who's just a young guy – God forbid you should call him for a chat or because you want something. He hardly replies at all – he's huffy and sulky, as if offended, miserable and gloomy.

Like the guy from the history section at the tourist museum. I want to have a chat, so he comes out to meet me in the lobby, and sits down, but says he is awfully busy. So off I go, and when I come back an hour and a half later, he's still sitting in the same spot and in the same position, staring at the wall. Russians call these people *sovoki* (a contraction of *sovyetsky chelovyek*, meaning 'Soviet man'). The people here are different, as if December 1991 had never happened and the USSR had not collapsed.

I must get out of this city.

But for the time being I'm looking around it. On the corner of Karl Marx Street and Parkova Street stands the former Dalstroi management building, converted into a shopping centre, a temple to the market economy and capitalist labour relations. There's a shop called Klondike (not selling gold, but shoes), Mango which sells trendy clothes, the Church of Christ the Saviour (one of hundreds of sects active in Russia), a lawyer's office, the Brave Step consultancy, the Your Choice advertising agency, Audit Services, Express Printing and the Oasis café-bar.

A few minutes away down Parkova Street comes the most shocking discovery. Standing on a granite plinth outside the Magadan administration building there is a bronze bust of Eduard Berzin.

The townspeople paid this honour to the manager of Dalstroi in the summer of 1989, at the height of perestroika, a time when the system under which hundreds of thousands of innocent people had died had already been totally dismantled in Poland, and was almost gone in Russia. It is more or less the same as putting up a statue at Auschwitz of the brilliant doctor and anthropologist Josef Mengele, or of the distinguished chemist who invented Zyklon B.

Tomasz Kizny, an excellent Polish photographer and reporter, has already written about the statue of Berzin. He was amazed by the Russians' readiness to forgive, and wrote that the city of Magadan is suffering from a kind of schizophrenia.

But that was fifteen years ago. I thought a decade and a half would be long enough to get over it.

It hasn't been. I must get away from this city.

Right next to Berzin I take a terrific photo of four schoolboys at a bus stop. Judging by the down on their upper lips, they're about fourteen or fifteen years old. I ask them who Berzin was. None of them knows. One of them is Chinese, a representative of the most recent wave of immigrants, who came here with his parents ten years ago. Another is an

Even, an ancient people that settled these lands long before the Russians got here. The third boy represents the conquerors – he's Russian – and the fourth is an Ingush, from the Caucasus. The Ingush have a weakness for gold and a talent for dealing in it. In the 1970s they had already monopolized the black-market trade in gold, and for years they have been one of the most populous Soviet ethnic groups to be living here, although the climate is murderous for them.

Apropos things that are murderous, I'm thinking of the shot fired in broad daylight, killing the Magadan governor Valentin Tsvetkov. The trigger was pulled and the governor was assassinated in October 2002 on Moscow's Arbat, the smartest street in the Russian capital. Suspicion fell on his two deputies, Viktoria Tikhachova, who even went to prison for four years, and Yuri Kotov, the biggest local oligarch. He *otmazalsya* – as they rather crudely say here, meaning literally 'unstained himself', but figuratively 'wriggled out of it', though the entire local electorate knows he bought his way out. The inquiry against him is still ongoing and the prosecutor has forbidden him to leave the city, but this does not prevent him from being a deputy to the oblast Duma (the provincial parliament).

Kotov is the owner of a firm called Sea Wolf which trades in crabs, lobsters, fish and caviar, and in Kolyma that is just as dangerous and shady as drugs, and as profitable as gold.

The murdered governor was nicknamed 'The Bulldozer', because he was fierce, tough, tyrannical, and fanatically dedicated to Kolyma, while the present governor, Nikolai Dudov, is neither fish nor fowl – or as the Russians put it, 'neither meat nor fish' – a man moulded from mist and jelly (that's my own metaphor).

The local journalists say the murdered Tsvetkov was a colossal thief and that 'everyone knew all about it'. He let others get rich, too, but only those who shared with him, so apparently he amassed a gigantic fortune in foreign bank accounts. He had his own fishing fleet and several fish-processing factories in Vietnam, which were registered in his lover's

Four schoolmates: a Russian, an Ingush, an Even and a Chinese.

name. But for all that, he was a superb administrator of Kolyma. He built several plants, opened a Special Economic Zone (business parks offering tax breaks to encourage enterprise), and above all built a state foundry for precious metals. Since then gold sand and ores have been bought and smelted into twelve-kilo bank ingots on the spot, and not shipped off to Moscow, which means the prospectors don't have to wait months on end for their money.

In Russia the state has a monopoly on the prospecting, extraction, purchasing, trading and processing of precious metals. All gold and silver prospectors have to buy a licence and sell their output back to the state. In the Magadan oblast in 2009 thirteen tonnes of gold were mined (in Tsvetkov's days it was thirty to thirty-five), and about seven hundred tonnes of silver.

All this means that in Magadan no one is allowed to say a bad word about the former governor. Not even the gold prospectors, who were cheated blind at Tsvetkov's foundry because payments were 'for purity', in other words measured against ore known as 'three-nines fine' (a so-called millesimal fineness of 999, equivalent to 24 carats). In Kolyma, gold sand has a purity grade of 600–940, each measure of precious metal delivered to the foundry is different, and only there can it be tested; it was in these tests that the gold prospectors were cheated. Yet the assassinated governor is remembered with affection and a sense of loss. For me it is yet another example of that Russian readiness to grant absolution, that legendary forbearance. The man in power only has to let the people live, and at once they're fond of him.

I *have* to get out of here. Get on the road, on the Highway.

'I was twenty-four years old when I got a sentence of twenty-five years in a labour camp. They arrested me on the third of March 1953, the day Stalin died.'

'Were they still handing out sentences of that length in those days?' I wonder.

'What do you mean?' gasps Miron Markovich Etlis, tangling me in the silken threads of his smoke-wreathed gaze (to quote Isaac Babel). 'They were still shooting people in those days! Several of my friends were put against a wall. They were the so-called Leninist groups, the children of victims of the Great Purge, shot in the late 1930s. Every last one of them was arrested, because they were opposed to distortions within Party and public life. They wrote programmes and leaflets and produced propaganda, while I was studying medicine in Ryazan. As I was chairman of the student council, they suggested that I should join them, but I refused because I found their programme disgracefully liberal, but that was enough for me to get twenty-five years.'

'Under which article?'

'Article fifty-eight, paragraphs eight, ten and eleven: terrorism, group activity and anti-Soviet agitation. They threw me into a camp attached to a coal mine in Kengir, Kazakhstan, the place where *One Day in the Life of Ivan Denisovich* is set. I worked in Solzhenitsyn's brigade just after they released him. I got to know the prototypes for his characters. Then they made me a paramedic at the camp hospital. I am probably the only zek in the history of the Gulag to have completed my degree while I was there. It started when I treated the

54

deputy head of my camp for psoriasis. After that he took me out of the convoy. I could leave the zone without any guards, but only for two hours and no further than two kilometres from the fence. It was fabulous, because my wife had followed me into penal servitude. She had brought my wonderful grey suit with her, so I changed clothes and hitchhiked to Pavlodar to see the man in charge of all the Kazakh camps.'

'Wasn't that more than two kilometres, Miron Markovich?'

'About a hundred and twenty. I reckoned they'd let me in, because they'd think I was a journalist. I reported to the boss and asked him to call my camp to tell them I wasn't on the run, but with him. The height of insolence! I thought the guy would bust a blood vessel, but he made the call, and I asked him to let me take the doctors' exam at the Medical Academy in Karaganda, because they'd taken me from the sixth year, just before my final exams. He cursed me out – *vymateril* – abominably.'

'What a lovely word!' I say in delight. 'Derived from the word *mat*, meaning "foul language".'

'And he took a sheet of paper and a pen, and he wrote that "z/k Etlis Miron Markovich is on leave, with the purpose of sitting a state examination". He stamped it, and off I went to Karaganda. I had no trouble passing the exam, because the entire body of professors at the Karaganda academy were deportees. So I got my medical diploma, number 120/56, then at the end of 1956 there was an amnesty and I was released, and a year later rehabilitated.'

'Your wife followed you into penal servitude,' I say, in delight again. 'Like the wives of the Decembrists.'

'Yes. She got a job at the canteen attached to the mine where I worked.'

'How very romantic.'

'Terribly. We divorced three years later. So I needed to escape as far away as I possibly could, and the furthest place to go was Kolyma. I've been married again three times here.'

Professor Etlis still works at Kilometre 23 of the Kolyma Highway in a large psychiatric hospital. In his spare time he is writing his memoirs – about his father who took part in the October Revolution and the civil war, and about his friends, the generals Blyukher, Yakir and Tukhachevsky, the old revolutionaries who used to spend time at their family home on Malokuznetsky Lane in Moscow.

His father was the head of a bridge-building trust, and the *narkom* – people's commissar – for the inland fleet was Nikolai Yezhov, who at the same time held the post of people's commissar for state security. Inevitably their interests were often contradictory. The two gentlemen would very often pore over maps and water-related investment plans at the Etlis home, and when they did, it often came to bar-room brawls between them, because neither man was exactly tender-hearted.

'One time a rumpus of this kind erupted at our dacha,' Professor Etlis tells me. 'It was getting dangerous, because both men were armed, so my mother quickly served vodka, brought the dinner and invited in the Gypsies who lived next door. Everyone began to dance. I remember my mother dancing like mad with Yezhov. They made a beautiful couple,' he says, laughing. 'He was 1.51 metres in height. During the Great Terror, he gave orders for all our family friends to be killed, with Blyukher, Yakir and Tukhachevsky at the top of the list.'

'Apparently he shot Marshal Blyukher in person during an interrogation.'

'When my father sensed that his turn was coming next, he disappeared, and stayed hidden in Crimea until Yezhov's fall.'

I am visiting Professor Etlis in hospital. He's resting in the surgical ward, in a smart single room.

'What does your work involve?' I ask.

'Since 1984 mainly research, on a preparation called *kaprim* which was jointly devised by Soviet scientists from the Caucasus and Vladivostok. It's a drug to treat alcoholic psychosis. My job has been to test it on people. I added it to alcohol, and gave it to people to drink. The result I got was that it doesn't cure them of alcoholism, though it does make the rate of progress three times slower, and prevents the appearance of psychosis, but if it's already there, it removes all the symptoms. So in principle it isn't a therapy, but a prophylactic. *Kaprim* should be added to all alcoholic drinks.'

'Then why on earth isn't it being introduced worldwide?' I ask.

'My friend,' says Miron Markovich, tangling me in the silken threads of his smoke-wreathed gaze, 'why is there no justice in this world?'

'Does a wise old Jew always have to give the sort of answer a simple man can't understand?'

'*C'est la vie.* And if it's this life we're talking about, they've just removed a tumour from my bowel. Thank God they didn't have to make an extra hole. That's three operations in a row – through the anus.'

Day VI

Ola, thirty kilometres east of Magadan

I spend the next night at – I never would have believed it – at the home of Yezhov's daughter. That Yezhov! Nikolai Ivanovich, known as Stalin's Iron Fist, People's Commissar for Internal Affairs, the top official in charge of the NKVD, the Soviet secret police, who had on his conscience hundreds of thousands, no, *millions* of human lives.

Do you have any conception of what that means? He was the successor to the monstrous Yagoda, and the predecessor of the dreadful Beria, but surpassed them both in cruelty. He was a booze-swilling degenerate who tortured and murdered prisoners with his own hands. The period of the Great Purge, when he was running the secret police, is called the *Yezhovshchina*, 'the Yezhov era'. Who knows, perhaps those were the most horrific twenty-six months in Russia's entire thousand-year history. The final year of the period, 1938, is known as *rasstrelny* – 'death-by-firing-squad' – year.

Yezhov was a megalomaniacal psychopath. He was nicknamed the Bloody Dwarf – possibly the most appalling monster humanity has ever produced, and here I am at his daughter's place, drinking my twenty-seventh glass of tea.

I know that she lives at No. 37 Lenin Street, on the central staircase. So I go up the stairs and bang on all the doors. None of the bells works, and all the doors are fitted with a solid sheet of metal. None of the tenants knows who lives here with them, and the name Yezhov means nothing to most of them.

Natalia Nikolayevna only has one room. I spread my mattress for the night in the corridor, under a portrait of my hostess's daddy, and nip out to buy something for supper.

The only food outlet in Ola is a sort of little shop with a deli counter and a very-fast-food bar where you can have a beer or a cup of disgusting Chinese three-in-one coffee (instant coffee, milk and sugar in a single bag). I have a jar of caviar from the fishing trip, but we need bread and butter. Natalia Nikolayevna is very poor.

In the process I discover that I haven't yet become completely *obrushaly*. *Obrushaly* is an offensive word to describe someone who has 'gone Russian'. It is used by the non-Russian peoples of the Russian Federation with regard to their compatriots who have lost their own language. When they want to show their disdain for someone of this kind, the Yakuts call him 'a marginal'. That's someone who has cast himself out to the edges of society.

For the first two weeks of my stay in Russia the relevant areas, or perhaps ganglia, of my brain have to translate everything I hear and say into Polish for the other ganglia. Later on I start thinking in Russian. But here and now I can tell it hasn't happened yet.

I buy some butter and some bread, and ask if they have anything hot to take away. Tongue fricassee or roast meat – *piechen* – and onions. Of course I congratulate myself on getting the roast meat, but at Natalia Nikolayevna's it turns out to be liver. Of course! The Russian for 'liver' is *piechen* – it only means roast meat in Polish. Of the two evils I'd have chosen the tongue.

Ola is an estate consisting of several dozen five-storey prefab concrete blocks, known as *khrushchevki*, because that's how they were built in the USSR in Khrushchev's day. Many of the courtyards have ice-hockey rinks that haven't been surfaced yet and stands for drying the washing, which nobody uses because it gets stolen. And all round there are big, waist-high weeds and bushes.

Natalia Nikolayevna lives in Ola because she got a flat of her own here for the very first time in her life when she retired in 1991. She has one daughter and six grandchildren, four of whom live on her estate. She is an accordion player, but since having a stroke she can no longer support the heavy instrument, and her left hand can't fly up and down the keyboard the way it used to.

I spend almost all night chatting with my hostess. And finally I'm laughing! Fit to burst, although it's freezing cold in the flat. The heating isn't on in Ola yet, though at night outside there's frost, taiga, and snow-covered hills. We sit there in our coats and hats.

Natasha and her mother.

'And what's this?'

'Chocolate.'

'What for?'

'For you.'

'For me?' says Natalia Nikolayevna in amazement. 'Chocolate? Do you know how old I am?'

'Thirty-two.'

And we're both giggling. Her laugh is very infectious. It takes us a few minutes to calm down, until Natalia Nikolayevna has a coughing fit. It lasts for ages. There's a thick, gurgling noise coming from her chest and throat, as if something has broken off in there, and she grabs an empty Maxwell House coffee tin and spits a small green dollop of her lungs into it. Maxwell House is her favourite coffee. And she must like the tins, because they're everywhere in her tiny little flat. Half of them are for cigarette butts, the other half are for spitting into.

'I don't need your compliments,' she wheezes, wiping her eyes. 'I've got through seventy-nine years, although I smoke an awful lot. But then I don't drink. At all! And the photo behind you is of my papa. You know, don't you?'

'Yes, I do.'

'Well quite – why else would you be coming to see me? Yezhov's daughter. My God, how dreadful that sounds.'

'So Khayutina is your surname from your husband?'

'From my mother. In fact it's from her first husband, whom I never knew. Daddy was her third husband, and Mummy was his second wife.

62

They weren't my birth parents,' she says, though she always refers to Yezhov and his wife, Yevgenia Khayutina, as her mother and father. 'They couldn't have children, and neither of them had any when they met. They got me from an orphanage in 1935. I was five months old, and my real, birth parents had been put in prison or shot a short time before. They were friends of my new mother. But when Yezhov was arrested early in 1939 I was renamed – instead of Yezhova they made me Khayutina and took me off to the city of Penza, to another orphanage, where everyone was terrified of me. I was six years old and I could sense the fear, but I couldn't understand the reason for it. I walked down the corridor, and on the wall there was a calendar, with a portrait of my father, so I cried: "Papa!" All the carers keeled over in sheer terror. They hadn't had time to take that calendar down yet.'

Natalia Nikolayevna is bursting with laughter, and once again starts coughing appallingly. She spits into the coffee tin, lights up, and takes two sips of coffee.

'The first night they brought me there I talked about myself in the day room. I told them about my father, my nanny, the servants, the guards, the cars, our guests, the dacha, our flat in the Kremlin . . . The children, aged five or six, sat listening, afraid to let out the slightest squeak. In those days even children understood the terror of that name. The woman in charge made up a bed for me in her office. For a month I slept in there. The name Yezhov was an awful thing then. But like all the others, I went by a number.'

'My God,' I gasp, 'that's how people referred to each other in the camps.'

'So did we. I was number 144. Shirts, knickers, gloves, all the clothes and even the winter boots had numbers. And they used to summon us by number, like in a prison camp. Every assembly, morning or evening roll-call, or work assignment was always by numbers.'

'What was it like in there?'

'They hated me there. They quite simply *hated* me. They bullied me, teased me and hit me non-stop. It was dreadful! The carers.'

'Why?'

'At first I had no idea,' says Yezhov's daughter. 'Take for instance the compulsory afternoon nap. A carer comes into the room, silently points a finger at me, I leave the room, and she pincers me between her knees. "Just try and squeal," she hisses, with real hatred. And furiously whacks me with a broomstick. For nothing! For no reason. She hits me so hard the stick breaks, and when I start to howl she blocks my mouth. Strangers used to come and beat me – carers from other groups, cooks, drivers, the night watchman, the administrative staff . . . What I feared most was that rest period. And nights. My God! I was only six years old. And I didn't know what had happened to my father. I felt as if I'd been kidnapped. Snatched away from my lovely, wonderful world and thrown into this hell. I had never seen so many children in my life before. I was always alone. The only one. For hours, whole days on end, I used to sit on a windowsill staring at the road. It took me years to recover. On top of that I had a shaggy mop of curly black hair, and they were all bald. The lice were awful.'

'And didn't they shave your head?'

'Oddly enough, no. And anyone who wanted to could yank my hair. They sometimes lifted me up by it so my feet weren't touching the floor. Nobody ever went past me without pulling my curls. Every single one of them did it! The older children imitated the adults. They didn't cut my hair for ages, not until they brought in the evacuees, war orphans, and their heads were crawling with lice, so then I finally got them too. There were an awful lot of us then – more than six hundred kids. Three of us slept in a single bed. Atrocious. The beds were made of iron, very narrow, and then there was the cold and the hunger. Awful! Colder than in my flat now.'

'But the war was on then.'

'And straight after that they came to take us away for adoption,' Natalia Nikolayevna tells me. 'Frontline soldiers in parade uniforms, festooned in medals, and their wives. We were dressed up too, and the soldiers chose children for themselves for good, for ever, like their own, because in our home there were only actual orphans. Wartime ones. Not the children of alcoholics. They chose the ones with the prettiest faces. They even looked under our clothes and at our teeth. There were two sisters among us, one as lovely as an angel, the other one not so pretty. That can happen if one child takes after the father and the other after the mother. So they took Julka at once, but she said she wasn't going without her sister, but they said they didn't need the second girl.'

'And did they pick you out?'

'Yes! This army man leaned over me and asked if he could be my father. Of course not! I'd never agree to that! I had a father of my own! I really did believe he was out there somewhere, alive, and missing me, and that one day he would come to get me. But the woman in charge shouted out that I was "an orphan!". And when they had all left, the woman took me into her study, took off my dress, stripped me naked, and whipped me with it. It had a row of big, rock-hard buttons – God, it hurt so badly! In the end I got her finger in my mouth and almost bit it off. I ran out of her study down to the cellar. They kept coal in there, and there was a barrel full of water. I hid there for four days. I slept on the coal, completely naked. I didn't eat anything, I just drank that filthy water out of the barrel. We were used to being hungry.'

'Didn't they look for you?'

'And how! They even called the militia. I could hear the carers running along the corridors looking for little Natasha. They hated me, but they were also afraid. They were responsible for me. Now I know that all my life I was under NKVD surveillance. If anything had happened to me, they'd immediately have held an inquiry.'

'But lots of children were dying in those days.'

'I was no ordinary child,' says Natalia Nikolayevna, tangling me in the silken threads of her smoke-wreathed gaze.

NATASHA THE REBEL — THE MOTH SYNDROME

'Who told you that you weren't an ordinary child?'

'When they arrested my father, and I was taken away, nobody in the family knew where I'd gone. My mother's whole family was looking for me, but they refused to say what they'd done with me. My uncles and aunts wanted to take me in to live with them. My nanny Marfa Grigoryevna Snyeragina wanted me too. She had worked for great, important people all her life, and I was the last child in her care.'

'Did she have trouble with the secret police?'

'By some miracle they didn't touch her,' says Natalia Nikolayevna. 'And she never stopped looking for me. During the war she was a nurse at a hospital. One time she spent the whole night sitting by a sol-dier, not a young man any more, who was in a serious state. It turned out that in civilian life he'd been an official at the Ministry of Health, who sent children off to orphanages. They agreed that if they survived, after the war they would look for me together. And that's what hap-pened, but they were looking for Yezhova, and by then I was Khayutina. So they started looking under all my mother's surnames, her maiden and married names, and they found me. How dearly she loved me! She travelled to Penza immediately, but the man was arrested and sent to a camp for betraying a state secret.'

'Didn't they do anything to your nanny?' I ask again.

'Nothing. It's very strange. I have no idea how she could have so much good luck. After all, it was a terrible time, Stalin was still alive — I kept writing him letters asking for them to give my father back. I always got the same answer, saying "rehabilitation not applicable". I didn't understand any of it, and the older girls kept asking if I wasn't afraid. But I was afraid of nothing. Nothing at all! And two years ago, just imagine, they rehabilitated *me*.'

'What on earth——?'

'Saying I'd been a victim of repression. They gave me a certificate.'

'But it was your father they shot,' I say in amazement, 'not you.'

'But they'd persecuted me my whole life, they'd made an orphan of me, and deprived me of a home.'

'What about the nanny?'

'I saw her in the courtyard. I was in the seventh class by then, I was fourteen, with a bald head like everyone else, and she said: "Oh, my dear little curly-haired child", and took me by the hand. But in a different way from anyone else. So warmly, somehow. And off we went together. Nobody had taken me by the hand like that for eight whole years. Whenever they took me, it was just to escort me somewhere or to see someone. But we just walked along, plain and simple. That was when I found out the truth about myself and my family. The man in charge gave us his office so we could stay there in peace and quiet, and he even put up a bed, so my nanny lived in there for several days. But I was a different child by then. They'd made me so walled in, so introverted and wild that I pushed everyone away from me, I didn't like anyone. Even towards my nanny I was gruff and rude. She couldn't believe what they'd done to me. Her sweet little Natasha had turned into a hooligan, such a little thug. She said she wanted to take me away for good, to bring me up, but I would have driven her into an early grave. So I stayed at the orphanage.'

'What about your mother's and father's families?'

'A year later they invited me to Moscow. My Aunt Manya was waiting for me at the station, the wife of my mum's brother, but there was an enormous crowd of people there, a real crush, typical on the railways after the war. Everybody was rushing to get somewhere, pushing

67

with their bundles and shouting, while I was standing to one side, waiting. A woman came up and asked if I was Natasha, but I didn't like the look of her, so I said "No." I was so stupid. So I went on standing there, and once the platform was empty, she came up to me again. What could I do? I had to tell her the truth.'

'You had no choice, my dearest Natalia Nikolayevna,' I say, and we both fall about laughing.

'I was an awful rebel,' she says. 'Even worse than when I was younger. I snarled at everyone like an animal. Mummy's entire family had come there to get to know me again. My mother's three brothers and their wives, her sister and her husband too. My mother, who was born Yevgenia Salomonovna Feigenberg, was the youngest of the siblings. She was Khayutina by her first marriage, Gladunova by her second, and Yezhova by her third. She was thirty-four years old when she died. In that entire great big family there wasn't a single child. They all had this problem. And then I came along and sulked at them all. I said I didn't like being with them and told them to take me to my nanny's. So they did. I preferred being with my father's family.'

'Did anyone from Yezhov's family actually survive?'

'Yes. Miraculously, all of them. They were ordinary people. Good, strong, proletarian Russian folk, simple working people. My father was like that too, so I felt happy with them, but the other lot I simply couldn't understand at all. They spoke so strangely, their words were so—'

'Maybe they were speaking Yiddish?' I wonder.

'It was Russian, but the way doctors speak. They were all doctors, mainly psychiatrists. Intelligentsia, cultured people, they took me to the theatre, to concerts and exhibitions, and they all wanted me to be at their place. Whenever I went to my father's people, they were angry, and when I went to my mother's, my dad's lot resented it. It was great because no one had ever cared about me before.'

'So how had your mother's family weathered the Great Purge?'

'Very well. Only one of her brothers was arrested. He got ten years with no correspondence rights. Aunt Manya used to deliver tins of food, tobacco and sugar for him, but he'd been dead for ages. They'd given him ten years and immediately executed him.'

Natalia Nikolayevna's adoptive mother, Yevgenia, died early in 1938, ten months before her husband's fall from power and her only daughter's deportation to the orphanage in Penza. Her family believes that she was poisoned in hospital; Russian historians cannot confirm this version of events, though they regard it as probable.

'It definitely wasn't my father's doing,' says Natalia Nikolayevna, and starts to cough. 'It was someone else! He tore his hair out, I remember it well. He was in dreadful despair. At first the family thought he'd done it, but then they saw how beside himself he was, which meant it wasn't him. Poor Daddy. I always felt so sorry for him, because it looked as if he was always carrying out somebody else's orders. He was so small and thin. He used to joke that he was scared of my nanny. She was such a great big woman.'

Natalia Nikolayevna shows me some old photographs which her nanny had kept. There is only one picture of her mother, and one of Natalia herself on a boat, which had also featured her father, People's Commissar Nikolai Yezhov, but he had been cut out by the nanny. She'd been afraid to keep an image of a man who had been shot on Stalin's personal orders.

The pictures are from Yezhov's dacha outside Moscow.

'We lived there the whole time,' says his daughter, 'although we had an official apartment in the Kremlin which was our registered address. I've still got my old address in my documents: Moscow, Kremlin building three, flat thirteen. Or the other way around. We had four rooms, and there was an infinite number of toys in mine. But our real life was at the dacha. My nanny was there, and Pola the maid, a cook and a

69

footman. There were guards at the gate, and a man and a woman living in a second house, who took care of some of my father's business. For five beautiful years we lived there. I was obsessed with playing tennis, I used to play with the cook.'

'And your father played billiards with Isaac Babel, the brilliant Soviet writer and journalist. All just to tear him away from the company of your mother, who in the 1920s – forgive my frankness – had briefly been the lover of the young Isaac. While also being the wife of Khayutin.'

'How do you know that?' says Natalia Nikolayevna, frowning.

'From Ilya Ehrenburg's memoirs. Babel was drawn to your home, to your mother, because he wanted to fathom the mystery of the Stalinist terror. It's called moth syndrome. The insect voluntarily flies into the embrace of death. And he got there. Your pathologically jealous and suspicious father gave orders for his arrest. He signed a very large number of death sentences on that billiard table.'

'It was more than seventy years ago, but I can still remember how my mother kept saying: "Kolya, pull out of it, get away, escape before it's too late!" Either way they would have executed him, but at least he would have remained a human being. But he couldn't leave Stalin. For him the man was an icon. He actually prayed to him! To the spirit of a living person!'

'Unbelievable!'

'Me too, I can't fucking— Oh, excuse me. I can't believe it either. But so his family said. Then I read in the papers my father's final words in court. He asked for Stalin to be informed that he would die with his name on his lips, for his family to be left alone, and for his daughter to be taken care of.'

Natalia Nikolayevna wipes her eyes and her nose. She lights a cigarette.

'He was on the point of death and he thought of me,' says the monster's daughter.

'Did you know that I was christened?'

'You can't have been!' I reply. 'Your mother was a Jew and your father was a Bolshevik who had priests shot.'

'My nanny arranged it. She was very religious.'

She had taken care of it during the girl's first visit to Moscow in the summer of 1946, but she had been very scared, and made Natasha swear by all that she held sacred never to tell anyone, not even, or perhaps especially, her family. The very next day the NKVD turned up at her flat.

'Several officers in uniforms,' says Natalia Nikolayevna, starting to cough. 'Even I, who wasn't afraid of anything, almost had a heart attack. But they had come to ask my nanny to be nanny to Joseph Stalin's grandson, little Joe, who had recently been born to Svetlana. And you know what? She refused! She said no to Stalin! We spent months living in terror after that.'

After seventh class Natasha submitted an application to a high school specializing in music, but the school declined the application, without explanation. She was kicked back like a football – that's what she says about herself. Instead, she was sent to a technical school for workers, even though she was an excellent pupil. Then she spent four years on a compulsory work assignment on the production line at a watch factory. And she was accepted as a member of the Komsomol, the young communists' league, but there was no question of her joining the Party.

'Because of my father and the suicide attempt . . . I'd broken something, and as a punishment our foreman forbade me to perform at the factory concert marking the anniversary of the October Revolution. My first public performance, and he wouldn't let me do it. I grabbed a rope and ran out of our department. Everyone raced after me, and

I quickly tied a noose, threw it over a tree, jumped and … the rope snapped. They led me like a goat on a tether right through the entire factory to the manager. He threw me on the sofa and screamed that the entire management team would be put in a prison camp because of me. Do you get it? Someone around me always had to answer for me. Wherever I lived or worked, they would come along and tell someone they were responsible for me. My whole life! It was appalling, because I could never just worry about myself – I had to worry about those who were answerable for me too. My whole life they were watching me.'

In 1953 Stalin died, and Natalia was accepted at the music school she had been longing to attend, though she hadn't applied again. They had been waiting, and now they sent for her. Then came four more years of study and another work assignment, but this time she could choose the location. She chose Kolyma. She can't say why.

After a tiring journey from Penza lasting several weeks by train, steamship and passing lorries, Natasha the young accordion player arrived in the town of Yagodnoye at the very heart of Kolyma. It was five in the afternoon on 23 August 1958 – one year, two months, three weeks and four days after the closure of Dalstroi, the prison-camp gold-mining trust.

'And at ten o'clock the next morning I was questioned by the NKVD, which was called the KGB by then. "You must show your face, work hard and gain standing for yourself." I asked how they knew who I was, and they said they were waiting for me before I even left home. Of course a few weeks later the whole town knew who my father was, so I went even further, to Chukotka, to Pevek, the north-ernmost city in the world. After only a week the manager of my cultural centre sent for me. He had big, round, terrified eyes and he asked if it was true.'

'If what was true?'

'I didn't even ask, and rapidly left for Ayon Island in the East Siberian Sea. I played the accordion in an *agitbrigada*, a propaganda team, though we called it a *kultbrigada*, a culture team. We used to go out into the tundra to perform concerts for collective-farm brigades of reindeer herders, to give people some contact with culture. Songs, recitals, sketches . . . That was my favourite way of life, my best years, but even in that wilderness they came after me to ask how I was behaving. But there was nowhere else to escape to. That was the end of the continent.'

'What about your husband?'

'I haven't got one!' Natalia Nikolayevna bursts out laughing, and of course it ends in a coughing fit several minutes long. 'They were all afraid of me. They didn't want to live with me, or get tied up with me, let alone marry me. All my life I've been on my own, it's awful. I was twenty-seven, and I thought at least I'd have a child. I chose the most handsome man I could find, our film projectionist, an Armenian. He was a good, normal man, but he was married. I told him right away not to worry, because I had no intention of turning his life upside down. I just wanted a child, not a man!'

'What did people say?'

'They didn't say anything at all. In the Soviet era it was quite normal. There was moral freedom. My daughter was born in 1959, sixteen months after I arrived in Kolyma. She's called Zhenya, after my mother Yevgenia. She grew up at workers' collectives, on the road, in the taiga and the tundra, on the trucks and helicopters that took us to the concerts. I adored that job.'

'What about the other woman?'

'His wife?' asks Natalia Nikolayevna. 'I didn't wait for people to gossip. As soon as she got back from leave, I told her everything. There was an awful row, but she calmed down and told me to hand the child over to them. What a nerve! She couldn't have any of her own. She was head of the Pioneers' Centre. Klara Alexeyevna. A Ukrainian. She disliked me intensely. But when he died, and there was nobody to keep us apart, she invited me round for tea, and we came to like each other. She died quite recently. People used to describe her as "a pensioner from the front, a pioneer from behind". She had a plait down to her bum and a great figure.'

'Have you ever been in love?'

'Of course I have! My first sweetheart . . . If it weren't for him, I'd never have written any poems.'

'Such as?' I ask, and she writes her life's creed on a piece of paper.

> I wasn't in a prison camp
> but imposed my own arrest,
> and now I live in Kolyma,
> an exile at my own behest.

'He's my inspiration,' she says. 'An angel. I write for him, but I don't even know if he's still alive. We met in Penza. He was a student at the polytechnic. We couldn't live a single day without each other. And it was like that for three years. Dear Yuri. He didn't know how to kiss. And he wasn't handsome, but I was terribly in love with him. And then finally someone told him, and he disappeared. He took his final exam and vanished. He didn't even say goodbye.'

'Now I know why you chose Kolyma after school, Natalia Nikolayevna. You can't imagine how many people have told me they came here to get as far away as possible.'

'And do you know what the ship that brought me to Kolyma was called? The *Nikolai Yezhov*.'

Day VII

Snezhny, Kilometre 21 of the Kolyma Highway

Today I cut my fingernails. Sixteen days have gone by since I left home.

For a week and a bit I hung around in Moscow, waiting for my press accreditation. I sweetened the pill by taking part in the thirtieth Moscow Peace Marathon. Everywhere else the competitors in these races are fed bananas, chocolate and dried fruit along the route, but in Moscow it's black bread and salt. Every time I eat it I'm reminded of the Russian saying from the 1930s, that white bread on the Black Sea is better than black bread on the White Sea. In those days white bread was a rare delicacy, and the first Soviet prison camps were on the White Sea, but maybe I've got something muddled up, because it seems hopelessly obvious. It would have been much wiser to say I prefer black bread on the Black Sea to white bread on the White Sea. We've lost a subtle play on words . . .

Before leaving home I couldn't do any solid training, so my time wasn't great – three hours, thirty-five minutes and fifty-five seconds. I came in 276th place, forty-fourth in the over-fifties age group.

But I began with my fingernails. I wonder if everybody finds that on trips away their hair and nails grow more slowly? My toenails will probably remain unclipped to the end of the trip, and that will be two and a half or three months.

Finally I'm getting away from Magadan. I haven't gone far, but it's better than nothing. The first driver who picks me up is another Yura. And once again I encounter someone from the criminal world. He refuses to betray his *klichka*, meaning his tag or nickname. I love the richness of Russian slang. It's very rare for a word to have only one equivalent in jargon. A nickname can just as well be a *klikukha*, *pogoniala*, or *pogremukha*.

Yura is a guy who doesn't let rip with the *mat* (that is, doesn't swear), and doesn't use the criminal slang known as *fenya*, though he must be perfectly familiar with it – this is a sign that I'm dealing with the aristocracy.

He takes me to a settlement called Snezhny, to the Komar family's enormous farm. They are people of my age, and they come from Belarus. They're the biggest farmers in Kolyma, but their house is a tiny little crumbling cottage in the middle of a vast open area knee-deep in mud. There's an office there too, the so-called *vagonchik* – 'the trailer'. It's a sort of circus caravan, or rather a PortaKabin, with two little rooms four by five metres each. I spend the night in the one where the woman in charge has her desk. The sofa is only one and a half metres long, but I don't have to stretch out, do I?

Thirteen years ago Sergei Komar bought a dilapidated collective farm without a single cow, pig or hen. He only paid 100,000 roubles for this ruin (about £2000), but he got 64 hectares of personal property, and 3000 hectares that he can put to use. Whatever they may lack in Siberia, there's plenty of land. Now the Komars have more than a thousand head of cattle, and are building a dairy and an abattoir.

The owner employs 150 workers, but they only include three Russians – his wife Tatiana, who is the accountant (when she was forty-eight he sent her to agricultural college in St Petersburg to attend an artificial insemination course), his daughter, who is the manager, and his son, who knows about large, expensive machines. All the rest are contract workers, Uzbeks and Kyrgyz from several villages near the city of Osh in Kyrgyzstan. Not long ago there were some violent feuds between the two communities there, leading to pogroms. In their homeland many of them were neighbours, they know each other and have one single agent, who arranged work for them in Russia. But when the ethnic cleansing began at home, the

Sergei Komar's Uzbek and Kyrgyz workers in the canteen.

Uzbeks ran away to neighbouring Uzbekistan and they are still afraid to go back – these people are incapable of living together. But on neutral Russian ground it's all right, they can forget their traumas and sleep under the same roof, eat from a single pot, and work in harmony.

The farmers bring them in for the summer season, or for an entire year. They buy them return air tickets, feed and house them, and each one gets 25,000 roubles per month (£500). None of the locals is willing to work for so little money. Definitely none of the men. In any case, the Komars prefer teetotal Muslims to boozy Russians. When they hire seasonal workers to pick the potatoes, they never dream of paying in cash, or the next day nobody would come to work. They pay in kind. Of every ten sacks of potatoes picked, one is for the worker, and that's thirty kilos, worth 45 roubles a kilo (the local market price, because the hideous mutants in the Chinese shops are sold for 55). This is a job for which mainly women from Magadan are hired. The strongest ones pick up to thirty sacks per day, so at the end of the day they have three sacks each, which they lug to the bus to go home to the city, more than four thousand roubles richer in kind.

Yura's parents were zeks. His mother was a political prisoner who got eight years for sabotage, known in those days as economic counter-revolution, because two cows which she was looking after at a collective farm had dropped dead. She was fourteen years old, and the cows had an inflammation of the udder.

His father was a common criminal.

'An Odessan.'

'From Odessa!' I say excitedly. 'Jewish?'

'Judging by a picture of my grandmother, his origins were complicated,' says Yura, but I won't write that he tangles me in the silken threads of his smoke-wreathed gaze, because he hasn't got one. Maybe because his grandfather was Ukrainian, and his mother pure Russian. She also had him baptized.

'My father was four years old when he was left on his own,' he continues. 'My grandfather was killed during the Revolution, and my grandmother died of starvation in the 1920s. He became a *brodyaga* [tramp], a Soviet *bezprizornik* [homeless child], a *banditets* [child bandit]. He was barely an adolescent when he ended up in a camp.'

'Why did the criminal prisoners in the camps persecute the political ones?'

'The *blatniye* may be lawbreakers, but they love their country. They were told the politicals were traitors, saboteurs, spies and vermin. The worst scum on earth. Everyone believed it, the whole Soviet Union. But that didn't stop my father from marrying a political. He was born on the coast and he was a tramp, and I was born on the coast, and I started off as a tramp too. Except that he was born on the Black Sea, and I was born on the Sea of Okhotsk. I started as a *karmannik* –'

'From the word *karman*, meaning a pocket,' I confirm. 'In other words, a pickpocket.'

'And a few years later I became an expert *medvezhatnik*.'

'From *medved* meaning a bear, or a large safe.'

'Who'll neatly open any safe, but who won't destroy anything, just find objects and remove them. That's the aristocracy, not like those dreadful thugs who extract protection money from the old biddies at the bazaar with knives and axes. They're the new bandit riff-raff. They're changing our old laws, which were written in blood. Before now a major thief, like me, couldn't have anything of his own, not even a wife, children or a home, because today he was here, but tomorrow he could be in prison or at war in the bandit world, where he could get killed, and the family would suffer.'

'What if someone like that falls in love? And wants to start a family, or have children like everyone else?'

'He has the right to come and say he's leaving. Ceasing to be an *avtorytet*. He can no longer make decisions or be in command. He has respect, but he's discharged from the system.'

'Do you have a family?' I ask Yura.

'Recently the time came for me too. It's tough on your own, just having casual girlfriends. People don't ask my opinion any more, nothing depends on me. But we're on friendly terms, I do help out . . . It's no longer my duty, but I want to. I contribute to the joint fund for my pals, the close friends I've worked with, and the ones who are in prison now. Every *blatnik* should provide his share of every job, every bit of income. There's a special cashier for that, and the *avtorytety* share it out. The main thing is to have something to eat, something to smoke and some tea to drink in the nick.'

'And something to get drunk on, or to shoot into a vein. That comes from your illicit fund too.'

'If someone has to do that, then yes,' says Yura. 'A large number of our lot are heavy drinkers. I used to be like that too. My mates wanted to get me off it, so they put me on a ship which wasn't going to call at a port for a whole year. It was a huge, floating fish-processing boat on the Sea of Okhotsk. You're not allowed to drink there, and there's nothing to drink either. So they thought up this therapy for me, but after a year the ship finally came into port in South Korea, and I went into town with all the others. I thought I was going to die. In a week I swilled down as much booze as I usually drank in a year.'

'And now?'

'I'm free of it. God helped me. Without any therapy, intravenous drips or meetings. I just went to church every day to find the strength, sometimes morning and evening. For half a year it was just home and church. The first time I went to confession, I had all my sins written on sheets of paper. There were twelve of them. It took me ages to read it all out!'

'Did it include taxes?'

'What about them?'

'That you hadn't paid any?'

'Is that a sin? I don't think that was on the list. But there are poor people in our bandit world too, so when I contribute to our fund, you could say it's a sort of tax. I think I'm a little less of a bad man now.'

Day VIII

Kilometre 23 of the Kolyma Highway

I arrive at Kilometre 23 in Valera's twelve-year-old Isuzu Elf 150 van. It's a veteran from Japan, with four-wheel drive, and the steering wheel on the right. Valera stops to give me a lift even though I didn't hail him – I had felt like walking the two stupid kilometres from Snezhny to Kilometre 23.

'Kilometre 23' is the official administrative name of a particular location, as well as the distance along the Kolyma Highway separating this place from the start of the road, in other words Magadan. Round here and all over Russia there are plenty of place names like this one.

There's only one reason for coming to Kilometre 23 – for a visit to the oblast neuropsychology hospital.

But before Valera takes me there, we make a detour into the taiga, where his mother went missing yesterday. She'd gone to pick berries. Earlier today, after spending the night in the woods, the old woman reached a spot within range of the mobile network and called her son. We drive to the place where they have agreed to meet. Valera goes off to find his mother, and I spend several hours waiting by the car, but I'm not complaining, because with me is Tamara Tikhonova, another hitchhiker.

It's not easy to chat to her because she never stops shielding her mouth with her hand. She hasn't any teeth, and it looks as if she's deeply ashamed of it. She's a very thin, wiry, energetic woman, with that something that's instantly recognizable on her face, a youthful fire in her eyes, but she's gone stale, she's been used up by hard work, endless grafting, nagging worries, privations and frequent malnutrition too. She's quite simply been worn out by life, by slogging away with a hoe although she went to music school, studied philology at university, writes poetry and reportage, sings romances, and spent twenty-three years working as a journalist.

Now she has a monthly pension of 10,000 roubles (£200) and has to maintain a twenty-seven-year-old son who's a rake, a lush and a womanizer – so to survive the winter each year she has to pick mushrooms and berries to sell, trade in caviar, and dig up potatoes. Yesterday she set a fantastic record. She picked thirty-eight sacks of potatoes, five more than the strongest man. She could keep four for herself, a whole supply for the coming winter.

Tamara only has one shortcoming – she has inherited her father's aversion to dogs. Aversion is definitely putting it mildly. He has infected her with a phobia, encoded her with uncontrollable fear at the sight of any dog. If it's a German shepherd, Tamara begins to suffocate, and red blotches appear on her face.

A lopsided, playful-looking mongrel sidles up to us, very gentle and flirty, and she screams, 'Get away!' To which I say it's just a puppy, because it's got big paws, floppy ears, it's seven or eight months old at most, but she's begging me to keep it away from her. It hasn't even gone up to her, it's just tussling with me, but she's leaped into the driver's cab, slamming the door shut.

I'm sorry, my mistake – Tamara has one other shortcoming: the same sort of phobia towards black gloves, also inherited from her father.

Valera comes back with his mother, and we're finally on our way to Kilometre 23, to the *psykhushka*, as the psychiatric hospitals are called in Russia.

In the corridor there's a sofa with a sign on it saying: 'Announcement. Dear Visitors, we humbly request you not to sit on the sofa. The

Administration'. I'm extremely curious to know what sort of a sofa it is that you can't sit on.

The ward I'm in was recently transferred from an old building, and hasn't yet been furnished. The sofa is from the manager's room, and is only in the corridor temporarily. What on earth would happen if everybody sat on it?

I'm out of luck. Nobody can talk to me today, because it's Friday, which is doomsday in the hospital. They're bringing some prisoners here under police escort for psychiatric observation, ordered by the courts. But they are letting me stay overnight. They want to give me a bed in the ward for treating depression, and thus among quiet people, but I'd rather sleep on that sofa in the corridor.

Tamara Tikhonova, daughter of Ivan, on the way to the potato harvest.

Whenever one of them put on black gloves, Ivan Tikhonov would scream like a madman: 'Take them off, take them off!' and run out of the house. One of them meaning Tamara, his other daughter Irina, or his wife.

During the war Ivan ended up in Nazi captivity. He escaped, but was caught and transferred to a concentration camp deep inside Germany.

'It was a camp with gas ovens, where they burned people,' says Tamara. 'There was this big, fat wardress there, a tough monster of a woman, a fascist. They would make the prisoners stand in line, then she would put on a pair of leather gloves, take an iron bar and whack each of them in turn. "If you can stay standing, Russki Ivan," she'd say, "you'll live." She called all the Russians "Ivan". Anyone who fell down was carried off to the crematorium. My father was tiny, and always very skinny. He went through this test several times. By some miracle he survived. He was active in the camp resistance movement and escaped twice more. Each time he was caught by the dogs. German shepherds, of course.'

In 1946 Ivan Tikhonov came back to Russia and was sent straight to a Soviet labour camp.

'From one hell to another,' says his daughter. 'There were four million of those poor wretches. Many of them couldn't stand it and went out of their minds, or committed suicide. In the 1990s they let me go through my father's camp records. One of the prisoners informing on him reported that he had said it was easier to survive in the German camp than in ours. The camp NKVD agent summoned my father and recorded a statement: "There we had an enemy, and the hope that once we were freed, we'd gain our liberty. But I'm in a camp again, you're talking to me in Russian, and you, my compatriot, are tearing me to pieces like a dog.'"

That was in 1951, and the next August Ivan left the camp. Apparently his French, German, Polish and Czech comrades from the communist underground in the German camp had begged Stalin himself to set him free. He served six years in the Soviet camp, two more than in Germany.

He was a linguistic genius, and knew seven languages. Before the war he graduated from the elite Moscow Institute of International Relations. He was a translator. He wrote books. He played the guitar, piano and accordion. He never used swear words. The most insulting word he ever used was 'dog'.

TIKHONOVA THE EDITOR – THE
SYNDROME OF SILENCE

'I grew up, finished school, then college, became a journalist, had children, and only when I was thirty-five did I find out where I was born. In a labour camp! Inside the zone! It was my parents' great big, sacred secret. The syndrome of silence. A ban on bringing up the most painful topics, dictated by fear. We weren't the only ones to have it. So did the whole Soviet Union. Why torment yourself when you can't do anything about it?'

Tamara shows me her 'veteran of political repression' booklet. She's probably the world's youngest victim of Stalinist persecution. 'Date of birth: 7 March 1952,' I read in the little box on the first page. 'Deprived of liberty: 7 March 1952. Released: 11 December 1952. Period deprived of liberty: nine months. Rehabilitated: 15 June 2004.'

'How did you find out about it?' I ask.

'By letter. We lived in Yagodnoye, here in Kolyma. My father was a junior official and my mother was a teacher.'

When Tamara finished school, the family moved to European Russia, to Saratov on the Volga, where she went to college. She can't explain it, but something drew her back to Kolyma, to the north. However, it's a closed region, so without permission from the authorities, or a job referral, it was impossible to go there. So she settled above the Arctic Circle, but in Igarka on the Yenisei river. In 1984 they opened up Kolyma. In a few weeks Tamara had packed up her stuff and her children, parted from her husband and flown to Magadan . . .

'Just a moment. Not so fast' – that's me speaking. 'This chapter is about you. What children? What sort of bloke was he?'

'There's nothing to say,' replies Tamara, turning up the corners of her toothless mouth. 'A sailor. Half the year at sea, and when he came home he wouldn't leave the bar for a month. He'd spend a month getting over it, and then he'd be off again. Back to sea. And that was all we'd see of each other. My son was eleven months old, I was three months' pregnant and we went to start a new life in Kolyma. I got a job at the *Severnaya Pravda* [Northern Truth] newspaper. What a wonderful twist of fate! In my hometown, Yagodnoye. Two years later my father sent me a letter. "Go and look for your mother's grave." My mother? I thought my mother was living with him in Saratov! My God! I must have read that letter a thousand times over! I know it by heart to this day.'

In his letter, Tamara's father told her how he had ended up in Kolyma in 1946, how he had been in a column of several thousand prisoners, and about being a prisoner at the Shturmovy labour camp near Yagodnoye. He also wrote that at the women's camp in Elgyen he had met Irina Vasilyevna Stepanova, Komsomol secretary at the polytechnic in Leningrad, who had become 'an enemy of the people' because she hadn't informed on her friends who were involved in spying activities. That was paragraph 12 of Article 58, which was called 'not reporting a crime'; in common parlance 'knowing but not saying'.

Irina had also covered the 531 kilometres from the port at Magadan to Elgyen in a column of female prisoners. It was an experimental march. The Dalstroi management wanted to check whether they could avoid the costly transport of female zeks by motorized vehicle. The same experiment was conducted on the men in the winter of 1938. Of a group of five hundred prisoners, about forty reached the final destination. Of the 2500 women in Irina's column, about five hundred got there. It was late autumn, with a strong gale blowing, and terrible sub-zero temperatures.

'The old, the young, and the city women died on the way,' says Tamara. 'My mother was both young and from the city, but she survived. This story made my heart ache so badly that I couldn't get on with anything else. In his letter my father wrote that he had deliberately encouraged me to study philology so that one day I'd be able to tell this story. I moved to Magadan and wrote historical features, and I made a programme for local television called *Our Fathers' Secrets*, but in our part of the world everyone had soon had enough of these tales, and they didn't want to hear any more about it.'

'Tell me about your mother.'

'It all happened in 1952. I was born in March, and in April my mother was seriously beaten up by the block "elder" – she was an old bandit, of course. My mum ended up in hospital, and in August my father was released. In December my mum handed me over to my dad, who was free. She was afraid that if anything happened to her, I'd be done for. At that time there were some incredible things going on at Elgyen. For four years an anti-Semitic campaign had been raging in the USSR, so Jewish children were being put down like kittens. Also, the children of the gentry, of aristocrats, white officers, factory owners and various rich people were being stolen. The camp governors were doing it. The mothers were murdered by criminal prisoners, and the governors were adopting the orphans as a way of getting hold of the property they had piled up in Swiss banks, in years to come.'

'How do you know?' I ask.

'From the KGB archives. I dug around in 1989 and 1990. They don't let journalists in any more.'

'How come there were so many children in the women's zones?' I ask.

'Do you know how badly starved people were of love? Elgyen was a collective-farm camp. The men came out to see the women prisoners in the fields. And do you know how many children were born of rape? It was often gang rape, or total, mass rape, when the male prisoners bribed the guards and invaded the women's zone or barracks in a drunken horde, raping anyone who tried to run – or didn't – often to death, regardless of age, state of health or looks. The speciality of the criminal prisoners.'

'They called it "choral rape".'

'The whole of Russia was raped in chorus,' says Tamara bitterly. 'And I and all Soviet people are the result of that rape.'

'Tell me about your mother.'

'I looked for her in the security police archives. And I found her. She died in hospital in 1954 at a settlement called Rybny. She didn't live to see freedom. I went there. The old women took me to the cemetery and showed me the grave. That settlement isn't there any more. It died out.'

Two years after Irina's death, Tamara's father got married, and his second daughter was born, to whom he gave the name Irina. They couldn't leave Kolyma, because Ivan Tikhonov was categorized 'with no right to leave'. This was a highly mysterious classification which many zeks were given at their trial, or when they were released from the camps. In practice, it meant a life sentence. The prisoners had no personal identity cards, without which it was impossible to buy tickets for travel in the USSR or within Russia. They only had so-called *spravki* (certificates) confirming their release from the camp, stating where they should live.

'They kept him until 1971,' Tamara tells me. 'Until his retirement. There were lots of people like that in Kolyma, mainly those who came under the first paragraph of Article fifty-eight, so-called traitors to the fatherland, who during the war had served in the Vlasov army [Russian anti-communist forces under Nazi command] or in other military and police units subordinate to the Germans. They were shown no mercy. They were kept in exile until the 1970s, and many of them even until the 1980s.'

'Perhaps your father collaborated with the Germans in the concentration camp?'

'Out of the question! They wouldn't have given him back his medals, his officer's rank, and above all his Party membership card! He would never have been rehabilitated. They restored all that to him in 1961, but they only released him from Kolyma ten years later. It's a mystery.'

Just like his death. In 1994 he left the house in Saratov and disappeared. He vanished without trace.

Tamara too would like to leave Kolyma, but to buy just one small room on 'the mainland' she would have to save her entire pension for ninety years. She has put her name down on Magadan's list of those willing to leave, to whom the governor assigns flats 'on the continent', meaning closer to civilization. She is in 3107th place on the list.

'How many flats do they assign each year?' I ask her.

'Two or three. It's just as if I were here with no right to leave either.'

Day IX

Stekolny, Kilometre 65 of the Kolyma Highway

I'm furious, because I've already been to Palatka, 10 kilometres further on, but I've had to come back to Stekolny at Kilometre 65. Fifty years ago this settlement was at Kilometre 74, and the whole Kolyma Highway was almost two hundred kilometres longer. In recent decades it has got shorter and straighter. It was built with the aid of nothing but picks, shovels and wheelbarrows, so to make things easier the road ran along the hillsides, and was cut out of the slopes, so it was very winding. Now it is being straightened and runs along the bottom of valleys.

It's a long time since I last failed to find a place to stay for the night. I walked about Palatka, asking people where I could stay, putting on a pained expression, but it was impossible. In the end someone at the office of a corporation called Arbat, the property of Alexander Alexandrovich Basansky, gave me a car and driver to Sokol, thirty-four kilometres away, because there's a hotel at Sokol airport. Basansky is the local oligarch, a gold magnate, a Kolyma rich man whom the FSB Colonel Dima (see Day II) affectionately calls 'Basania'. Basania specializes in gold. He has mines and jewellery shops, plus a department store in the centre of Magadan. I tried to meet with him, but today he has flown off by helicopter into the taiga and it's impossible to get in touch with him.

A real millionaire, but his office is just two connected flats in an ordinary, shabby prefab block.

But when they gave me the car, I told them to take me to Stekolny at

Kilometre 65, where there used to be a glassworks (hence the Russian name of the place – *steklo* means 'glass'), where up to two million green bottles used to be made each year. The colour came from copper, because there's an awful lot of it in the local volcanic ash, the main component of the local glass. Many of the Kolyma hills have volcanic origins.

But I'm not going to Stekolny because of the bottles. In 1943 they opened a unit at the glassworks where they renovated burned-out light-bulbs.

The glassworks is no longer there. It collapsed in the 1990s, like most of Kolyma's industry, and the settlement went after it. Of five thousand residents, only two thousand have stayed. And sometimes it's 1999 people, or worse yet, 1998, but it only matters to the chairman of the *poselyok* administration (a *poselyok* is a settlement, an administrative unit in between a village and a town). Two thousand residents is the lowest population figure above which the chairman receives a salary of 54,000 roubles per month. If there are fewer residents, he only gets 40,000 (£800). Alexander Nevmerzhitsky, the present chairman, used to be a PE teacher and a judo trainer. The only instance known to me of a statue of Lenin being brought down in Russia took place during his term of office in Stekolny. Lenin's statue is still standing in Moscow to this day, more than one of them. But here they pulled it down. The electorate resisted, especially the older people, and most of all the women, but Alexander stuck to his guns. Get it off the pedestal! He said that after repairs the revolutionary leader would be able to return, but for the time being there was no money to give him a facelift.

This Lenin was made of plaster, painted silver, and stood in the main square of the settlement outside the local administration and cultural centre. After coming down from the plinth, it made its way to the regional administrative centre, Palatka, where they took it in with open arms at the headquarters of the local Communist Party. But there too it was in the way, because whoever heard of a statue standing indoors, in an apartment? What's more, a statue of the leader of the peace-loving Soviet nation, which no longer exists. So the plaster Vladimir Ilyich Ulyanov, aka Lenin, went back to Stekolny and is kicking around in a warehouse at the former glassworks (the one that made the light-bulbs). Next to the warehouse there are several former camp barracks. They're miserable constructions – two layers of wooden planks with insulation made of sawdust or moss in between them. They're some of the last remaining buildings from the Gulag Archipelago, but people are still living in them. For greater warmth they have 'plastered' them in clay mixed with straw.

Irina lives in one of the last prison-camp barracks left in Kolyma.

The light-bulb-renovating unit at Stekolny was a bit like Kolyma's version of a sanatorium. *Dokhodyagi* were sent there – criminal slang for zeks suffering from muscular dystrophy caused by starvation, goners who had reached the limits of human endurance. They no longer had the strength to drag their feet along, but somehow it took them ages to die, even on 'penalty' bread rations (for failing to achieve the work norm) of 300 grams per day. A *dokhodyaga*, also known as a 'wick' (because the last remains of life were burning down in him), was the equivalent of a *Muselmann* in a Nazi camp.

But even someone that weak can reconnect burned-out tungsten filaments. You drill a hole in the light-bulb, and patch it up afterwards. This sort of light-bulb doesn't work for long, but even so the invention brought immense savings, because light, and thus electrical energy and light-bulbs, were as strategic a product for this region as barbed wire and the prison guards' guns. Except that the wire and guns hardly ever got used up.

Let's just think about it. There were 160 Kolyma camps with hundreds of metres of wire-fenced, illuminated zones, hundreds, or maybe thousands, of illuminated barracks, guard turrets with floodlights, endless mine corridors and pit faces which had to be lit too. That's thousands, millions, tens of millions of light-bulbs with a wattage ranging from 100 to 1000.

The technique was invented in 1943 by a prisoner called Kipreyev. Engineer Kipreyev was a brilliant scientist from the Kharkov Institute of Physics and Technology, who in cooperation with Igor Kurchatov (known as the father of the Soviet atom bomb) tried to solve the mystery of nuclear reaction in the 1930s.

In Kolyma Kipreyev invented a way of renovating light-bulbs, for which NKVD General Ivan Nikishov, in command of Dalstroi, received the Order of Lenin.

Although he was only a slave, a talking instrument, Kipreyev became head of the renovation unit at Stekolny. Shortly before the end of his five-year sentence, a celebration was organized in honour of all the bosses involved in the invention. They were showered with medals, and each one got a wonderful package from the Lend-Lease programme, American war aid for the Land of Soviets as it fought against the Germans. This was the object of desire of every Soviet small-scale bigwig – a suit, a tie, a shirt and a pair of thick-soled red-leather boots. There was a package for Kipreyev too, but he refused to accept it, saying he didn't need American cast-offs. For this he was immediately arrested (yes, you could be arrested while already a prisoner) and got eight more years added to his sentence (for anti-Soviet propaganda). A witness stated that Kipreyev had said that Kolyma was Auschwitz without the ovens. He ended up in a very tough camp for recidivists. He survived, and after serving his full sentence he voluntarily remained in Kolyma for the rest of his life.

Alexander Nevmerzhitsky was born in 1955, but he has a perfect memory of those people.

'We only had one bathhouse for the whole settlement. The day when our house's turn came was the finest day of the week for me. I loved looking at the undressed men. Half of them had their life stories inscribed on their skin – war scars or prison tattoos. They often talked about them, and I would listen in. It was a thrilling experience.'

Alexander has a vivid memory of the two Vladimirs who lived in his house. They both had war scars and prison tattoos, but there, apart from their names, the likeness ended. They were like fire and water – irreconcilable.

But fate, or perhaps the mindlessness, the soullessness, of Soviet officialdom led to them being billeted in the same communal flat, which meant they had a shared hallway, kitchen and toilet. The problem was that one of them had been a Belarusian policeman in the service of the Nazis, fighting partisans and pacifying remote villages, while the other had been a Belarusian partisan. There were no two more ardent adversaries in the entire history of the Second World War.

Both fell into the clutches of the enemy. Vladimir the partisan was a prisoner of the Nazis, and Vladimir the policeman was a prisoner of the Soviets. The partisan was freed in 1945. A few months later he was arrested and sent to Kolyma, where Vladimir the policeman had already spent a year.

They were both well over 1.9 metres tall, so in theory, after ending up in a gold mine, they should have only survived a few weeks or months. In the Gulag it was the rule that a normal, full-sized company horse got more fodder than a little Yakut pony. With people it was different. The rations didn't take the size of a man into consideration. This meant that the small, skinny intellectuals lived longer than the big workmen and peasants, who were used to physical labour. Size mattered; the bigger the man, the quicker he died.

But the Vladimirs survived. The partisan was freed in 1953 during the mass liberation following Stalin's death. For the policeman, as for all traitors, deserters and Vlasov army men, there was no mercy. They had to serve their full sentence, usually a very long one. In Kolyma there were about three thousand of these prisoners, who remained to the end of the 1950s in the camps. In time they were let out, because the camps were gradually closed down, but they had no right to return to the European part of the Soviet Union.

So Vladimir the policeman came to live in a communal flat with

Vladimir the partisan. They both started families, and one had a daughter, the other a son.

'And when the children grew up,' Chairman Alexander tells me, 'they fell madly in love with each other. Whereas their fathers always went for each other with axes whenever they got drunk.'

'Shakespeare couldn't have thought up a better plot.'

'Definitely not. Because it was vodka that finally made peace between them, not the children. They both drank themselves to death, and the young people got married and they're still living here among us to this day.'

'Are there any stories like that in your family too?' I ask.

'My father-in-law had been a prisoner of the Germans. He had a medal for Stalingrad, but it didn't save him from the Soviet camps. I wanted to commemorate these people. Last year we put up a memorial in honour of victims of the Second World War, and I thought it should also be a monument to victims of Stalinist repression, but most of the residents didn't agree. They held a referendum. Amazingly, it was the women who objected the most. So the monument is only for the seventy-four residents of Stekolny who were killed on the faraway European Fronts. To make sure, the people had their names carved on the stone. And in the camp section of our cemetery there are about fifteen hundred zeks' graves. Half of them were Red Army soldiers too, but they were captured, and then sent to the prison camp nearby.'

Day X

Sokol. Kilometre 49 of the Kolyma Highway

What a great day. I'm in Sokol, at Magadan's airport, even further south than yesterday. They've driven me in the wrong direction away from Palatka again, because there's a hotel in Sokol with the world's most expensive Internet connection, as far as I know – 500 roubles (£10) per hour. It's the fourth time I've travelled this stretch of the Highway now (and soon there's going to be a fifth).

But one thing at a time. This morning I set off from Stekolny, heading for Palatka, and along comes the driver who took me there yesterday evening. So I get in his car, and the guy lets slip that Alexander Basansky, the Kolyma gold king, is back from the taiga. Great!

The oligarch wants to receive me at once, but he's very busy. He promises to devote the entire day to me tomorrow, and has me taken to the hotel in Sokol.

I'm as furious as a rabid dog as I make the thirty-four-kilometre journey back to Sokol, but then at the hotel I discover something truly phenomenal.

Damn – I'd promised myself I wouldn't bother with odds and ends of history, sad tales of martyrdom and desperate reminiscences of the camps, but what am I to do, when here, standing before me, is a real, live Russian aristocrat? And in Russia that's a greater rarity than a Siberian tiger or a snow leopard.

And so here is Marianne Igoryevna Juquelier, née Verigina. A lady, a thoroughbred noblewoman, as you can hear and see with the naked eye, but she's no shrinking violet. Madame Marianne has come to Kolyma on her own. She is a representative of the old, pre-Revolution Russian émigrés. She speaks with a very slight French accent, because for sixty-three years she has been living in France, but conversation with her is a luxury, like reading Leo Tolstoy in the original.

Her family was exiled from Russia by Tsar Nicholas II after the 1905 Revolution. They settled in Finland. Madame Marianne's father was an émigré activist, a staunch opponent of the Bolsheviks and of Stalin, and during the Soviet–Finnish war of 1939–40 he was fully committed to defending his new homeland. He served at the Front as a volunteer, working as an interpreter.

But the Finns surrendered to the Soviet Goliath and signed a humiliating agreement with it, as a result of which they had to hand over part of their territory and sovereignty, as well as a group of the Soviet Union's greatest enemies of Russian origin.

Madame Marianne was five years old in April 1945, when at three in the morning two NKVD agents entered their flat in Helsinki, accompanied by some Finnish policemen. They searched the flat, and took away her father.

By the afternoon of that same day her father was already in Moscow's Butyrka Prison. Then he was locked up in the infamous Vladimir Prison outside Moscow. A year later a letter came, in which Igor Verigin wrote to his wife that one of his arrested comrades had been shot, and the rest were probably going to die too, so they should get divorced. And so it was.

A few years later his ex-wife and daughter left for France, where after a few more years Marianne met Marc, the love of her life.

They had plenty of love, as well as wealth, a successful business, three happy children, and a very faint sense of something missing. Madame Marianne took up a job at a hospice, so four years ago, when

Marc was diagnosed with liver cancer, he had wonderful professional care at home. But he refused treatment. He didn't want chemotherapy. They both agreed that what matters is not how long your life is, but how beautiful. They spent their final weeks together skiing in Finland, but when Marc died, Madame Marianne lost the ground under her feet. She didn't know what to do in life, where to live, or even who she was – a Frenchwoman, a Russian, or perhaps a Finn?

She decided to go to Kolyma. She wanted to search for traces of her father, and to gather her thoughts. It is the most extraordinary story I've heard here – and every story I hear in Kolyma is more extraordinary than the one before.

Madame Marianne spent a year and a half preparing for her journey, and now she finds everything here immensely to her liking. Everything here? Apart from nature there's nothing likeable here at all. Almost everything man-made is hideous. Magadan and all the settlements scattered along the Highway consist of nothing but large, ugly, messy tower blocks, but she, a Parisian, is delighted.

She's mesmerized by the magical light of the north, the colours of the larch trees, the Indian summer, and the beautiful, sunny autumn weather.

After spending the day together Madame Marianne and I come to an agreement on this matter. Here there is spirit without beauty, and there, in her French homeland, there is beauty without spirit.

The picture on Igor Verigin's grave.

VERIGIN THE CONVICT AND THE
COLLECTIVE-FARM WORKER WIFE

In 1955 Mademoiselle Marianne received a letter from the USSR. It was from her father. She and her mother had been sure he was dead, but now, ten years on, they discovered that for a year he had been free. He had been given a ten-year sentence, and was sent to Kolyma. They had released him a year before the end of the sentence, because he had promised to stay in the USSR and take Soviet citizenship. He had wanted to go to Moscow, but they wouldn't let him do that.

'At the end of the letter my father wrote that he had married,' says Madame Marianne. 'A woman called Zoya Ivanovna. I don't know her surname.'

'Surely it was Verigina?'

'My God! My father also wrote that the woman had a son, Mikhail, and that they were giving him the surname Verigin too. Mama was outraged, and told me to write a letter to my father, saying you couldn't give your surname to just anyone like that. Our surname! Mama used to make me lovely little dresses. She chose one and sent it with the letter.'

'What was that supposed to mean?' I ask.

'I'm not entirely sure. I was fifteen years old. My father replied, telling her not to write such awful things. "It's too complicated, but one day you'll understand me." My mother destroyed the letter and all the rest that followed. I was terribly upset, I even tried to commit suicide.'

'Could your father come and see you?'

'I think so. A year or two later he could have left the Soviet Union, but he didn't want to. Now that I've come here, I finally understand. He loved Russia. In one of his letters he wrote to me that when he was in prison he asked the guard to bring him all of Lenin's books, and he did. The light was on day and night, so my father was able to read almost without interruption. He wanted to understand what he'd been fighting against all his life.'

After his release from the prison camp, Igor Verigin became head bookkeeper at a fish-processing plant, producing tinned fish, and in the evenings he performed at the Magadan People's Theatre, because the theatre was the great passion of all the Verigins. He and Zoya did not have any children. He died in 1968 and was buried at the old Magadan cemetery. The funeral was arranged jointly by the managers of the factory and the theatre. On his grave they put a typical gravestone with a portrait and a red star at the top, such as one could buy at any scrap metal yard.

'I spoke to Tamara Igoryevna, who acted with Papa at the theatre,' says Madame Marianne. 'He was a good soul, she said. The leader of the local intellectuals. Good and gentle, with great class. Because that wife of his . . . Very Soviet, severe. I've seen pictures of her. The collective-farm type. A Soviet worker.'

'Not an aristocrat.'

'Not a bit. My grandmother and aunt, who lived in Moscow, actually received her as a guest when she went there after Papa's death. They said she was such a – peasant. She died in Leningrad ten years after my father. Her daughter-in-law, who lives in Magadan, says that Zoya was cremated when she died, then her son brought her ashes here and unofficially buried them in Papa's grave. And why not? Let her lie there.'

'It sounds as if she loved your father very much.'

'Very much,' says Madame Marianne. 'And after the camps he needed someone badly. I can understand that. Her son drank himself to death in 1995. He was forty-seven. He had left his wife and child earlier on.'

'And what are you doing today, Madame Marianne?'

'I'm waiting for the evening flight to Moscow. Then I'm off to Paris.'

'So may we go to Magadan, to the cemetery once again?'

'Wonderful. Minibus Number One will take us there.'

MADAME MARIANNE — THERE IS NO DEATH

'When I was here yesterday, I met a woman in tears,' says Madame Marianne, leading me down the cemetery paths. 'I asked what was wrong, and she said they'd killed him. She was a mother. They'd killed her only child. Bandits. She'd brought her son beer, sausage, sweets and cigarettes—'

'She'd brought him breakfast.'

'There are containers of food and drinks on the graves all over this place. When we tidied up Papa's grave, Tamara from the theatre took two of those cups, washed them and gave us tea. Then we left them on the spot.'

'Poor people come here to eat.'

'So do dogs,' says Madame Marianne. 'While we were drinking our tea, one of them came along. They all look like wolves here – big and dangerous, wild and mistrustful, but this one lay down near us and began to whine. He was crying, softly, but awfully. "What's the matter?" I asked him, but he didn't answer. I gave him something to eat, he took it and went off. When I went back, I found him lying in the main avenue, dead. He wasn't injured.'

'His time had come. And he was whimpering because he could already see death. Dogs can see it.'

'Possibly.'

'Definitely,' I say. 'In my former life I was a dog, so I know.'

'And the first time I came here I could feel that Papa wasn't in here.' Madame Marianne points to an old rowan tree near her father's grave. 'He was standing over there. I talked to him quite normally, just as I'm talking to you now. I said: "Your daughter's come, are you pleased?" And he said he was very pleased – "I've missed you terribly." I know he's been helping me here every step of the way – at the offices and archives, and at the police.'

'Were you afraid?' I ask.

'Why should I be? It was my papa. I very often talk to the dead. I can see them. I have a large number of friends in the other world, because I spent ten years working at a hospice. I talked to my father for ages. During that time I was absent, I'd gone off to that other world. Tamara, who was with me, said it was almost as if I had disappeared, become blurred in mid-air.'

'What does your father look like? Like the portrait on his grave, or as you remember him from childhood?'

'He's the spitting image of my son,' says Madame Marianne. 'I'd recognize that long, thin Verigin nose anywhere. It's exactly the same as in the seventeenth-century family portrait that's hanging in the Tretyakov Gallery in Moscow. Papa is forty years old, like all the dead. In the other world everybody stops at that age. That's how the world is arranged. All my friends from the hospice are forty now. It's wonderful to see them young, strong and healthy. When my mama was dying, I saw her sister and my grandmother, who had been dead for many years. They were sitting beside us, waiting for my mother. I told her they were there and that she was going to join them. And when she took her last breath, breathed her last sigh, she simply left her body and went off. She flew off to the other side.'

'To join her mother and sister.'

'She didn't even look at me. I thought it was my imagination, my psyche playing tricks on me. I told a very wise, old priest about it, and he said there are people who see ghosts. Since then I've known that life continues. There is no death.'

'And do they say that in Kolyma, Madame Marianne? This is a place where death has reaped thousands at a single blow. Like nowhere on earth.'

'That's why I feel a very strong, powerful energy here. It's emanating from every hill, every paving stone, like a pillar of light. I can feel all the bones that are lying here, the blood that has soaked into the ground. An immense energy.'

'Negative energy!'

'Nothing of the kind,' replies Madame Marianne. 'It's positive energy. There are good spirits watching over this land. Here the bones are even lying on the roads, just under the asphalt, yet we can walk over them. Even I can. Now I can go back to Paris and live out the rest of my life quietly. I am an entirely different person now. My soul is at peace, because I know my father died a happy man. I have closed the book of my life. That is a great joy.'

Day XI

Sokol. Kilometre 49 of the Kolyma Highway

This day cannot be described on a piece of paper smaller than a map of Russia on a scale of 1:100,000 (and that's a sheet as big as a parachute). Sky-high similes, I know, but I've just flown here – virtually. And I'm smashed. The fact that I got drunk is nothing, but the guy who drove me here ... Horrors! He raced along at 190 kilometres an hour, as excited as a kid on a roller coaster. Of course there was no question of wearing seat belts. He quite simply wouldn't let me do it up.

He drove at that speed along the Kolyma Highway, which as far as Palatka is still concrete or asphalt, but even so it undulates like the Sea of Okhotsk in a strong wind. Every road built on permafrost ripples like that. The earth partly defrosts each year, and then freezes again, so it shifts, and the whole road moves with it. I wonder how the Canadians cope.

I'd already had a curious night. I was sleeping in a twin room with a stranger (it's quite normal here for them to add company to your room), and the man got up in the middle of the night and started 'walking' his hands along the walls. He got as far as a mirror in the hall, took it down and 'walked' on. I'd never seen a somnambulist before. But what if he was a lunatic who was going to suffocate me in my sleep with a pillow? I got up, took him gently by the arms and calmly led him back to bed like a child. In the morning he couldn't remember a thing.

After breakfast I'm off to Palatka again. It's my third day trying to hunt down Basansky, the gold oligarch, who has sent a car for me (it's the fifth time I've travelled this stretch of the road to this town). We meet, and the oligarch loads me into his *kruzak* (a huge Land Cruiser V8, registration number 00300 – he boasts that the police have no right to stop it) and we race to his restaurant, Khutor, in Magadan (my sixth journey along the road between Palatka and Sokol).

It's a tremendously expensive eatery, lavishly furnished, but completely empty. And right there, in a room set aside for the exclusive use of the owner, I witness yet another ritual – a whole series of strange scenes.

Like this one, for instance. Basansky's phone battery runs down, so he looks for a new, charged-up one, but he can't find it. He bemoans the fact that he has millions of roubles, but he hasn't got a battery, and to prove it, while apparently looking for the spare one, he takes some plastic-wrapped bundles of cash out of his briefcase. There must be millions of roubles in there! Why the hell does he carry that briefcase around with him all day?

At his restaurant my host plainly feels like a pig in clover ... What am I saying? Like a god in heaven. He adores basking in his wealth, and hasn't yet had his fill of it. But he hasn't got the fanciful urge to go off skiing at Courchevel with an army of tarts, or buy a royal yacht, or a football club. Steaks, caviar, appetizers, deluxe vodkas, gold watches and hunting trips are enough for him ... And driving at breakneck speed in his Land Cruiser. Bloody hell, he's got everything! But he needs spectators, an entourage, a public.

I spend all day being that audience.

For all that, he is a very secretive, self-contained, mysterious person. I have to steal information from him, spy on him, work it all out for myself. The only personal items he shows me are the scars all over his body, but how he got them he won't say. He fought in Afghanistan and Angola, as a high-ranking officer in the Soviet special services. He is a retired lieutenant-colonel of combat units in the GRU, the military intelligence corps of the USSR and the Russian Federation. In Russia, the millionaire businessmen are as often as not from intelligence – you can only get into the oligarchs' club via the secret service.

Basansky comes from Ukraine, he is a mining engineer, and as befits the Kolyma gold king, a quarter of his teeth are made of that precious metal – to be precise, the entire upper right side of his dentition. He has two open-cast mines and one under ground, mining gold and silver ores, and three large companies sluicing gold sand at seven enormous gold-bearing plots. In Russia they're called 'polygons'. He employs 800 workers, of whom 550 are miners. In 2010 they extracted 1.2 tonnes of gold and 23 tonnes of silver, worth two billion roubles (£40 million). Every month Basansky pays two million dollars in taxes, though he doesn't hold his spoon in three fingers the way everybody else does, but in his entire fist.

All day long his phone is red-hot. It rings non-stop. Basansky is constantly running things, issuing orders, giving instructions, and making inquiries ... He summons Igor Dontsov to the restaurant, a deputy to the oblast parliament (Basansky himself is its deputy chairman), to put their friendship on show for me. Dontsov ranks Number Three in Kolyma in terms of wealth and range of business interests. He builds roads, catches fish, and obtains caviar. Basansky ranks second, and first among gold prospectors.

Then comes the drunken drive back to Palatka. Basansky races along as if seeking death, mainly on the left-hand side of the road as well, even when he's going uphill and round corners, and even though the right lane is completely empty. Why does he drive like that? Because the right-hand side belongs to him anyway, so he's got to conquer the other one. He's got to take possession of it. Literally, to 'take it under him', as they say here. Just as a dog takes a bitch, a man in need takes a whore and a *blatnik* takes a sucker from the next cell. It's a concept of control. The guy who accepts this sort of deal 'lies down' under the taker, and if he doesn't, there'll be war. And in principle there's nothing you can't 'take under yourself': a public office, a governing body, a company, a town, or a person. Including a journalist. And even the road.

When we were going in the opposite direction, before all the drinking, Basansky drove the car just the same way, maybe a touch more slowly.

The gold oligarch Alexander Basansky (right) and his friend Igor Dontsov.

I ask for coffee, and as usual I have a problem because the cup is small and the sugar lump is big, so I try to break it in half, but I can't do it. I ask Basansky to do it for me, because the guy's as tough as a bridge support. He manages quite easily.

'That's another test,' says the oligarch. 'It's obvious you graduated from the intelligence academy. You're testing me the whole time.'

'What do you mean? I just couldn't break it in half.'

'Nonsense,' he replies. 'Who takes so little sugar?'

'I do.'

'But I live in Russia and you can't fool me. You even noticed that the ashtray is stamped with my sign, and that I'm a Taurus, born in May.'

'I'm a reporter. I pay attention to details. I was born like that.'

'You cannot be born like that. They teach it at schools for agents. We'll drink one more bottle of vodka and I'll find out what rank you are. But for now let's drink to friendship between nations.'

So we drink. It's Beluga, the most expensive of the local vodkas – 2100 roubles a bottle (£42). My host takes care to make sure that in keeping with Russian tradition I leave nothing in my glass. We drink an equal amount, except that he is almost twice as strong as I am.

We snack on Sea Wave crab salad for 420 roubles and tuck into my favourite Russian soup, solyanka, for 440. The menu has thirty-three pages. The most expensive dish is stuffed fish for 1600 roubles, two hundred more than a glass of the most expensive cognac, but I order blinis with caviar for 280, because I love them.

We have another drink, and Basansky pulls up his trouser leg to show me a scar on his calf. Then he pulls up his other trouser leg, and takes off his shirt. There are several scars in a line on his back – from a burst of machine-gun fire.

'They recruited me when I was still at technical college,' he tells me. 'They needed guys who did sport, and I was a keen boxer. Then I turned out to be an excellent shot. There wasn't a single mission where I ever met a man who was a better shot than I am. I'm able to shoot guided by hearing alone. From fifty metres I can smash a bottle that's swinging on a string.'

'Dersu Uzala could cut that bottle off its string with a single shot.'

'Not bad! Is he in your unit?' says the oligarch, taking an interest.

'No, he's in literature – yours, in fact. Vladimir Arsenyev wrote a book about him, and Kurosawa made the film.'

'When President Putin awarded me a medal in 2007 for my business success, he shook my hand and said: "Our people are always at the top."'

'He's an agent too,' I say, 'but from the KGB.'

'Vladimir Vladimirovich Putin is my idol and model. I am an active supporter of the United Russia Party. I have stood three times in elections to the oblast parliament on United Russia's list. Last time I got sixty-six per cent of the votes, more than all the other deputies in Kolyma put together. In a couple of weeks we're going to win the election too. And we bloody well won't surrender the victory to anyone. None of those communists, opportunists and populists. Over my dead body! Let's drink!'

'How did you get the wounds on your back?'

'You what? So do you work for intelligence or a newspaper? There was some fighting. Always fiercest in Kandahar. We were few, they were a swarm. And we completed our assignment with honour.'

'Is there anything you fear?' I ask him.

'Yes, that I've put on weight. And after all those wounds and general anaesthetics, towards evening my eyes are a bit blank. Meaning I can't see as well. But let's drink to Polish–Russian relations.'

Igor Dontsov arrives, Basansky's deputy friend. They yarn away about money, business and the forthcoming elections. They establish which of them is the more powerful.

'With your monthly income of two million dollars you're the richest candidate in the elections,' says Dontsov. 'I come second, and Volodya Khristov from Susuman is third, but if you add share dividends to that income, then I'm first.'

'My cash reserves are immense,' says Basansky, makes a call and switches on the speakerphone. 'Irina, how much credit did we get recently from Sberbank?'

'Four hundred and ten million dollars,' replies a woman's voice. 'No, sorry, four hundred and twenty million.'

'And by the way,' says Dontsov, 'there's a deal to be done. A delegation of businessmen has come to see us from St Petersburg. They're looking for a present for their governor, because it's his birthday at the end of October. They went to your jewellery showroom, but everything there is too modest for them.'

'In a week there'll be a gold cup full of nuggets,' says Basansky, and over the phone he instructs someone to bring a copy of this souvenir to the restaurant. 'We only make them to order. The price depends on how many nuggets we throw in. The last cup cost one hundred and three thousand dollars.'

'Oh, that would suit them very well. So let's have one for the road – I've got to get going now, I've got a lot of travelling ahead of me. God grant you good health, Alexander.'

We drink up. Basansky checks to see if I've left anything in my glass, says goodbye to Dontsov and summons a man by phone, who for several hours while we've been chatting has been waiting in the Magadan office, next door to the restaurant.

The man is forty-seven, the same age as Basansky, but he's small, thin and worn out, with a sort of cross-eyed honesty in his face. He's instantly likeable, even though he has no teeth, his ugly face is covered in old scars, and his hands in tattoos – and not just the sort of wimpy tats free people have, but typical army or prison scrawls. He fought in Afghanistan too, and has probably been in more than one jail.

The story is this. (But let's have a drink first.) So the story is that Basansky bought a ten-year licence to mine gold over an immense area on the eastern coast of the Kolyma Gulf. It's an entire peninsula between the Obo and Congo streams. There's a sea of gold in there. The oligarch has already bought a ship, because that's the only way to get there. The problem is that Mr Honesty here has a tiny three-man lumber-and-sawmill business on that territory, so he has come to ask the potentate to let him live, and not to destroy him. It's not as if they're in competition, and Basansky hasn't bought the whole peninsula, just a licence to mine it.

'Well, I don't know . . . ,' says the potentate, scratching his head. 'My directors are in favour of resettling everyone, every last man. But somehow I can't do that. First I want to meet with the people, and then I'll decide. Because most of all we like to have our terrain to ourselves. And that's probably what will happen this time too, because we've got colossal reserves of cash, and that solves all sorts of problems.'

'Ho-how-how's that?' stammers Mr Honesty.

'We can come to an agreement, pay a bribe or buy someone out. Whenever there's a prospecting firm standing in our way, I buy it, and we make the former owners directors. That's our system. There's also the method involving force.'

Basansky has a very powerful security service, in which he employs former KGB and FSB agents, as well as ex-members of the Ukrainian Berkut Spetsnaz (special forces) unit, the equivalent of the SAS. The former Ukrainian president Viktor Yushchenko had this unit disbanded, because it had supported his rival during the Orange Revolution at the end of 2004, when public protests against a rigged election result led to Yushchenko coming to power. Now they are the armed wing of the Arbat corporation.

BASANSKY THE ENGINEER — A RUSSKI MIDAS

Alexander — Sasha — Basansky is a boy from a farm in Dikhanka, in Ukraine's Poltava oblast. He came to Kolyma as a twenty-one-year-old veteran of the Afghan war. He was a simple locksmith, then a master one, then a mechanic, and three years later he finished night school and was instantly made chief mechanic at the Karamkinsky Mining Conglomerate. That's the sort of power to build a career (interrupted by long and frequent journeys abroad for combat missions) which the Soviet special services had.

After a year Basansky became director of the conglomerate, and the year after that he bought it. He was twenty-seven years old.

'Where did you get the money to buy an enormous open-cast gold mine?' I ask. 'After working for only six years?'

'I was a rationalizer. I patented twelve inventions and submitted eighty-seven proposals for rationalization. For each proposal I got six thousand old Soviet roubles, and that's serious money. At that time a worker here earned four hundred, and a director nine hundred, roubles a month. A Zhiguli cost five and a half thousand roubles. But I didn't buy cars, just lottery tickets for all I had, sometimes for as much as twenty thousand. I used to carry the coupons away from the sales point in suitcases. And the prize money can be enormous. I earned a vast amount of money like that.'

'Are you trying to tell me you earned the money to buy a gold mine through gambling?'

'No, through rationalization. And I gambled, but it's the rule for me that whatever I do, I'm successful. Always. Even the time I went to Gdańsk with the governor as part of an official delegation – they all went off to dinner with our hosts, while I went to the casino and cleaned it out completely. That was the first and last time I have ever been to a casino. I didn't even collect all my winnings, because they didn't have enough hard currency, and what use would zlotys be to me? I only played the lottery for three years. It doesn't tempt me. I have immense willpower.'

In a few years the deposits at his mine were exhausted, so he closed it down and bought a drinks production line in Poland. He was the first man in Kolyma to sell drinks in plastic bottles, so he gained control of the entire market at lightning speed.

'I sold twenty-six kinds of sweetened water for a million dollars a month,' he recalls. 'I earned a clear forty million dollars that way. On water and sugar. And when others started doing the same, I sold it all and invested the money in mining. Privatization was going at full steam. I bought the mines when an ounce of gold cost two hundred dollars on world markets. Today it costs more than fifteen hundred, and it's still rising. In 2010 the price shot up thirty-five times, and the Russian central bank kept on buying and buying. From 2007 to 2009 it increased the country's gold currency reserve from one hundred and twenty-one billion dollars to five hundred and sixty billion. What will you have for dessert? I'm going to have cherry dumplings with kiwi-flavoured ice cream, and *syrniki* [pancakes made with soft white cheese] with *sgushchonka* [sweetened condensed milk]. I love sweets.'

'I'll pass on dessert.'

'Have you got any passions?' asks the oligarch.

'Work, sport, I like to have a drink, to be on the road, to make love—'

'Well, quite,' he says, livening up. 'What about your women?'

'Nothing too modern – just the one wife.'

'The ice-cream flavours are fruit, cream, coffee, chocolate—'

'I only eat vanilla.'

'You poor guy. Come on, let's drive into town.'

His true nature emerges after drinking. He hoots at everyone like a man possessed, hurls insults, opens the window and screams abuse at the entire street. Even at women. He goes looking for fights, and he breaks all the traffic rules. I get the impression he doesn't do it for convenience, or out of carelessness, but out of obligation, so that his right to do whatever he wants won't be wasted.

We go back to Palatka (my seventh journey along this stretch of the road). I fetch my backpack, which I left there, and Basansky drives me to the hotel in Sokol (that's my eighth!).

On the way, over the phone, he discusses action to be taken against a man whom he calls 'a rat'. He almost takes his foot off the accelerator out of sheer emotion.

'He's got to be dealt "the full programme" with FSB assistance,' I hear him say. It's to do with settling a score between businessmen, but it only involves a small sum, just one and a half million roubles (£30,000), not even half a cupful of nuggets.

We say goodbye, and as a souvenir Basansky tosses me a nugget, which he took from a display case at his jewellery showroom on Karl Marx Street. It's almost pure gold, more than twenty carats, a stone weighing 8.81 grams from the Berelokh river.

I try to ward him off and get away, but there's no escaping him.

'I can't!' I shout at him. 'I don't want it, I'm not allowed—'

'Give it a rest!' he says, and forces the stone into my pocket. 'You're an agent, not a journalist. You can take it.'

PART TWO

Battlefield Syndrome

My life is set in this far place
And lived in silence, by God's will
For I have seen Cain face to face
And could not bring myself to kill.

V.P. Tarnovsky, quoted by Alexander Solzhenitsyn in
The Gulag Archipelago (translated by Harry Willetts)

And now for a joke, a paradox of history. The explorer who discovered Kolyma, its unusual geological qualities and unimaginable, inexhaustible riches, was a Pole called Jan Czerski, a freedom fighter exiled to Siberia for taking part in the January Uprising of 1863, which aimed to win Polish independence from the Russian empire. He was the first European to travel across this boundless wasteland. In 1924 the Russians honoured him with the most splendid natural monument in the world, something not even Lenin himself ever got. This particular memorial is 1500 kilometres long, 200 kilometres wide, and more than three kilo-metres high. Its highest peak bears the derisive name Pobieda – meaning 'victory'. He also got a second, slightly smaller, mountain range in Transbaikal, the mighty Chersky Peak in the eastern Sayan Range, a lake, a valley, a waterfall, a boulder at the source of the Angara river, a street in Moscow, a crustacean in the order of Amphipoda endemic to Lake Baikal, and the town of Chersky on the lower Kolyma river, where in 1892, in the arms of his Russian wife and son, he gave up the ghost. He was buried there too.

It was on the slopes of the Chersky Range that forty years later the camps and gold mines were established which were to be the graves of millions, 'which under the name Kolyma,' as Ryszard Kapuściński writes in *Imperium*, 'will pass, together with Auschwitz, Treblinka, Hiroshima and Vorkuta, into the history of the greatest nightmares of the twenti-eth century'.

The aorta, the central nerve of Kolyma, was and is the Kolyma Highway, the Route. And like many of the older residents of Kolyma, I write the words 'the Highway' and 'the Route' with capital letters.

Because this road, which runs for more than two thousand kilometres, is paved with human lives, built on bones. And that is not a metaphor. Why isn't there a single old graveyard the entire length of the Route?

Because the dead lie about half a metre below the road surface. Thousands of them. Apart from mining gold, constructing the Highway was the worst job in Kolyma. Anyone who fell dead by the roadside had his camp rags pulled off him (they would still come in handy), then he was turned face up and covered in the Kolyma soil from which the Route is made.

In the first few days, I can't help wondering how I am to empty my bladder here. I get out of the car, and my mind aches at the thought that I'm pissing on some poor wretch's head.

It could be one of ours – a nineteen-year-old soldier boy from the September 1939 campaign, a boy from my native Warsaw under my grandfather's command, a boy who never had a girl in his life, and as he was dying of hunger, whispered . . . Well quite, what could he have said? And now, old cynic that I am, I feel ashamed for writing romantic twaddle like that. But when you're alone in a shabby hotel at the end of the world and you feel like screaming because the MS has got you, you write like that (MS isn't multiple sclerosis, it's Memoirist's Solitude).

Construction of the Route began in 1932, when the Dalstroi trust company was brought to life. By the end of the decade the road had been laboriously extended as far as Ust-Nera at Kilometre 1007. In the 1940s they took it further, to Khandyga on the Aldan river, at Kilometre 1605. This was the western limit of the trust company. The last stretch, to Yakutsk at Kilometre 2025, was completed in the early 1950s, but it was a so-called *zimovik* – a road that's only fit for use in winter, when the marshland freezes. The entire Kolyma Highway only became driveable in summer in the 1990s.

I'm travelling along it in the footsteps of Varlam Tikhonovich Shalamov, and his thousand-page collection of *Kolyma Tales*. This is a classic of Russian literature, the most shocking, extraordinary picture of prison culture, which Shalamov compresses and summarizes in three commandments: do not believe, do not be afraid, never ask for anything. And one more prison-camp virtue, without which you won't survive: know how to steal, starting with your fellow prisoners' bread. In Shalamov's camp a man only becomes worse. Everything is always bad. In the camp God dies too, whereas for Alexander Solzhenitsyn the Gulag is a test of character, from which the prisoner can emerge redeemed.

Shalamov spent eighteen years in the camps, and another two as 'free' but with no right to leave. Altogether he spent seventeen years in Kolyma. He was released in 1953, but to the end of his life he remained obsessed with the camps.

He is my first, my permanent, *poputchik* – one of my favourite Russian words. It means a fellow traveller, a man who is on the road (*po puti* in Russian) with you. Literally and metaphorically – the person with whom you travel the same road, in the same train compartment, someone who shares your political views or aspires to the same goal. This book is about the people I travelled with, but it is also about the people I met along the Route.

In this part there will be quite a lot about drivers. The lorry drivers in Russia are called *dalnoboyshchiki*, meaning people on a 'distant [*dalno*-] throw [*boy*-]', that is, a long route. Sometimes they are called *kamazisty*, even if their lorries are not Kamaz trucks, or *ugolshchiki*, if they are transporting coal, because *ugol* means 'coal'. But in Kolyma they had already worked out their own word in the days of the Gulag – here they call the local drivers *trassoviki*, based on the word *Trassa*, meaning 'the Route'.

The Route is a dangerous road, made out of yellowish Kolyma soil, in which there are more stones than earth. Beyond Palatka the road has no hard surface, so any heavier-than-usual downpour washes it away. It is cracked and crumbled by permafrost, and in winter there are vast amounts of snow; when there isn't so much of it, the frozen surface is like an ice rink. In summer the problem is a horrible yellow dust, which hangs in the air for ages. Cars crash in it as if it were fog. There are a lot of makeshift memorials along the road. Instead of a cross on a stake, they hang a broken steering wheel, and instead of stones there are arrangements of tyres or a radiator full of holes.

At many points on the hard shoulder there are the remains of fences designed to hold back snowdrifts. They were woven out of larch sticks by Gulag prisoners. Although the Highway is dangerous to drive along, living on it is safe. There isn't much common crime. Out here, even in the terrible 1990s there was none of the *rekiet* ('racket') which agonized Russia, in other words the highway muggings and extortion of protection money for safe passage.

Kolyma went through its worst times with regard to crime after 1953, when the camps were emptied, and thousands of people were set free, including a lot of criminals, who in spite of their release were not allowed to go back to 'mainland' Russia (that is, closer to civilization) for several more years. To be safe in the towns, people went about in groups, and men escorted their wives to work, because many of the newly released prisoners hadn't seen a woman for years.

At this point a former political prisoner called Ryabokon set out on the Route, an old soldier from the anarchist Revolutionary Insurrectionary Army of Ukraine, led by the ataman (Cossack leader) Nestor Ivanovich Makhno. Shalamov devotes one of his tales to Ryabokon.

In the story, the veteran anarchist forms a gang of four men. They recklessly rob and murder anyone they can, but they argue over the division of the spoils and give each other away. Each of them gets a twenty-five-year sentence.

Those days are long gone. Nowadays, every encounter on the Route is a pleasure, and I love the roadside bars. There are about fifteen of them between Magadan and Yakutsk. I can sit in them for hours, gazing at those ordinary, genuine, honest faces, at the people of the taiga dressed in camos, at the drivers with their large hands covered in car oil (machine dirt is not dirt, they say), and the rheumatism-twisted gold hunters. I'm happy that I don't have to look at the red faces of overfed oligarchs, or the bulging eyes of booze-soaked secret-police officers. Finally I hear 'please', 'thank you', and the woman wiping the floor with a dirty rag at the bar in Lariukova at Kilometre 386 even says 'Sorry' to me. You don't often hear that among the city people, in Magadan.

The woman wants to wipe under my table too, but she realizes I'm a foreigner so she sits down beside me and tells me about the first foreigner to cross the threshold of her bar a few years ago. He was a huge bald fellow in a leather waistcoat, and covered in tattoos from head to foot.

'*Day-vid yoo-ess-ey*,' he said, pointing at himself.

'Larissa, Rash-en,' the lady replied in English.

'*Problema kaltso* [Wheel problem],' he said, and to make an impression, tried to curse: '*Yop tvy-oo mat* [Fuck your mother].'

Larissa didn't answer, because she didn't know any more words in English.

'*Skolko paloo-chay-esh?* [How much do you earn?],' the bizarre guest asked, just to talk about something.

'Fifty dollars,' the woman replied truthfully in Russian.

'*Vryosh! Konyeshno bolshe* [You're lying! It must be more].' Now he had used up his supply of foreign words too, so the conversation came to an end.

David had come to Magadan by ship, and was travelling west on his motorbike, with the dream of reaching Moscow, but in Lariukova at Kilometre 386 of the Route he'd broken a wheel rim and that was the end of his adventure. Larissa sent him back to Magadan by lorry, where he sold his Honda for 2000 dollars and flew to Moscow by plane.

There are fewer tourists in Kolyma than at the North Pole or on Mount Everest. I didn't meet a single one.

The Route, somewhere between Susuman and Ust-Nera.

Day XII

In the taiga. Twenty-two kilometres south of Kilometre 438 of the Kolyma Highway

Today I'm going to write about reporter's luck.

Małgorzata Szejnert, former head of the reportage section at the Polish daily *Gazeta Wyborcza*, says that the reporter who has no fortune has no future in the profession. By fortune, she means professional good luck.

So this is about luck. I write up my diary, and before noon I finally get out of the bloody hotel at Sokol, which I haven't been able to leave for so many days. My dream for today is to reach Debin at Kilometre 448 of the Highway.

I make my way from the hotel to the road. In a small shop I stock up on provisions for two days, then stand on the hard shoulder, open a little carton of juice and ... I haven't had time to drink it before a vehicle stops, the second one I've hailed. I've been waiting less than five minutes. It's 11.50 a.m.

It's an old Russian Gazela (a Gaz microbus, the company that makes the legendary Volga cars), and behind the steering wheel is Andrei from Magadan, with a set of gold teeth. He's my first *poputchik* of the day. With him I make my ninth journey along the stretch of the Highway to Palatka.

Andrei is driving to Seymchan, so he's leaving my road at Lariukova, at Kilometre 386, but there's a busy bar by the Route at that spot, so I'll have no trouble finding my next *poputchik* there.

Andrei is going to fetch some Spanish hunters who came for elk. They couldn't endure life in the taiga, camping out in tents, so they have to be evacuated, even though they haven't got their trophies.

In the car we're carrying a tremendous supply of petrol, but we tank up everywhere we can, because there can be problems with fuel. There are deposits of oil and gas in Kolyma, but they haven't yet been exploited, so fuel is brought in from mainland Russia and is very expensive. The further away from Magadan, the more it costs.

At Kilometre 164 there's Yablonov Pass, and a change of weather, to snow and frost. Today is the first day of October, and I'm driving into the Kolyma winter. At Kilometre 202 I let out a joyful Hurray!, because that's ten per cent of the Route done. I'm starting to count out the journey the way I do during marathons, when after the fourth kilometre I'm glad I've already covered ten per cent of the distance. Andrei brings me down to earth by saying it is indeed ten per cent, but it's also the easiest bit.

In the bar at Lariukova we have dinner, and my driver finds me a new *poputchik*. This is Borya – forty-nine-year-old, slightly stuttering *staratyel* Boris Aryekhov, Andrei's childhood friend. *Staratyel* is the Russian for 'gold prospector', and it also means a keen person, a fanatic. Borya is driving into the taiga, where he and a friend have a partnership, one of the 250 Kolyma-based gold-sluicing cartels, which is also not far from my goal, Debin. Borya offers me his hospitality, which I am happy to accept. I'll go to Debin later.

On the way we stop off at his hometown Orotukan, at Kilometre 390, for supplies. It breaks Borya's heart to see how the settlement of his youth is dying. Most of the houses have smashed-in windows which stare eerily, like empty eye sockets. The remaining residents are gathered in the last five four-storey blocks. Each of them has two or three little shops on the ground floor. Every single one. And in every single shop they sell vodka, though the licence for it costs 120,000 roubles per month

(£2400). Borya and I wonder what sort of turnover they must have to earn enough for the payment.

Outside the house where Borya used to live is a mountain with a lovely long slope and the remains of the only ski-lift in Kolyma. Metal hunters are cutting it up piece by piece for scrap.

Scrap-metal scavengers are modern-day Neanderthals, savages, barbarians. They have stolen the bronze plaque from the monument to Tanya Molandina, which stands near the disused cultural centre named after her, and they've gouged out one of the girl's eyes, even though she's made of concrete. Judging from the statue, she must have been very beautiful. She was a Komsomol activist. In 1937 a gang of criminal prisoners who had escaped from the zone raped her to death.

As we drive into the taiga, Borya points out the totally extinct settlements: Yasny, Spornoye, Pyatiletka and Razvyedchik, as well as Utinka, Dorozhka, Tayozhka, Pribyl, Rybny, Shturmovoy . . .

So here I am at the gold prospectors' tiny community, twenty-two kilometres into the depths of the taiga from Kilometre 438 of the Route, on the right bank of the Kolyma river. With no electricity, no phone connection, and no Internet.

I spend the night with Vitali (Vitya) in his trailer, a little hut on wheels. Vitya Marku is Borya's business partner. He comes from Moldova, so they call him 'the Moldovan'. At our feet stands a little safe containing the roughly twelve kilos of gold which they have sluiced in the past month, and between our bunks there's Vitya's Kalashnikov. Life in the taiga is impossible without a gun. The bears are particularly dangerous right now – not long ago they devoured the cook from the neighbouring cartel. Every now and then gold prospectors are attacked and robbed by bandits, too.

I've just had breakfast (buckwheat and chicken thigh in a thick sauce – a fairly typical Russian breakfast), and Marina is treating me to a bread roll she has baked. She is the cook, the only woman in this ten-person team.

It's an incredible brigade. There are nine guys, including five Vladimirs – a geologist, a driver, a bulldozer operator known as 'Grandpa', and two sluice-box operators – all people who've had interesting fates. The tenth is Marina. She used to be the cook at a hospital, but she only earned 15,000 roubles a month, on top of which she found it awfully boring because she never saw any people there, just pots and pans, so she joined the gold prospectors. It means half the year out in the taiga, the middle of nowhere, and there are only men around, sometimes as many as fifty or sixty blokes.

Marina is not the Valentina Teryeshkova of the frying pan. By this I'm trying to say that she's not a high-flyer like the first woman in space, but she can do everything that matters. She bakes bread, boils potatoes and cabbage, and won the team's greatest respect when Vitali shot a bear, which she skinned and made into steaks. This is an extremely foolish thing to do, because bears are carrion eaters, omnivores, so they carry in their flesh countless parasites harmful to humans. However, the team reckoned they're used to the bugs of Kolyma, just like the Koryaks and Evens who have lived here for thousands of years, and who aren't affected by them. Bear meat has a strange, spicy, woody taste, the flavour of pine nuts. You have to season it very strongly to get rid of that.

The prospectors' cook isn't familiar with the method described by Varlam Shalamov in *Kolyma Tales*. If the meat of any animal is buried in the ground for one night, it loses that horrible smell. Even crow, mouse, dog or fox becomes edible like that . . .

That isn't the only miraculous property of the Kolyma soil. In summer, it can help you to get rid of your lice. You just have to bury your clothes, leaving a tiny corner of cloth above ground, and within a few hours all the parasites will emerge onto it. They're trying to escape from the cold of the permafrost, though pubic lice stay behind, so it's only a temporary method. Pubic lice can survive the Kolyma frost in the seams of clothing. They can only be finished off by boiling or with an iron.

According to Shalamov, there are only two things a person cannot get used to – the cold and the lice. I don't entirely believe him. What about the hunger? He forgot to mention the hunger. After all, it's the main character in his tales.

Marina hasn't got a husband or children, but she has been known to cast her spell on one of the team occasionally. For two seasons now Volodya, a driver for Borya's cartel, has been living in her trailer. The privy has no door, and provides a fine view of the taiga and the Kolyma river. For her, the guys set up a seatless chair, but with a piece of plywood nailed to the front legs so the lady won't pee on her own boots.

And the view is stunning, because the larches have just dropped their needles, but the first snow has already fallen, so it looks as if the earth is on fire, as if glowing lava were pouring from under every tree – thus can one sit and meditate on the throne set up for Marina.

The gold prospectors live at their camps from mid-April to the end of September, the period when they can sluice gold. The season will end in a few days' time, because it's already seriously cold. Last night it was fifteen degrees below zero, the water needed for sluicing the gold froze, and so work is becoming impossible.

My God, what wonderful faces there are here: plain, good, honest, bright, open and bold, furrowed by life. Their eyes are wise, attentive and inquiring, but also cheerful, playful even. I love these people. How fortunate I am to have left the city.

In the trailer. Borya (left) playing backgammon with his friend.

'GRANDPA' THE BULLDOZER DRIVER — THE NARK'S BURIAL

Volodya, known as 'Grandpa' because he is already sixty, operates the bulldozer. This is a caterpillar-tracked, computerized, fully electronic thing of wonder weighing ninety tonnes, a machine the size of a two-storey tenement, which can shovel 2000 cubic metres of mined material in a twenty-four-hour period, and which costs a million dollars. That's the price of a new machine, but in Kolyma hardly anybody buys one of those. The prospectors import used Komatsu and Caterpillar bulldozers from North America, because they only cost twelve million roubles.

Volodya's profession is the most coveted mining job, and also the best paid. Bulldozer operators are the aristocracy among gold prospectors. 'Grandpa' gets a monthly wage of 60,000 roubles (£1200) from Borya, and thus he earns 20,000 more than the digger operator, and twice as much as the cook and the man who operates the sluice box.

Each of the two three-man shifts lasts twelve hours, seven days a week, throughout the season. The bulldozer operator's task is to expose the seam of gold. On Borya's plot it is buried from sixteen to twenty-one metres below ground and is forty centimetres thick. Volodya has to dig down to it, which means working in permafrost.

The bulldozer pushes the gold-bearing soil, in other words the seam, into one spot, and then the digger loads it into the sluice box. Every scoopful contains a cubic metre of frozen, stony earth, in which there is on average one gram of gold — such is the productivity of Borya's plot. The average productivity in Kolyma is two grams, and the richest seams are in Chukotka, where in a cubic metre of soil there can be up to ten grams of precious metal.

Each of the two shifts working at the plot sluices two hundred scoopfuls of soil, so in one day on average they sluice 400 grams of gold. However, there are days when Borya and his partner mine a whole kilogram of gold from the machine, though while I was keeping them company it was only 100 grams – a small handful of gold sand and one little nugget resting on a large sloping channel lined with grooved rubber matting where the heavy ore collects.

In 2010 Borya's team sluiced sixty-five kilos of precious metal on this plot. There were fifty more left, but they would deal with that once the next season came.

In Soviet times 'Grandpa' Volodya worked at the Burkhalinsky Mining Conglomerate, about a hundred kilometres further along the Highway. In 1982, at a plot named after Kalinin, and known as Kalinka, his machine dug a human body out of the ground. It was almost intact. Human beings buried here can be preserved in the permafrost for hundreds, or even thousands, of years. It was a zek in prison-camp quilted clothes, with a sack over his head, which had been smashed by a pickaxe or a crowbar. In his pocket he had a *spravka*, meaning a certificate releasing him from hard labour – a highly coveted little document, every zek's dream for years on end.

'He must have been a nark,' Volodya reckons, 'an informer whose colleagues did him in, or else the guards killed him instead of releasing him because he'd seen too much. The name on the *spravka* was legible, so we wrote a letter to a national newspaper, which they published. A woman from Moscow turned up, who was the sister of our stiff who almost attained freedom.'

The woman came to Kolyma and took her brother home. Thirty years on, at the mining conglomerate's expense, the poor wretch went back to the mainland.

At Kalinka it was full steam ahead. The prospectors moved on up a stream until they came to a clearing covered in waist-high weeds, among which they found some wooden stakes in rows with numbers burned onto them. They'd come upon a zeks' graveyard.

'And the work stopped,' says Volodya. 'We were told to go around it. But the whole place has been dug up and excavated now. All the bones have been sluiced. We're living in bloody nasty times. Nothing's sacred any more.'

Day XIII

In the taiga. Twenty-two kilometres south of Kilometre 438 of the Kolyma Highway

A change of plan. The gold-sluicing season ends tomorrow. The last shift will go out to work tonight.

In the summer thaw it's possible to sluice up to seventy per cent of the ore. When the frost returns, three-quarters of the gold escapes through the sluice box. This is the sort of thirty-per-cent productivity level produced by the equipment used in the days of Stalin and the Gulag – wheelbarrows and shovels. Many of the plots that were worked then are being washed through again now. In some places, old heaps of earth and stone are being washed for the third time.

Part of the plot where Borya's partnership operates was worked in the 1970s by the state Pyatiletka conglomerate, from the settlement of the same name.

State licences for prospecting are obtained through tenders. They are valid for a few years (Borya's is for five), and the winner who works the plot has to deliver the gold he mines to the state, or else the tax office will take away his licence. He makes the first annual payment before entering the auction. The price depends on the plot's resources.

And that's my greatest disappointment, because after reading Jack London I thought a gold prospector was someone with a tendency to gamble, doomed to move about in a fog, someone who stakes his entire life's savings on a single card. Nothing of the kind. Each plot put up for tender is precisely valued through geological research.

Borya shows me the geological site plan for his plot. It was drawn up in 1946. It shows the places where test boreholes were drilled, and the measure of gold content in each spot. The best research and maps were produced in the Stalinist era, because any geologist who estimated the deposits wrongly ended up in a camp. The worst maps were created in the last decade of the USSR and the post-Soviet years. The geologists faked them because they couldn't be bothered to do the work; they drilled test boreholes but overvalued the deposits, because they were being paid according to the value of the seams discovered.

So you can go bankrupt, says Borya, just because someone pulled a fast one thirty years ago. Or if one of your machines goes wrong – extraction comes to a halt and the prospector can't pay back his loan. The machines are bought on a mortgage, so the bank can repossess and sell them. All prospectors are up to their ears in debt. Borya took out a loan of twelve million roubles to buy the bulldozer.

But the biggest nightmare for prospectors is bureaucracy. To start up, they must go to a great deal of trouble, obtaining consent and all the relevant documents at fifteen different places, including the Agency for Technological Safety at Work, the Agency for Nature Protection (prospectors do terrible damage to the environment, and they are not obliged to clean up the plots after use), the Hunting Agency, the Central Office for Utilization of Waste, the tax office, the police, the foresters, the firemen ... And at each of the fifteen places they have to pay money.

And now let's take a look in Borya's and Vitya's pockets.

Their mighty bulldozer consumes (as they say in Russia) one and a half tonnes of fuel oil a day at a cost of 25 roubles a litre. The digger and the electricity generator use up 400 litres each, so in total, in each twenty-four-hour period they burn 2300 litres of fuel at a cost of 57,500 roubles (£1150). On top of that, add engine oil, wages for the workers, food, cigarettes, licence payments, loan repayments . . .

It easily comes to 100,000 roubles a day.

On their final day the partners sluiced out 100 grams of gold. When I was with them, the price was 1350 roubles per gram of ore ('three-nines fine', in other words a fineness equivalent to 24-carat). My prospectors' gold is 21-carat, so they'll get less for it, and they'll also have fifteen per cent of the value subtracted for smelting, purifying, taxes and bank charges. So they will get 950 roubles for each gram, 95,000 roubles in all. Seventy per cent of this sum will reach their account three days after delivery, and the rest after a week.

So Borya and Vitya end the first day of my visit on a slight minus. And they must close the season to avoid running up costs.

A gold sluice.

Varlam Shalamov, in whose footsteps I am travelling across Kolyma, mined gold here for ten years before managing to get another job. It was the worst, fastest-killing work in the entire Gulag Archipelago, even though those doing it were the best fed, comparatively speaking. On site a prisoner could only have one of three jobs. If he was lucky, they made him a *trapovy*, the guy who nailed planks together along which the *tachkovye* — the wheelbarrow men — carried the output. The *tachkovye* were the old equivalent of the digger. The bulldozer's job was done by the hackers, who smashed up the permafrost with pickaxes and loaded it onto the wheelbarrows — that was the worst job in the world.

The hackers' daily work norm grew by the year. In 1933 it was 0.8 cubic metres, and by 1936 it was five cubic metres in the course of a single twelve-hour shift. Volodya's bulldozer is today's equivalent of two hundred zeks.

How much did that 'machine' consume?

At the museum in Magadan I found Order No. 377 issued by Berzin, the head of Dalstroi, on 22 November 1937, 'on setting the bread ration for individual categories of worker depending on percentage of work norm completed' — meaning how much of those five cubic metres of soil they managed to work.

The first category included those who completed the set norm. They were to get 300 grams of bread per day. The second category were those who completed from 131 to 175 per cent of the norm, which earned them half a kilo of bread, and the third category, who completed from

176 to 200 per cent, got 800 grams. Those in category U, for *udarniki* (super-productive workers), had to smash up more than 200 per cent, but they got a whole kilo of bread. There were some of these, but they wore themselves out very quickly, working themselves to death in only five weeks. Most zeks had trouble completing the norm.

Nine days after issuing this order, Berzin was recalled to Moscow and shot. Of course it had nothing to do with Order No. 377, it was just that Yezhov's purge was picking up speed and Berzin's turn had come. Just as a year later, in 1938, it was Yezhov's turn, along with some twenty thousand other NKVD agents.

How much did that 'machine' consume? Two hundred zeks completing one hundred per cent of the norm, and breaking as much earth as Volodya's bulldozer on a twelve-hour shift, comes out at 60 kilos of black bread. These days a loaf (800 grams) of the cheapest black bread costs 30 roubles in Kolyma (60p). Sixty kilos is equivalent to seventy-five of these loaves, or 2250 roubles (£45). Such was the cost of the basic ration for two hundred people, plus a morning and evening bowl of watery soup made with a cabbage leaf, a carrot, or peelings.

In twelve hours the bulldozer consumes 750 litres of fuel oil at a cost of 18,750 roubles (£375).

But there were some pleasures in the Gulag. Prisoners who found a gold nugget were supposed to get a cash reward – one rouble for each gram of gold over 51 grams. In those days a packet of the cheapest cigarettes cost 10 roubles, but a 50-gram nugget was an extreme rarity, a stone the size of a small walnut.

In the course of ten years spent in the gold mines, Shalamov found very few nuggets that could have earned him a reward, and only received something on two occasions. The first time it was a coupon for an extra dinner, and the second time it was a pinch of tobacco.

'Can you steal gold on the plot?' I ask Vitali the next night as we're getting ready for bed in his trailer.

'It's impossible to steal from the conveyor belt in the sluice box, because it's padlocked shut,' says the man who before becoming a gold prospector was a crime-fighting policeman in Magadan. 'And if somebody were mean enough to break the lock, the most he could steal would be one day's output, because we collect it daily, and getting caught would mean a five- or six-year stretch in prison, because in Kolyma sentences for stealing gold are no joke.'

'But if your workman who operates the sluice box sees a nugget, could he just pocket it?'

'Yes, but I've never heard of anybody seeing a nugget on the plot. I've never seen one myself. It was possible in the days when they worked manually, but now everyone's using machines. How can you spot a tiny little stone covered in mud in a cubic metre of soil?'

'How much do the Ingush pay for gold?' I ask, because as long ago as the 1970s they had taken absolute control of Kolyma's black market in gold.

'Eight hundred roubles,' says Vitali.

'Then why the hell do business with them if the state purchase price is better?'

'Because they pay up right away. It's a salvation for anyone who needs money immediately. But our biggest problem isn't money – it's people. Give them a few roubles in advance, take your eye off them for an instant, and they'll send someone to the nearest settlement to buy vodka, and then they'll all get dead drunk. Now they're not drinking, because out in the taiga they've got nowhere to buy it, and I'm on their case the whole time. I'm like a prison-camp guard, dammit! I do nothing else.'

'Does everyone drink?'

'Yes! They drink all winter long. They blow all their money in the summer. Then in the season they detox a bit, and then they spend the whole winter boozing again. Every spring I go and fish them out of their settlements, get things moving, make arrangements, sign contracts and get them on their feet . . . When they meet up again they're really happy because they haven't seen each other for six months, and they celebrate by drinking away their last few kopecks together. Then I hurry them off to the plot, where somehow they sober up and recuperate, because there's no drink.'

Day XIV

Debin. Kilometre 448 of the Kolyma Highway

This is the place where the curse of Kolyma began. It was right here in 1929, during a geological expedition, that one of the members went to wash in a stream one morning, and, while he was about it, gathered a whole cap of gold nuggets.

The gold prospectors are taking me there this morning. We're travelling in Vitali's twenty-six-year-old Kamaz truck, which they describe as 'just like brand-new'. The truck is three years older than my son, but with fewer miles on the clock, because it spent twenty-five years 'under conservation'. It didn't go anywhere, it just sat in a warehouse waiting for the outbreak of war. But it never happened, and a quarter of a century on, the army sold off its old equipment.

I have to get to Debin. Firstly, because this is the site of the only bridge across the great Kolyma river, which crosses my path to the west. Secondly, because Varlam Shalamov spent several years working as a paramedic at the local hospital for prisoners. The writer was already a *dokhodyaga* – a goner – when he was brought to the hospital from a gold pit. Another prisoner, a doctor, saved his life by sending him on a paramedical training course.

A kilometre before the *poselyok* (big village), the massive bridge stands on the high crutches of its piers. The dates of its construction are marked on one of them: '19 VI 36–19 V 37' – bloody fast for a bridge built by prisoners without the aid of machines. To me it looks horribly likely that it was a Soviet-style 'heroic feat of production': 'We'll deliver the completed bridge ahead of deadline!' They cut exactly one month off the allotted year.

And the next spring, along came the worst flood in the history of Kolyma, known as the 'eleven-metre flood'. Water poured over the top of the bridge.

For eighteen months Kolyma had had a new man in charge. Berzin's place was now occupied by Colonel Karp Pavlov. He gathered all the available lorries, had them loaded with stones, and parked on the bridge. It had to be weighed down to the maximum. Then he sent off all the drivers (they were free people, not prisoners), and spent the entire night standing alone in the middle of the bridge until the water began to drop.

Pavlov was a primitive, uneducated man who successfully applied the method devised by Berzin of forcing high work productivity out of the prisoners by means of hunger. The era when he was in charge at Kolyma was the worst of all.

To me it is obvious why Pavlov stood on the bridge. He wasn't brave, as the citizens of Debin tell the story. He was fully aware that one way or the other he was bound to share the fate of the bridge. Either they would both survive, or he would come crashing down with it. If the water had carried away the structure, he would have been shot for failing to protect a priceless investment. The bridge stayed put, and Pavlov went on running Dalstroi for almost two more years. He shot himself in 1957, when people in the USSR started talking about Stalinist crimes.

There's an even more curious construction in Debin, and that is the large edifice housing the oblast TB hospital. It is a vast hulk of a building in the shape of a trident, or the Russian letter . It was built in 1936 for the secret police. Dalstroi's garrison had its headquarters here, and there was also a jail and barracks for the Kolympolk, the Kolyma NKVD regiment, which had the job of guarding all the camps. In 1945 the regiment was put on its feet and sent to war against Japan, and the Central

Gulag Hospital was established in the barracks for prisoners, with a thousand beds. The nurses and doctors were prisoners too, very often academics or professors, the flower of Russian medicine, a vast wave of whom ended up in the camps after the anti-Semitic campaign unleashed by Stalin in 1948.

Shalamov describes the man who gained the greatest fame in his day. He was a paramedic in the neurosis ward, who one day boiled a large tomcat in a sterilizer and ate it in one sitting.

In 1955 the hospital was turned into a normal district hospital. I'm eating breakfast in the hospital kitchen with the head doctor, Georgi Goncharov. Shalamov lived in a tiny room behind us – at last he was close to food, and could eat his fill. Never the same again, for the rest of his life he ate and hoarded food without restraint.

Eighty-three-year-old Galina Nikolayevna Gogolyeva remembers him well. She was a nurse at the hospital for fifty years. Shockingly, she was given a six-year sentence because in the postwar famine she made patties for the children from the glue with which she assembled paper toys in a factory. Not her own children, but homeless ones. The glue contained a bit of flour.

Galina Nikolayevna lives with her son. She used to have her own flat, but she gave it back in exchange for compensation. Some twenty years ago the Russian state decided that the north is overpopulated, which costs Russia a great deal. Why should gold prospectors and their families live here all year round when they only dig for gold for six months of the year? So they have switched to a shift system. Local people are being resettled on the mainland, and prospectors are brought in for the season. It is particularly expensive to support retired people who have to be given heating, medical treatment, and finally a burial, while everything costs far more here than in the rest of Russia.

So the authorities pay compensation for resettling. There are plenty of willing applicants, but old people take precedence, as do residents of the most expensive, most loss-making settlements, where there is no work. These places are being 'frozen', meaning that they are being totally depopulated. The electricity and heating get cut off, and even those who refuse to leave are forced to move out. This fate recently befell Spornoye, twenty-three kilometres from Debin.

But according to the Russian Federation constitution you cannot forbid people to live wherever they wish, so Galina Nikolayevna accepted a million roubles (£20,000) from the state for her two rooms and a kitchen, and moved in with her single son in the rabbit hutch next door. She used the proceeds to buy him a car, then bought a second one for her grandson, and a flat in Magadan for her granddaughter.

Sasha Trofimov from Spornoye came to live in her old flat. He bought it from the local administration for 200,000 roubles (£4000). Flats are very cheap, because everyone is leaving. For his old flat, Sasha received 1,100,000 roubles in compensation from the state.

Thus the state bought two flats for an exorbitant price of over two million roubles, but failed to rid Kolyma of a single resident. However, they are making progress. There are now 715 people living in the *poselyok*, three times fewer than twenty years ago.

I leave Galina Nikolayevna's place. Outside, near the Tibet *zakusochnaya* (snack bar), a character with a dark complexion hails me and invites me in for tea. This is thirty-six-year-old Mustafa Nalgiyev from Ingushetia, and it is his bar. Dealing in gold is his destiny, a family tradition.

Mustafa and I quickly make friends. As proof of his affection he gives me an oral insurance policy. In his own name, in that of his brothers, his entire family, his friends and all his compatriots he solemnly guarantees me safety within the entire Yagodninsky administrative region. I gratefully accept.

Soon after, I get ready for bed. I'm staying at the *shinomontazhka*, Vitali's tyre-repair shop, which is also his home. The place has all the charm of a drinking dive and a resident of equal charm and beauty called Sanka. The workshop has one or two customers a day, who get service as long as they can find Sanka, who spends most of his time trailing around the settlement, hardly able to stay upright from morning on.

The fellow hasn't got a single tooth, but he does have a broken nose and a livid purple and red face, like a tropical fish, or coral. He's dirty, stinky, drooling and festering – simply atrocious, a wreck of a man, a shell, but a well-known figure in Debin, because, now aged thirty, he has a son who is eighteen. It's true! Sanka became a father at the age of twelve. He is a real physiological phenomenon – if only because he hasn't yet managed to drink himself to death.

I am to stay with him. I ask him to light the stove, but he doesn't want to. He says his favourite temperature for sleeping is ten degrees, and that's what it is now. Except that it isn't, because the tea in our mugs has frozen.

Before going to bed I try to bash out an account of Day XIV on the computer, but my hands are too cold.

Debin. Breakfast in the hospital kitchen. Varlam Shalamov, author
of Kolyma Tales, *lived in a tiny room off the kitchen.*

MUSTAFA THE RESTAURATEUR –
THE PROMISED LAND

For ten years Mustafa ran a snack bar on the Kolyma Highway, but last year he closed the business.

'Because I am a civilized guy, and above the bar, upstairs is my private home, so I'd like people to behave in a civilized way round here. But there's nothing but drinking, fighting, screaming and swearing. Even though I didn't sell vodka. Because of my religious principles, because I'm a Muslim. I don't even want to get the Russkies drunk. Because they all drink like mad here. The women too, the young people, fathers . . . I didn't even sell wine. I did have beer. I wasn't the one who sold it – that was a woman, a Russian. I refuse to serve people like that. I can't stand that sort of work, or that foul behaviour.'

'So how do you make a living? From gold?'

'Yes.'

Dealing in gold is his destiny, as well as a family tradition. It started with his father, who came to Kolyma for the money, because they paid two or three times better than anywhere else in the Soviet Union. He worked at a gold-mining conglomerate. Mustafa was born here.

'In those days there was internationalism and people took no notice of your ethnicity.' Mustafa gets excited easily, and nervously stirs the tea which he has sweetened three times already. 'But now there's no way they'll take an Ingush to work with gold. I was a child, but I can remember that there was no thieving in Kolyma. Can you believe it? Now they've all learned to steal. It's like a disease.'

'They don't steal, they just take things left lying about in the wrong place' – I repeat my favourite Russian saying.

'My father had a small business on the side. Buying and selling. He'd buy gold, take it to the south of the Land of Soviets and sell it. He built a fine house in Ingushetia on the proceeds and we went back to our homeland, but my father continued to go to and from Kolyma for gold.'

Later he usually took it to Ashgabat in Turkmenistan, because they paid the best price. The Turkmens adore gold. Every young man has to have some in order to get married, to pay the bride price. But eventually on one of his trips Mustafa's father was caught.

'How much gold did he have on him when they stopped him?' I ask.

'Two kilos. In those days that was an immense amount, about fifty thousand old roubles, and a new Zhiguli car cost five. Now it would be more than a hundred thousand dollars. In the USSR there were two very severe articles of the penal code for gold – illegal financial operations and *rasstrelnoye* economic damage.' *Rasstrelnoye* means 'punishable by death'.

'Meaning?'

'For economic damage you could get the chop for only one kilo of gold. But my father was lucky, because he was caught by the KGB, the secret police, not the militia, and they gave him lenient treatment. They realized he wasn't a bandit, just an ordinary guy with six kids to feed. So they met him halfway, and gave him five years.'

'And you were left without a father.'

'It was an awful childhood,' says Mustafa. 'Degrading. The communists weren't bad, people lived well, but we only ate once a day. My father served the entire sentence, to the very last day. He came out, and returned to Ingushetia, the Soviet Union collapsed, his savings ran out, and for the first time there was unemployment, loss of hope, despair, and war with neighbouring Chechnya, so we went on starving, but in a large, fine house. We suffered like that for another five years, until in 1994, when my father decided we were going back to Kolyma, to our promised land. And once my father had spoken, there was never any discussion. If he said "Die", you'd have to die.'

'And so here you are.'

'The whole family. We started from zero. We buy gold by the tonne and take it south. But the gold gets stolen by Ukrainians, Georgians, Armenians and the Russkies themselves – most of all the regular policemen, the secret-police chiefs, and the heads of state mines and conglomerates. But the Ingush get all the blame.'

'But you just buy and sell,' I say.

'That's the business.'

'Who do you buy it from now?'

'From prospectors and thieves.'

'Yesterday I was with some prospectors, removing the gold from a sluice. I have no idea how you could steal any, because they secure the thing with a hundred bolts, locks and padlocks.'

'There are thousands of ways to do it,' he assures me.

Day XV

Debin. Kilometre 448 of the Kolyma Highway

Vitali arrives from the taiga and gives the wretched Sanka the sack, for drunkenness. And all because of me. Instead of taking care of me, a guest, by tidying up the room I slept in, and not bringing shame, Sanka has been drunk as a skunk the whole time.

Debin shouldn't be poor. For eight decades they've been ripping fabulous treasure out of the earth here, but the place looks as if a hurricane went through it. In Chukotka, where they also mine gold, the towns are no different from the ones in northern Canada. The same is true of the Russian towns in the Yamalo-Nenets Autonomous Okrug [region] in the Far North, where they extract gas and crude oil.

If a hole appears, usually you fill it in, and if weeds start to grow, you cut them down. If something overturns, you pick it up, but here (and not just in Debin, either) nothing gets done if it's possible to avoid doing it. Take, for instance, this electricity pole which has fallen over right beside the Route, though by some miracle none of the cables has broken. The pole is hanging by its wires, pulling them right down to the ground so that you can touch them, but the current is still flowing, so why the hell move it? The problems will start when one of the cables snaps and someone is left without power, or when a child on his way to school tries hanging on them, or a drunken trucker drives a Kamaz lorry into them and gets fried in his cab.

But this sort of philosophy sometimes bears good fruit, because

Debin's waterworks, installed in the 1930s and replaced in the 1990s with a new one, was not dismantled, thanks to which it could be put back into operation when the new one broke down after twelve years on the job.

Yet there are eight full-time officials working at the local administration – one for every eighty-nine inhabitants. To keep things in proportion, they'd have to cram 160,000 civil servants into the Moscow mayor's office.

I ask all eight of Debin's officials about the statue of Lenin. Just imagine, here, as in Stekolny, the revolutionary leader has disappeared from his plinth. It happened in 1991, just after the collapse of the USSR. Nobody knows where he has gone, but I conduct an inquiry at lightning speed, and in half a day the riddle is solved.

Vandals were constantly ill-treating the statue, until one night they simply knocked it off its plinth. But then along came Yura Rybakov, who loaded Vladimir Ilyich's cast-iron head onto the firewood cart he was dragging behind him, and went on his way without being observed by anyone. Yura says he took Lenin away to spare him further humiliation, to protect him and save him from the scrap-metal scavengers, and that when better times came he was going to return him to the community with honours. Except that nobody misses Lenin, and there is a stone flowerpot standing on his plinth.

Long-haired Yura is Debin's most colourful inhabitant. He used to be a gold prospector but he went bust. He is seventy-two years old. And he has an irrepressible desire for collecting, a need to amass things and take them under his wing. It was this passion that prompted him to toss Lenin's head onto his cart and transport it to his workshop in the former barracks of the military guards who protected the Kolyma bridge. Yura's workshop should really be called a store for all manner of junk, a museum of mess, a country fair of curiosities, a warehouse full of thingamajigs and whatsits. What isn't in here?! Besides the most fabulous library in Kolyma there's a collection of old maps, uniforms, minerals, and eleven stones with holes in them, which bring good luck, and if you look through them you can see into the future. There is the Lenin, a tin of American Spam dating from the war, some stuffed birds, shamanic talismans, portraits of communist notables, pictures of astronauts, and saints in old icons. There are a vast number of prison-camp mementoes: spoons, bowls, lamps, kettles made out of old food tins, and a metal wheel for a barrow with four spokes, which weighs twenty kilos.

In the prehistoric zoology section there are some huge mammoth tusks, and the teeth, horns and hooves of an immense bison. Both species lived here in harmony, and died out in harmony ten thousand years ago, when the climate cooled down and the Siberian steppes became covered in taiga. Yura came upon the animals' remains while looking for gold. He dug the complete skeleton of a bison out of the permafrost, with bits of flesh and a large chunk of blubber, the whole thing coated with the creature's skin and hair. Yura gnaws a piece of rancid fat off the dark, shapeless lump, reeking of old age. He swallows it. I too cannot possibly refuse a bite of 10,000-year-old lard.

Luckily, Yura's wife serves dinner. Today it is borscht (thick soup with meat), and to avoid eating without drinking, my host fetches several huge plastic bottles of bitter, sour wine which he made himself out of bird cherry, rowanberries, blackcurrants and wild mountain currants, the leaves of which substituted for tobacco in the camps.

Over the wild-currant wine Yura tells me about his Lithuanian friend. During the Great Patriotic War (as the Russians call the Second World War) the man was in the Gestapo. Then he spent time in a prison camp until Dalstroi was disbanded in 1957, but they wouldn't let him go back to his homeland because people with a 'black mark' were not allowed to return to Europe. He lived in Debin, where he was an official at the administration, and everyone called him Slavka, although his name was Stanislavus. Nobody can remember his real surname, because to make his own life easier he had taken his Russian wife's surname. Every year, in the first few days of January he went to the regional KGB office to submit an application to return to Lithuania. The last one was dated 1983. That one was rejected too.

It was from Slavka that Yura inherited his fantastic library. The Lithuanian was killed before his friend's eyes during a booze-up. Yura tells me that after a few drinks, conflict had arisen between European and Asian culture, in other words Lithuanian and Russki. And the Russki kind, represented by 'the declassed, criminal element', as Yura puts it, could not hold back and went for the old fascist with a knife.

We drink to his soul, and then have one for the road before walking to the tyre-repair shop for my backpack, because tonight I'm shifting to a cosier place. I'm sleeping at the hospital. I get a room with a bathroom. At last. I haven't had a wash since leaving Magadan. For four days I haven't even washed my face. As I'm standing in the bathtub, I find myself looking at an extraordinary sight: the toilet is on a pedestal, almost half a metre high, so it looks like a monument to the crapper. When I sit on it, I can swing my legs, but my feet can't touch the floor.

Yura Rybakov, collector of junk, in his workshop.

Or to be more precise, a machine for mincing meat and industrially grinding bones, made out of a gold dredge. Vladimir Augustovich Naiman has been haunted by the image of this piece of machinery for the past thirty-six years. And also by the sight of a field strewn with human remains, with a bulldozer piling them up into a huge heap.

Where does this vision come from? After all, Vladimir was born in 1956, when the prison-camp gates stood wide open.

Vladimir is a geologist. Under the commies, as some here disdainfully call them, he was head of a state enterprise called 50 Lat Oktyabrya ('50 Years of October', referring to the anniversary of the 1917 Revolution), which was something like a collective farm for gold prospectors. Now the company is called Spokoyny ('Peaceful'), and is Vladimir's property. He employs forty workers, who in the past year sluiced sixty kilos of gold.

'I was a seventeen-year-old kid straight out of school, and for the first job in my life I was sent off to a plot at Serpentinka, not far from here. It was the site of a special camp for the investigation of offences that carried the death penalty. The secret police murdered tens of thousands of Kolyma prisoners there. They'd reinvestigate a zek, the NKVD military tribunal would pass the death sentence, and they'd finish him off. Using machine guns. In only two years of the Great Purge, from 1937 to 1938, they shot twelve thousand people there. And they buried them all somewhere in the vicinity. In 1973 along comes an order to rework those plots of land.'

'How were you paid?'

'Triple rates. Because it's a dreadful job, messing about with human remains. And while working with my geological research team I came upon another graveyard. Dating from the early 1930s. We could tell, because they were wearing boots. From the mid-1930s they buried them without boots. Without clothes even. The man who buried his mate had a right to his clothes. So we were taking measurements, calling in the bulldozer, marking out the plot, and in half an hour the machine had run into an entire graveyard. A little stream, and on both banks thousands of bodies were torn from the ground and gathered into a single heap by the bulldozer. That was where God gave me the first sign.'

'What sort of sign?'

'We'd just finished work, the bulldozer was sinking into a bog, driver and all,' says Vladimir. 'That was God saying not everything is allowed. But I didn't know there was a God. Then they brought the dredges, like huge meat-mincing machines, and they put everything through them.'

'Were the bodies intact?'

'No, not on my plot. They would have survived if they'd buried them a metre deeper, in the permafrost, but they were just under the surface. They must have defrosted every summer. On the neighbouring plot the bodies survived intact.'

'Shalamov wrote that every guest of the permafrost is immortal.'

'But they put them all through the dredges.'

'So what did God do?' I ask.

'He gave me several more signs, until finally He knocked me off my feet.'

'What for?'

'For using life the wrong way. For committing sins. For booze, women, arrogance, conceit, greed ... Not everything is allowed. It was some undiagnosable heart-and-vascular disease. Eight months in hospital while I continued to go downhill. They wrote me off as a goner. But three years ago I came back to my plot and put up a great big cross. And I got better. I've put up seven of those crosses at zek graveyards now.'

Vladimir takes me to one of them. I'm struck by the ingenious and simple method for mass burial. I finally understand the literal meaning of the prisoners' words when they said that the dead end up 'under the *sopka*' – *sopka* is the local word for a hill here. The dead were laid in rows on a hill slope, and then covered in earth from just above their heads. This created a small terrace, on which the next row was laid, and was then covered with earth from higher up. The graveyard we are visiting has eleven terraces of about 130 metres in length. It is easy to calculate how many poor souls are lying here. Eleven times 260 (two per metre) comes to 2860 zeks.

The graveyard is situated in a beautiful spot, high above the channel of the mighty Kolyma river. It's a south-facing slope, which drops its snow the moment winter ends, and Debin's young people have favoured this place for beery barbecues and bonfires for years. This is where spring emerges.

How do the young people amuse themselves here? Do they chat, laugh and fool around? Probably. Young people the world over typically don't want to look back. Like my parents, who a few years after the war would spend the long break running about the ruined Jewish cemetery in Sochaczew – which had suddenly lost the Semitic half of its population. There's a sort of ghoulish metaphysical quality to this, because the western Polish youth hung out in German graveyards, while the west Ukrainian and Belarusian youth still hang out in Polish graveyards, to this day.

'Why did you put up the crosses?' I ask Vladimir.

'Because when you put up a cross you stop being an earthly creature. You become a spirit. You connect with the dead people, for whom you're putting up those pieces of wood.'

Day XVI

Yagodnoye. Kilometre 522 of the Kolyma Highway

I arrive in Yagodnoye from Debin in an ambulance from the hospital. It's a 'Lazhik' (meaning a tramp), a bus made in 2002, known in Russia as a *bukhanka* – a 'loaf', in Siberia as a *tabletka* – a 'tablet', and in Kolyma as a *bobik* – a 'broad bean'. The driver is called Sergei, and like a typical Russian, he likes to 'make Tashkent' in the vehicle. That means making the water boil, which is what they say here when someone stokes up the fire. Sergei doesn't take off his overcoat or his leather cap, so there are streams of sweat pouring out from under it. The Russians rarely get undressed in cars. Our journey takes an hour and a half.

I feel privileged, occupying a seat in the cab, but after fifteen minutes I'm feeling jealous of the people in the back. They're sitting on stretchers and their teeth are chattering with cold. There's no heating in the back. Not because it has broken down – the designer didn't provide for it. Indeed, this is an ambulance, but a sick person doesn't have to be kept warm. What matters is that the driver doesn't freeze.

At Kilometre 481 we drive through the settlement of Rybny, where Tamara from Magadan found her mother in the graveyard. All the gold in the vicinity has already been removed, so ten years ago the settlement was frozen, but the compensation packages were so small that despite the cold the residents stayed put, until one night the whole place was set on fire and burned to the ground.

At Kilometre 507 I celebrate completing a quarter of my journey.

One-fourth of the Route. In marathons I observe this sacred moment at the tenth kilometre, and I enjoy it, because I feel better than at the start, I feel as if I could keep running for a week, although I know that after the next ten kilometres things won't be quite so great.

Yagodnoye is the county town, with 3800 inhabitants – less than a third of the population twenty years ago, but the local welfare office has twenty-seven employees. For each employee there are 140 inhabitants. Of its former forty thousand residents, the entire region has only ten thousand remaining. It is a vast territory – 200 by 300 kilometres (a fifth of the size of Poland), and it is policed by a hundred militiamen. In 2010 they had five murder cases.

One night a couple of years ago, someone toppled and destroyed the statue of Lenin here in Yagodnoye too. The local communists found a new one, but it was ugly, made of concrete (the old one was plaster), so to beautify it they covered it with *zlotol*, gold-coloured paint, and erected it in its old place.

The leader of the campaign to pick Lenin up off the floor is fifty-five-year-old Ivan Panikarov, a legendary figure throughout Kolyma. He was the first person, in the 1980s, to start talking out loud and reminding the locals about what happened here in the first half of the twentieth century. By profession a plumber, he founded a Gulag museum at his private flat in Yagodnoye. In 1991 he made a collection among the local citizens and put up a monument to the victims of communism in nearby Serpentinka.

In 2004 he enrolled in the Communist Party. Locally they say he did it to be contrary, out of spite, but he says he did it to defy the United Russia faction, the hegemony of the ruling party. And he hung portraits of Lenin and Stalin in his office (because now he is a journalist for the local newspaper) – he says they're just museum pieces, but it's plain to see that there's something wrong with Ivan. He's sad, embittered and discontented, and for some reason he has been publicly critical of Varlam Shalamov. He says he has no right to judge him, but he has found people who knew him, and were in prison with him, and now he knows that although Shalamov was a great writer, 'as a human being he was a bastard'.

What a town. Right now there are chevrons of wild geese flying over it, heading south.

And I've got a problem finding somewhere to stay the night. The only hotel, at the bus station, is full. They say it's full of Filipinos, but they turn out to be Australians, who want to buy a licence for a gold-bearing plot but don't trust the geological plans done by the Russians, so they've sent their own geological research team. The Filipinos were here before them, and gave up.

So I end up in a hovel for seasonal workers, a shabby block at No. 4 Lenin Street.

I undergo the obligatory registration, in other words I report my presence at the police station. I fill in an enormous form and submit a copy of my visa, my landing card and my passport. Every single page of it! Even the blank ones, and the ones with old visas from Mongolia, China, Russia and Vietnam.

I feel as if the deeper I venture into Kolyma, the further I plunge into the old, Soviet, suspended reality – the world of omnipotent officials who do everything to demonstrate their superiority, power, might, and authority over the person standing in front of their desk.

The alien registration procedure drags on into the next day.

I'm writing about these idiotic odds and sods, these trivialities, because they provide a good illustration of everyday life.

I'm sleeping in a room with four electricians who have come to Yagodnoye to do a job. Two of them snore monstrously, but at two in the morning we all jump to our feet. Outside all hell has broken loose. In front of the entrance to our block a pack of large dogs is causing an uproar. And I'm sleeping by the window, on the ground floor. There are dozens of homeless dogs in this town, and the bitches are on heat.

Bob, known as Bobik, on his way home from work.

Officially he's Bob, but everyone calls him Bobik. He's the most famous dog in town. A really big cheese, and a genius too, an aristocrat despite being a mongrel, but there must have been a laika in his distant ancestry. He doesn't talk, but only because he doesn't choose to.

This dog belongs to Viktor Andreyevich Smolyakov, editor-in-chief of the local newspaper, *Severnaya Pravda* (Northern Truth, affectionately known as the *Severka*). But you might as well say this man belongs to Bobik. Every morning they come to work together, go to meetings and interviews together, collect material for articles together, and, as they share an office, they probably write together too. They are only ever apart when Viktor goes on a business trip. Then the mongrel keeps an eye on everything at the newspaper office. When his master returns, he calls someone at the paper and asks them to tell Bobik that he's back. They say the dog opens the door by himself and goes home.

He can be sent to lots of places. You only have to say 'home', 'newspaper', 'post office', 'administration', or 'shop'. Bobik knows these words and places perfectly well. His master's wife works at the post office, and the local paper is the organ of the regional administration, so the editor-in-chief is very often there, and even more often outside the shop. Bobik has fetched him from there on more than one occasion.

Whenever Viktor goes on holiday to mainland Russia, Bobik moves into the newspaper office for the duration, even though Viktor's wife keeps calling him and saying 'Home'.

In the Far North, people have two months' leave each year, and every two years the state pays for all retired people, pensioners and state or local authority employees to have a free return flight to the mainland.

Viktor has been working at the *Severka* for thirteen years now. He's been in charge for a year. Ten years ago, Bob was born under the previous editor-in-chief's desk.

'I delivered the litter myself,' he says, once we've holed up in his office with some Dagestani brandy and snacks.

'But—'

'Let's drink!' he interrupts me, before I can add 'how?' 'One in the eye for the communists!'

Viktor grips his glass in both hands and tips it back, then battles with a slice of pork fat that gives him the slip. Because Viktor hasn't got any fingers. He has part of his right thumb left, in which he can grip a fork or a pencil whenever he has to tap something out on the computer. It doesn't bother him at all. On the contrary. He loves to wave his paws about. He absolutely has to greet everyone by offering his hand.

'What sort of team do you have here?' I ask him.

'A shitty one.' Viktor is very small and has the rare gift of being able to say awful things about anybody.

'But how many of them are there?'

'Along with the cleaning ladies, the IT guy and all the rest, fifteen. Including four journalists and a photographer.'

They mainly write about nature, hunting expeditions, fishing trips, and a bit of history. Not a word about the health service, education, the police, corruption or bureaucracy ... No criticism, because that would mean the regional administration, which owns the paper, is doing a bad job. But there is one exception – the chairman of the city administration. He's a communist, the only real opposition to the United Russia Party, which reigns supreme in the Yagodninsky region, the Magadan oblast, and the Russian Federation. By what miracle he triumphed in the most recent local election, no one knows, and in articles penned by Viktor himself, the *Severka* gives him a merciless drubbing in every single issue, branding him with all manner of infamy.

Viktor loves his work, his position, his office and his desk more than life itself. He's prepared to write and do as he is told, just to keep it all. He tells me this in confidence. He has done a wonderful job of fitting in with the provincial realities of the place, and has settled in well among the local aristocracy. But his even greater passion is *preferans*, a card game for at least three people. And here there's a problem, because in Yagodnoye there are only two players. There was a third, but he moved away to Magadan.

'Luckily he comes here on business for two or three days each month, because he has a shop here, and then we pounce on the cards like starving wolves.' Viktor rubs his hands together. 'We make a night of it, the soul takes wing, and of course we also have a drop to drink while we're about it.'

Viktor tells me to pour, and the whole time I'm wondering how he holds the cards. We've drunk an entire bottle of iced lemon brandy, but somehow I haven't the temerity to ask.

He tells me about his dreams. They mainly bring back his childhood and youth spent on the Don. As they set off for the river, he plays the concertina, and then they catch crayfish.

'Have you ever had crayfish in beer?' he asks. 'It's the best thing in the world! A Don Cossack can't survive without it. Have you ever caught crayfish? You do it with your bare hands. They grab onto your fingers . . . It's such a pleasant feeling! That's the main thing I remember from childhood. But there are no crayfish here. It's too cold.'

We walk each other home, Bobik showing us the way. It turns out we're living in the same block. On the way Viktor explains what a blessing the men are for Russia. Here they work until the fifty-fifth year of their lives (five years fewer than in mainland Russia), and four years later they die, because that is the average life expectancy for a Russian.

'In the north it's even less,' he says. 'And seven years ago on this little bridge I almost gave up my life. Some yobs were pestering a woman I'd never seen before, and although I'm small and skinny, I am a Don Cossack, so I intervened. They whacked me on the head with a bottle. I collapsed, and it was minus forty on the twenty-sixth of December. They took off my hat and gloves and poured beer over my hands. I was found by a man who just happened to come along, but my fingers were frostbitten.'

'Were you at all drunk?'

'Why wouldn't I be? It was seven in the evening. I was on my way home from work.'

'Had you had a drink at the office?'

'On my way home,' says Viktor.

'Had you bumped into someone you knew?'

'Of course! We all know each other here.'

'Did you know the yobs?'

'Actually I didn't.'

'What about Bobik?' I ask.

'He wasn't there just then. He'd gone home earlier because I'd been away on a trip. If he'd been there, we'd have done all right.'

Day XVII

Yagodnoye. Kilometre 522 of the Kolyma Highway

I thought I was going to drop dead. I go into the office, and there stands the Polish actor, Stanisław Mikulski, in a uniform, as usual. Though it's not a Wehrmacht uniform, but a Russian police one, and not a captain's but a lieutenant-colonel's, and he's not Kloss the fictional wartime double agent whom Mikulski famously acted on TV, but Kakhnovich. Viktor Viktorovich Kakhnovich, police chief for the Yagodninsky region.

I have a short chat with the lieutenant-colonel about his work and about the illegal trade in gold, but just a short one, because Russian civil servants are completely obsessed with the confidentiality of state and official secrets. It's a leftover from the days of the Soviet Union and heightened vigilance, the war against spies. Here in Kolyma not a day goes by without someone asking me straight out if I'm a spy. I say I'm not, and show them my Russian accreditation issued by the Ministry of Foreign Affairs in Moscow. It's my most valuable document. I couldn't take a single step here without it.

Then I ask the police chief if they caught the thugs who attacked the editor of the *Severka*.

They did – three drunken boys from pathological families. Two of them were minors. They saw an inebriated man carrying a parcel, so they whacked him on the head and robbed him. There was no woman in need of defence – that's just Viktor's favourite myth. The older attacker got eight years, the others got seven each, and when they grew up they were transferred from the young offenders' home to a prison. All three are still serving time.

We move on to politics, which I hate discussing in Russia, because it means I have to do some explaining. The Russians are pretty well clued up on world events, they watch television, buy newspapers and read a lot, but they can't possibly be up to speed on the nuances of what's happening in Poland. So I have to explain every foolish remark uttered by the most irresponsible Polish politicians, their idiotic insinuations that the Russians may have shot down the Polish president's plane over Smolensk, or deliberately damaged it, or released artificial fog, and provided an ugly Russki coffin, and so on. Russian television is all too willing to repeat this sort of tosh, and I get into trouble because of it. Seriously! Ordinary people in the provinces are hurt by such stories. So I explain to them that it's the political extreme, it's folklore, like the German politician Erika Steinbach, whom the Polish media love to write about because of her unfortunate remarks implying that Poland started the war. I tell them it's a basic principle of democracy that anyone can say whatever he wants, even if it's nonsense. The Russians can't understand this at all. They don't like the concept of 'democracy', which they associate with what they now think of as the worst period in their history, when the Soviet Union collapsed – in other words the 1990s, the Yeltsin era.

Ordinary Russians blame the democrats and democracy for the country's decline and for the indigence of the years that followed, calling it *dyermokratsiya* – 'dermocracy', because *dyermo* means 'shit'. Democracy ended over a decade ago when Vladimir Putin came to power, but all the country's failures are still blamed on the democrats.

It's extraordinary how in Russia everyday words can turn into insults. In the communist era the ugliest word of all was 'pacifist', then it was 'democrat'. Now it's 'liberal'.

And here's a small, symbolic curio: for many years Yagodnoye was called Yagodno, in honour of People's Commissar for Internal Affairs (head of the NKVD) Genrikh Yagoda, Yezhov's predecessor, the butcher, murderer and degenerate who started the Great Purge. Yezhov had him killed on Stalin's orders. At that point the name of the place was changed by adding one letter (-e, which transliterates as -ye), so that instead of reminding people of Commissar Yagoda, now it would glorify the local berries – *yagoda* means a berry – a whole sea of which grows in the surrounding taiga.

A second symbolic detail concerns the local Orthodox church, which is painted a hideous underpants-blue colour. It used to house the local *raikom*, in other words the district committee of the Soviet Communist Party.

Midday on the dot.

Maria Yakovlyevna Koshalenko is eighty-five and has lived in Kolyma for sixty-five years. She comes from the Urals, where they started forcing people into collective farms in 1937. Soldiers came into their farmyard, took all the grain and animals, and drove off. Maria's father, identified as a kulak, a rich farmer, died as a result, so his wife, son and daughter moved to the city. When the war began, Maria's brother was taken into the army, and her mother died too.

The girl was fourteen. She was completely alone. She went to work in a mine factory, then four years later the war ended, even the one against Japan, and a machine tore off her finger. Maria was laid off on medical grounds and went to live with her aunt in their home village. She arrived one day late for work.

'I got there, and at the gate the guards took away my pass and my Komsomol membership card, and arrested me,' Maria Yakovlyevna relates. 'I got six years under Article fifty-eight, paragraph fourteen, I think.'

In other words, economic counter-revolution, also known as sabotage – for what else is neglecting your job and shirking?

Maria was eighteen years old. She ended up in Kolyma, at a timber-felling site at Kilometre 43, then she worked on the wheelbarrows, mining gold at Kilometre 359. And that was in the terrible 1940s. They used to say 'sorokovye – rokovye', meaning 'the forties – fateful'. She couldn't bear it, and after eighteen months she escaped.

'A friend and I went running down to the Route, with shouts, shots and dogs barking after us ... We got to the road. Oh, I said, there is a God! There's a car coming! So we stopped it. But they were "operationals", a squad of runaway hunters. They took us to Yagodnoye, and then to the investigation camp at Serpentinka. A military tribunal, and they added four years for trying to escape. Also Article fifty-eight.'

And paragraph 14 again, because escaping also counts as shirking, and thus economic counter-revolution. And once you had tried to escape, you were bound to end up digging gold at a penal camp for women in Debin, a place which could be described as a women's hell. And she went straight to its very depths, into the ninth circle.

'I promised myself I'd never tell anyone what I saw there, what I went through. The guards were nothing, but the criminals, the *vorovki*, the ringleaders ... It was quite normal for them to kill other prisoners with axes, rape them, beat them up, steal their food ... They were horrendous. Worse things happened there than I've ever heard about in the war. It's a miracle I survived it.'

A *vorovka* (plural *vorovki*) is the female equivalent of a *vor* in the criminal hierarchy – a top-level thug.

Maria stuck it out. Then she was transferred to the huge women's camp at Elgyen, near Yagodnoye, where there was a vast collective farm. The years of extreme starvation were over for her. In the autumn drivers came to fetch the vegetables they grew from the Yagodninsky transport depot and deliver them to the neighbouring camps.

'That was how I met a boy,' says Maria Yakovlyevna. 'A free man, a driver. During the war he'd been in a tank crew. He was wounded in Poland, and came to Kolyma of his own free will to work. A good lad and a communist! He was always coming to see me. We'd meet in the fields, because from 1952 on I was no longer under escort, so it was easier, there was nobody keeping an eye on me. In the autumn Ola was born, our daughter, but a week later they took her away from me to the *dyetkombinat*.'

Literally that means 'the children's conglomerate' – the child factory. They were kept there until the age of three, and then they were taken away to children's homes in Russia. Any mother who wanted to could look for her child once she'd been released, but it didn't happen often, because many of them gave birth as a way of getting into a less severe camp, with a better job, and for the extra food to which pregnant women were entitled.

A vast number of women gave birth in the camps. Many of the pregnancies were the result of rape, including gang rape, to which hundreds of women fell victim. This was the case at Elgyen too.

A week after giving birth Maria returned to the zone and went back to work.

'Once a month I could see my daughter,' she tells me. 'But only in an illicit way, when we went to the bathhouse. I'd give the guard something and beg her to let me see my daughter. I'd rush there and maybe get to spend an hour with her, hold her in my arms, and then race back. I can't begin to describe what it was like to leave that child there and hurry off to the bathhouse.'

'And the tank driver, your daughter's father, didn't he want to take her?'

'How could he? How could he prove she was his?'

There were terrifyingly few women in Kolyma. On days when they were released from Elgyen, men would come down by the lorryload from all over the taiga, all the Kolyma mines, gold plots and factories, as if to a slave market. Almost all of them had once been prisoners too. They would wait for the women at the gates, and as soon as one appeared, they'd go up to her and ask if she had somewhere to go, and if she didn't, they'd say 'Come with me.' That was all. There was a terrible thirst for love.

The women who hadn't found a future husband would gather in the evenings among the bushes near a petrol station at the edge of town. They called this place the fiancé fair, where rapid matchmaking took place, and some thorough getting to know each other.

But Maria was still serving time.

'Then one day, to our surprise, they didn't drive us out to work,' she tells me. 'They lined us up in the parade ground. In the middle there was a pillar, and on the pillar there was a loudspeaker, which suddenly spoke in the voice of Molotov, saying that Stalin was dead. I remember that moment to this day. As I stood there, my entire family passed before my eyes. A wonderful, large family full of good people, which had disintegrated when I was ten years old. People who were always hard-working, God-fearing non-drinkers. I began to cry.'

'What about the others?' I ask.

'They were crying too. Some were silent, and some others were laughing, rejoicing. Because there were women there who had been imprisoned on twenty-five-year sentences since the war for nothing more than stealing a bottle of milk from the collective farm for a child. Their husbands had been killed fighting, and their children had been sent to orphanages. At Elgyen they counted as "enemies of the people". Then a couple of months went by, and they began to release us. At the end of 1953 the governor sent for me and said I'd already served my six years for being one day late for work, and they were going to let me off half the sentence for trying to escape. I collected my documents and went to fetch my daughter. She'd spent a year and a half at the *dyetkombinat*. And then out I went, through the gate. My God! To think what I'd had to endure in those eight years . . . Are you recording all this?'

'Yes, of course. I told you in advance.'

'But I haven't said much.'

'Not much,' I confirm.

'And I've had letters with best wishes from President Putin,' says Maria Yakovlyevna, showing me some official anniversary leaflets with a picture of the Russian president on them. 'And from Medvedev. I'm very grateful, because they send them every year on the ninth of May.'

'Why on the anniversary of the war?'

'Because I'm a war veteran. A behind-the-scenes combatant. I spent four years working a lathe in an arms factory. Shall I show you my medal?'

'Absolutely!'

'They gave it to me on the anniversary of the Great Patriotic War.'

'*Podvig vash bessmiertny,*' I read on the medal – 'Your heroism is immortal.'

LITTLE MOTHER MARIA – HUNGER FOR LOVE

'I had a whole wall of books, but I gave them away to my son,' says Maria Yakovlyevna.

'When was he born?'

'I got him from the hospital. We had our daughter, and my husband and I were very keen to have lots of children, but I couldn't have any more. All because of failing to fulfil the norm. They made three of us stand in a stream for an hour as a punishment. Barefoot. Water up to our waists. And a guard on the bank watching us. That was enough to make sure I never had children again. I was extremely ill after that. Inflammation of the ovaries. I almost died.'

'What month was it?' I ask.

'During the potato harvest. It must have been September, almost winter. But the water there was always icy, as it is in the mountains. In Yagodnoye I worked for the *Severnaya Pravda*, printing the newspaper. Next to the newspaper office there was a children's hospital, and in summer they used to bring the children out into a small garden, and one time I went out for my dinner break, but for some reason I didn't go home, I just sat and watched those children. And one of them seemed so isolated from the rest. A weak, sickly one whose mother had abandoned him at the hospital. The next day I went there again and had another look at him . . .'

Maria Yakovlyevna starts to cry.

'I'm sorry,' she sobs.

'It's all right. I'm happy to cry with you.'

'Because you see, I was fourteen years old when I was left without my parents, and there was that poor little chickabiddy, only eight months old and nobody cared. So I persuaded my husband, and we put in a request to the Party district committee asking them to let us have him. Three times they turned us down.'

'You asked the Party?' I say in amazement.

'Who else?' It's her turn to be amazed. 'The committee met and said "*Nyet*". So I came to an agreement with the doctor to let me have the child for Saturday and Sunday, and when I came to work on Monday I'd hand him back. So I took him home with me, and I gave him a good wash, a decent bath, and a proper feed, and put him to bed with us. Or with our daughter, our Ola, who was thirteen by then. He was called Yura, and I didn't change his name. And one Saturday in 1965, when my daughter had gone to summer camp, in the middle of the night I took my documents, some cash, and some spare nappies, sent my husband to fetch the taxi – there was only one in Yagodnoye – and we went five hundred kilometres to Magadan. I stole the child. In Magadan I bought an air ticket, sent my husband home and flew to Moscow. Then I went to Ukraine to stay with my husband's family.'

By some miracle Maria managed to travel the entire length of the Soviet Union without any documents for the child. In critical situations she pretended to be breast-feeding him. And he pretended too.

In Yagodnoye the militia spent two weeks going crazy looking for the child and his kidnapper. Her husband pretended his wife had run away and left him, but once the situation had calmed down, a few months later Maria came home. And she even got permission to adopt the child.

Five years later her husband died, leaving her on her own with two children, but as usual she coped. The kids were very good students, finished college, started their own families and companies, and are happy.

'And I'll tell you another thing,' says Maria Yakovlyevna, 'I'm very grateful to our governor from Magadan. Every year on the ninth of May he sends me a large fish by courier. He never forgets! Seven or eight kilos! It's enough for me for the entire winter. I just have to write and say thank you, so he won't think I've died and give my fish to someone else. Shall I show you my employment booklet?'

'Absolutely!'

'Just two entries. Printing at the newspaper office, and then at the bookshop. That's my entire record.'

'Every zek has a release certificate as well,' I say. 'The most important document he gets in his whole life.'

'I tore it up! I threw it away! I didn't want the children to see it! I didn't want them to be ashamed of me.'

'Ashamed? But Maria Yakovlyevna, you never did anything wrong! You were a victim.'

'Yes, but they were at school, they were in the pioneers, and a mother who's a criminal ... An awful disgrace. Now I don't hide it any more. Two months ago my son came from the mainland for a couple of days, and I even told him how dreadful it was in Debin. But he doesn't know he's not mine.'

GRANDMOTHER MARIA — TWO HUNDRED VOLUMES

Maria Yakovlyevna's little granddaughter was extremely ill. The doctors said the only hope was to move away from Kolyma to somewhere with a milder climate. But Yura and his young wife hadn't a penny to their names. The Soviet Union was falling apart, and everyone was in trouble, so nobody could even lend them the money to leave.

So Maria gave them her wonderful library to sell.

'The Empire was crumbling, and you expected people to buy books in this godforsaken hole in the middle of the taiga?'

'They did buy them! They spent their last kopecks, but they bought them,' she says proudly. 'That saved my granddaughter's life. We only took as much for the books as I had paid myself. If I'd paid four-twenty, then four-twenty it was. What mattered was to cover the cost of the tickets. Among the books there was a fabulous fifty-volume edition of world children's literature. What lovely illustrations it had! My daughter-in-law didn't sell it. They took it with them to the mainland. They had five suitcases and a backpack, because they were leaving for good, and two of the suitcases were full of books, children's literature.'

'They loved their child,' I say.

'And the books. They also left . . . It's the most wonderful thing the Soviet Union had alongside Shostakovich, Akhmatova, Gagarin and Vysotsky—'

'What's that?'

'A great two-hundred-volume edition of world literature. For adults. Everyone wanted to buy them because it's the greatest treasure you could have in the home, but we didn't know how much money we'd get, so we took down names for the two hundred volumes. More than a hundred people came forward! In such a small place with only a few thousand residents! In such hard times! But we reckoned we had enough for three tickets already, so we didn't sell them. They took the children's literature away with them, and my son only took the adult ones this year.'

'You didn't have to give them away.'

'But I wanted to,' says Maria Yakovlyevna. 'I love giving books to my children. I've been buying them all my life, and those two hundred and fifty volumes were on subscription. I used to get one volume a month. Can you imagine? I spent more than twenty years collecting the entire set. I used to pick them up at the post office. And I tell you, I'm very grateful to the chairman of our regional administration. He came in person on the ninth of May, offered me his best wishes and left gifts. The administration is good. They never forget, they treat me with respect.'

'How much is your monthly pension?'

'Nineteen thousand roubles, plus bonuses for being a veteran of labour and a war veteran. It comes out at twenty-one thousand [£420].'

'And the bonus for victims of repression.'

'No. I've never asked for it, I am not a victim. What do I need it for, anyway? I don't need rehabilitation either. I'm just grateful they let me go. And that I survived the 1940s. The fateful forties! My son wanted me to move to the mainland with him. But I'll live out my days here. I know every pebble of the earth here. It's my earth, my own beloved land. My Kolyma.'

Day XVIII

Yagodnoye. Kilometre 522 of the Kolyma Highway

Today I bought some deodorant. I walked all over town looking for a shop – there were dozens, but all of them were selling *produkty* only, in other words foodstuffs. Finally I found one with a toiletries section. I need deodorant now. To keep the weight of my bag down, I never take any on the road, and usually I don't need it. I might change my shirt every two or three weeks on a journey, but that's if I have the occasional wash, and right now I've gone rather a longish time without one. I'm not fussy, but there are bathrooms in this world at which you take one glance and know you'd rather stink. Even brushing your teeth is an act of heroism in places like that.

Human odours are a curious matter. When a friend and I travelled across the Gobi Desert by bike, we went the entire month without a drop of water except for the drinking kind, and the whole time we both smelled the same as when we set out. Mongolian nomads don't stink either, nor do the nomads from arctic regions of Asia – the Nenets, Komi and Evenks – not even in winter, although they wear furs the whole time and live in tents, without water or baths.

From the reporter's point of view I regard this day as a great success, because as well as deodorant I found a real diamond – a human one. A man with the sort of history every reporter dreams of.

How did I come upon Yura Salatin? By accident, of course. I didn't really know what to do with myself this morning. I felt as if my work was reaching an impasse, so in a downcast mood I trudged off to the cemetery. I had no idea what for. I often do that when I feel a crisis coming on.

From the road I saw an old Soviet IZh motorbike with a sidecar standing by a heap of scrap metal. I recently got my motorbike licence, so I found a way in there to examine this specimen at close quarters. Then Yura appeared, washed his face with snow, blew his nose in his fingers and invited me into his wooden garage, or workshop, for tea, which turned out to be brandy.

And what a handsome man he is! In an old airman's sheepskin jacket, an officer's cap and a blue polo-neck on his bare chest, with large holes under the arms. He's energetic, straight-backed and holds his head high. He's well built too. He's sixty-seven years old, his face is tanned almost black, and there's a defiant, rascally glint in his clear bright eyes the colour of his sweater. He's a real beauty. His hands are large, strong and rough. You can tell he's an officer from a mile away. But you'd have said he was the captain of a stricken warship returned from the battle of Trafalgar, not a scrap-metal dealer from Yagodnoye. Commander of a yacht, not of the local tip.

The inside of Yura's shed is like a continuation of the junkyard outside, except that its constituent parts are much smaller. Yura extracts a set of false teeth from a metal mug, puts them in place and takes me on a tour of his cave. Everything he has comes from the tip. He has just restored it all to life – machines, stoves, kettles. He single-handedly assembles motorbikes and furniture – he even made the officer's cap and the tank driver's helmet he wears when he rides his motorbike, on a sewing machine of his own construction.

But this must be the only junkyard in the world where there's nothing I'd like to have. There's nothing curious in it, nothing worth inspecting. It isn't like Yura from Debin's junkyard. That Yura collected trash, this Yura digs it out of the rubbish heap.

There's a huge box full of nothing but samovars, but they are not antiques from Tula, just Soviet junk, the plug-in kind. There are also dozens of electric engines, drills, accordions, hats, chandeliers, lampshades, phones, batteries, handsaws, mechanical saws ... And lots of radiators from demolished buildings, crappy high-gloss dressers, and old fridges, with hundreds of snake-like coils writhing about among it all. The coils of shower hoses.

There are several pictures on a rug fixed to the wall. The most important one is of Misha – a Red Army major like his father, he was a helicopter pilot shot down by an American Stinger over Afghanistan in the final days of the Soviet intervention there. He was decorated twice with the Hero of the Soviet Union star – three months before his death and at his funeral.

Below this are pictures of Yura's younger offspring – Galka, and Vaska, who is a diplomat in Holland. Each of Yura's children has a different mother.

But no photos of women, sweethearts or wives, of whom Yura has had nine (not counting Misha's mother, whom he didn't marry, and the women in between). He has worked his way through the lot of them in the thirty-six years since he first came to Yagodnoye. All of them still live here, and Yura is on friendly terms with them, especially when they need money. I ask him to list their names in turn, but after Natalia, Lucy and Olga he gets lost. He was with each of them for two or three years, and, even though they are divorced, the last one still lives with him because she has no place to move to.

I ask if he loved them, at which he makes a face and explains beautifully that it's the same with women as with rusks or sunflower seeds – you can guzzle away all day, but you can never eat your fill.

Yura is the local Croesus. He gets a monthly army pension of 30,000 roubles, plus 10,000 for working at the town tip, and on average about 13,000 roubles a month for the scrap metal he collects (a total equivalent

Major Yura Salatin at his rubbish tip.

to £1060). He accumulates it in old metal fuel drums. Once full, each one weighs seventy kilos, and once he has collected forty drums, he puts up a sign on the Highway to say he has scrap metal to be transported to Magadan. The Chinese or Japanese buy scrap metal at the port for 11,000 roubles a tonne (£220). The driver who picks up the metal from Yura gives him the money on his return journey. The whole system works on trust, and it has been fine for years.

So we sit and drink Caucasian Tradition brandy from Dagestan, and I wonder why people have never brought beautiful objects out to Kolyma. I don't get the chance to ask Yura about it, because my body is suddenly pierced by a bolt of lightning from the bare wires sticking out of the electric stove behind me. Until then I was sober, I thought, but after a few shots of brandy I'm losing my vigilance. The stove was built by my host.

The most exciting thing here is his motorbike. I want to buy it, because Yura has nearly finished building the next one, but we can't come to terms. Money is not the issue. Yura is worried I won't survive. With every day, and with every kilometre I travel westwards, it's getting colder. On a motorbike I won't even make it to Susuman at Kilometre 625. He's not going to sell it to me, and that's final. So we put on tank drivers' helmets and travel to the tip. I ride in the sidecar, but once there we fill it up with scrap, so on the way back I sit behind Yura. My seat is made from an old sterilizer for medical equipment, and to stop the stainless steel from freezing the bum, Yura covers it with sheepskin.

'How did you end up in Kolyma, Yura?'

'That's a very long story.'

'I love long stories,' I reply. 'Start from the crucial moment.'

'My mother died when I was eighteen months old.'

'So it was in 1945. That's a very long story indeed.'

'I can remember toddling underneath the horses in the stable, when I was just a tiny tot, and my father thrashed me mercilessly for it, because the stallion could have shied and trampled me. But I loved the stable. The horses never did me any harm. I used to creep under their bellies, and they'd nibble at my head. It was the sweetest thing. My first childhood memory. And I used to sleep in the manger all summer. I'd be asleep, and the horses would gently nuzzle my head. Because a child's head is sweaty, so it's salty, and they were trying to lick it, nuzzling me. And there was a clever one, Styopa, who would bend his leg the moment he saw me, to make a step to climb up, and then he would toss me onto his back. In 1947 Styopa and the whole farm were incorporated into a collective farm. We lived outside Tarnopol in Ukraine. Before the war it was part of Poland, and my father served in your army, but he was away for the whole occupation, because he was a *bandyuga*.'

'What's a *bandyuga*?' I ask.

'A thug, a *banderovyets* — a partisan in the Ukrainian nationalist movement led by Stepan Bandera. How the hell did I come to be born in 1943, when he spent the whole war in that gang? And I didn't look the least bit like him. Maybe that's why he hated me so much when he came out of the forest and thrashed me with that Polish army belt of his, until the blood splashed the walls. I wouldn't be surprised if he was the one who battered my mother to death. One hell of a thug. A real *banderovyets*. How he managed to avoid getting picked up by the secret police and sent to a camp I will never know. It's a miracle, because he was virtually a kulak, a former Polish soldier and a supporter of Bandera. Round our way everyone was with Bandera, but they were all as silent as the grave.'

'Did your father remarry?'

'Yes. She was Polish, just like my mother, with the surname Nakonieczna. She bore him a daughter, and they started thumping and abusing me even more. It's true I was a little rascal, but you can't beat a child every single day. I ran away from home. I was five years old, and I got all the way to Dnepropetrovsk on my own. In those days, after the war, nobody took any notice of vagrant children. There were thousands of us. The militia picked me up at the station. I wouldn't tell them where I was from. As I refused to say anything, they assumed I was a war orphan, gave me the name Sokolov and took me off to an orphanage. But seven years later I did a runner and went back home.'

'How did they greet you?'

'My father beat the shit out of me so badly that I couldn't sit for a week. But I wasn't a little rascal any more, I was a hulking great hooligan. Twelve years old, raised in an orphanage. My stepmother couldn't lift a finger to me any more. She just bawled whenever I knocked someone about, screaming that the Moskal was back, and trying to hit me. They called me "Moskal" – the term of abuse for a Russian – because I only spoke Russki now. They spoke Ukrainian. I only stuck it out for three years. I got thrashed with that Polish army belt again, so I thought fuck the lot of them! I ran out, and I had a fine bow of my own making, so I tied a wick made of hemp to an arrow, dipped it in oil, lit it and fizzzz! The house was on fire.'

'Whose?'

'Ours! With a thatched roof! What the fuck did they keep thrashing me like that for? I ran straight to the station and got on the first train. I was fifteen now, and I got all the way to the Urals. It was only at the station in Serov that the militia caught me. I said I'd run away from the children's home in Dnepropetrovsk, so they gave me an escort and took me back to the orphanage under guard. Then came special schools for thugs like me, then some tests, which I came out of superbly, and I was accepted at artillery officers' training school. I wasn't eighteen yet when my son Misha was born. Natasha, his mother, died in childbirth, so the officer in charge of our school adopted the boy as his own. But I was still passing myself off as a war orphan. We all were, for security reasons, because after a year we were all sent to a test site in Novaya Zemlya, and that's a terribly secret place.'

'What did you do there?'

'We tested various missiles. I was a radar operator. I guide a missile and follow its flight. They launch this sort of technical marvel in Kamchatka, each radar station passes it on to the next one all the way to us, and I whack it into the target. Or vice versa, we launch a rocket towards Kamchatka, and we guide it until it disappears over the horizon. I can't tell you any more, because I signed a confidentiality agreement. I was the only officer in the unit who wasn't in the Party. I dug my heels in. They actually wanted to throw me out for that reason, but then they'd spent seven years training me, so they hesitated to get rid of me just for that.'

'But you did leave.'

'We had a ballistic missile blow up on take-off. It exploded the second it left the launcher. It was a Pioneer, in NATO they called it the SS-20. It ripped apart a three-metre concrete wall as if it was cardboard. I was engulfed in a ball of fire. We were lucky the warhead wasn't armed and that only the eight tonnes of solid missile fuel blew up. I spent the next six years fighting for my life in Soviet hospitals all the way from Leningrad to Vladivostok. I had three blood transfusions. They needed to do it a fourth time, but perestroika or something came along, and they said I had to pay three thousand roubles per litre.'

'That was an awful lot in those days.'

'Where was I to get fifteen thousand roubles? I was on a pension. But leukaemia was the least of my worries. I had terrible burns which refused to heal for years. The worst were on my hands and feet, the parts of my body which were in leather boots and gloves before the explosion. They'd put out the rest of my clothing pretty quickly, but those leather boots and gloves had gone on and on burning. I tried living in Europe, then in Siberia, but the wounds kept on festering, worse and worse. In Siberia it wasn't bad in the winter, but in the summer, when the hot weather came, the skin on my hands and feet came off in patches. To the raw flesh. I couldn't walk, or touch anything. The doctors in Novosibirsk said I must move to a dry cold climate, and just then they were recruiting people for gold mining in Kolyma, so I signed up. They made me the foreman of a Komsomol brigade. Me, who fucking swore like a bloody trooper. And I was cured in a couple of weeks.'

'It must have been the morning dew,' I say.

'How do you know?'

'That's how Vitali from Debin cured the athlete's foot he caught from his army boots.'

'In Kolyma all skin diseases are cured that way. In summer I would get up early in the morning and crawl about in the dew on all fours. So my hands would heal too. It's best to search out a patch of wild *klevier* for yourself.'

'What's that? I don't know that word. Say it another way.'

'It's a weed with white flowers. Animals love it. In Ukrainian it's *konyushina* [clover]. And how bloody badly it hurt! Because they were open wounds, imagine walking on the ground on raw flesh. I'd leave bloody footprints behind me, then I'd wrap my feet in cellophane to avoid ruining my shoes, and go dancing. After five years they made me deputy manager of the Yagodninsky Mining Conglomerate. The summer came, the girls were in light frocks, running about without stockings, and I had to do annual reports, semi-annual appraisals, quarterly balance sheets . . . But I didn't give a shit about all that! I stuck it for eighteen months, then I went to see the boss and said I had a void in my head, I said my life was all about screwing women, not shuffling bits of paper. Make me a driver! And he did.'

'And now you're a discoverer. You discover scrap metal on the rubbish tip.'

'But when I put on my uniform on Missile Troops Day or on the twenty-third of July, Veterans' Day, and set off across town, I positively glow! Moments like that are worth living for.'

Day XIX

Burkhala. Kilometre 557 of the Kolyma Highway

Je-e-esus! What a day. At 11.25 I'm standing on the Highway at the exit from Yagodnoye. It's Saturday. Traffic's at a minimum. Maybe one car every fifteen minutes or so. Half an hour later, the driver of a factory minibus for transporting workers pulls up next to me and thrusts a massive chunk of greasy smoked pork into my paws. Greasy, because there's a large piece of fat attached to the meat. Altogether about two kilos, but as it comes, without any packaging – a solid hunk of meat to make me feel that I'm in Kolyma. That's what he says.

An hour later I'm still standing in the same spot. It's a lovely day, sunny, and yet frosty, so I'm a bit stiff with cold. I'm wondering whether to open my backpack and extract a jacket from it when the meat guy reappears. He's come specially for me. He shields me from the wind with his minibus and gives me a sheepskin coat. A rustic, seasoned labourer's coat, black in colour, with bits of cedar cones in the pockets (the seeds are edible). For keeps! And there's no wriggling out of it, no chance to explain that I've got something to put on, I just don't feel like getting it out of my pack. He shouts at me that further on, in Yakutia, I'll freeze in my *khrenovye* (shitty) European rags, and forces the sheepskin coat on me.

At once I feel nice and warm. His name is Sasha. He decides to stop there with me until I get a result, and if we don't get a ride, we'll go to his place for the night.

Sasha always has his faithful laika at his side, whose name is Rem.

This dog is famous round here because a few days ago he managed to track down a rogue bear which had been terrorizing Yagodnoye for several weeks. It started when a cook from the local school's car broke down on the Highway, so she started walking towards town. She never got there. Tracks in the snow implied that a bear had grabbed her.

During the first hunt the cook's remains were found. She was a woman of very generous proportions. According to her family, she weighed ninety-eight kilos, but the hunters only found about sixteen. The bear had eaten all the soft parts, and had buried the bones for later. And then gone on hunting.

It killed two gold prospectors out in the taiga and bit the feet off a third one, who had fled up a tree. Finally it seized a man from a small square in the very centre of town, and the worm turned. All the local hunters set off in pursuit of it, and that meant almost half the men in Yagodnoye. They were accompanied by dogs, the sharpest and quickest of which was Rem.

Stories like these help to pass the time, so I was disappointed when someone stopped. I wasn't even waving at him. It's 1.30 p.m. A smart Honda van, and inside there's Anatoli Romanovich from Burkhala at Kilometre 557, which is exactly where I want to get to today. He stops because he has recognized me. By my face! Honest to God. I felt like a star, and all because of an interview I gave to Magadan television before setting off on the Highway.

Together we arrive in Burkhala. It's the capital of Kolyma's *khishchniki*, the seat of their king, Vladimir Mikhailovich Lyskavyets, a legendary eighty-year-old gold prospector. In Russian the word *khishchnik* means a predator, and in the figurative sense a plunderer. The Kolyma *khishchniki* are illegal, freely operating prospectors who look for gold and sluice it without licences, and Vladimir Mikhailovich is their godfather, a man famous throughout Kolyma for his ability to scent out precious metal, an innate talent, or maybe an animal instinct for finding it.

And here's what happens in the first ten minutes of our acquaintance.

Vladimir Mikhailovich is sitting on a small bench outside a shop called Nadyezhda ('Hope'). My *poputchik* Anatoli Romanovich stops his Honda. Vladimir Mikhailovich and his good friend Vanya are warming their old bones in the sunshine. I introduce myself, and refer to a common acquaintance, upon which Vladimir Mikhailovich invites me to his place, and then goes into the shop. He buys brandy, vodka, wine (just in case a woman were to come by), and plenty of things to eat. By local standards he spends a whole heap of cash and there is no question of my making a contribution (which is always my experience in Kolyma anyway). Vladimir Mikhailovich reaches into his pocket and fetches out a wad of 5000-rouble banknotes in bank-issued wrappers. Half a million roubles (10,000 quid), though if you were to cast an eye over the old boy you'd feel sorry for him, going about in such shabby old boots.

Vladimir Mikhailovich roars with laughter and puts the money back in his pocket. He says he's got his pockets muddled up, and explains that he keeps his line of credit in the left one, and the company capital in the right.

He takes me to his house. Vanya comes with us. Burkhala is yet another dying settlement. Of three thousand residents, there are only three hundred living creatures left, including cats and dogs, because all the gold in this vicinity has already been extracted, to the very last speck of dust. But there is still a bit underneath the actual settlement. So Burkhala looks as if a war has passed through it. The *khishchniki* have been tunnelling under the streets, in the basements and the courtyards. Half the houses have lost the ground under their foundations and are collapsing, and the other half, which are empty, have been burned down by vandals and scrap-metal thieves. The streets are caving in, the bridges are cracking, the electricity poles and boiler-house chimneys are falling over, and the courtyards resemble a front line criss-crossed by trenches. The residents sluice their gold wherever possible.

I gaze in wonder at an electricity pole stuck into a mound of earth one metre by one metre in size, as if a giant's child had made a bun out of sand and stuck a stick in it. The prospectors have removed all the earth from around it, only leaving enough to stop the pole from collapsing.

Vladimir Mikhailovich lives alone, but we're carousing at his neighbour Tamara's house because he hasn't got any tumblers, shot glasses, plates or forks – it's an old bachelor pad. And Tamara is the model hostess, a retired nurse from the settlement's medical centre, who has been supplying Burkhala with exquisite home-made hooch for the past thirty years. The fourth of my companions, Vanya, is also retired, but he prospects because he needs the money. He's even going to work in the winter, because this summer he had no luck and hasn't got any savings.

Working in the winter is dreadful. The ground is frozen hard as rock, so you have to warm it with bonfires, and the same goes for the water for sluicing, which the *khishchniki* do by hand – amid savage frost. The only advantage is that the *mienty* – in other words, the cops – don't pursue them in winter.

Any *khishchnik* who lets himself get caught pays the police a bribe to turn a blind eye without any arguing, because in theory you can end up in prison for only two or three grams of gold. The bribes are paid 'in grams', depending how much illegal precious metal they find on you. It is generally twenty or thirty grams of gold dust. And from then on they'll give you a *krysha*, which literally means a roof, and thus a cover, protection; once in a while they will come to collect their share.

Vladimir Mikhailovich addresses Tamara and Vanya by their first names, but they very respectfully call him Mikhailovich, which is his patronymic, based on his father's name.

Now I'm sitting in his flat, on a mattress which I'll be unrolling for the night on the floor in between the dresser and his sofa bed. We're watching TV Rossiya Kultura, Mikhailovich's favourite channel. He shows me an eighteen-gram gold nugget found recently. He keeps it on the television set, in a bowl for odds and ends.

Vladimir Mikhailovich, king of the khishchniki – *illegal gold prospectors –*
(left) with Vanya outside Nadyezhda's shop.

'I was three years old, but I've never forgotten that night in the autumn of 1933 when they came and took my father away,' recalls Vladimir Mikhailovich. 'In our town, Borisov in Belarus, a militiaman had been shot, and the blame fell on him.'

The young Vladimir — Volodya for short — was left alone at home, because his mother was on a night shift. He grew up without his father, and ten years later his mother got married again. But she had no luck with men, because a few months later the boy's stepfather was conscripted and went missing at the Front, and then a few months later his half-brother was born.

On 7 August 1949 Volodya was conscripted too. As bad luck would have it, he ended up in the navy, where the basic service lasted for five years. Twenty-two days later he received a letter from his father, who had come home. They hadn't seen each other for sixteen years, and they'd missed each other by three days. In the letter his father wrote that he understood the boy's mother, had forgiven her for not waiting for him and was going to stay with her, and he was adopting her younger son as his own.

'He'd come home, but I was only going to get my first pass two years later!' Vladimir Mikhailovich rarely raises his voice.

'Had he never written to you before?' I ask.

'Not once! Not a single letter in sixteen years! Though there were people who sometimes wrote from the camps. But there'd been no sign of life from him, so when ten years had passed, his entire sentence, we were sure he was dead.'

Two years later Volodya got his pass. He arrived at the family home very early one morning. At the threshold he put down his bag and opened the door. Inside he saw a man pulling on his boots, clearly getting ready to go to work. His face was totally unfamiliar.

'Dad, hello,' stammered Volodya. 'Is that you?'

'Yes. Hello, son. I'm off to work now, but I'll get some time off and come back to see you.'

But he only came home in the evening. They hadn't seen each other for eighteen years.

'Did your father give you a hug, did he kiss you or touch you?' I ask.

'No. We exchanged greetings and said hello to each other. Verbally. And when he came back from work, we drank a shot of vodka each. Then he told me his story. And I told him mine. Just like men. We drank tea, ate food and chatted all night one to one, although everybody wanted to see me, but Mama kept them out.'

'Did you weep?'

'No,' says the king of the *khishchniki*.

'Because you've got tears in your eyes now.'

'I cried when I got my father's letter. I like to cry sometimes. Such as when the children's choir sings on TV. From the sheer joy of hearing them sing so beautifully ... Come on, guys! Trebles all round!'

'What did your father say about his forced labour?'

'One thing was that right after being arrested he was put in a terrible prison in Orsha, where he was shut in an isolation cell, and opposite was the death cell, from which they took people out to be shot every night,' Vladimir Mikhailovich tells me. 'My father couldn't stand it. He dug a big nail out of the bunk, put it against his forehead, took a run-up and banged it into his head. But he hadn't aimed well, and he survived. Later on, once he was in Kolyma, he'd tried to escape three times, and for each attempt they added two years to his sentence. That was why he wasn't home for sixteen years.'

'It was rare for a former zek to tell his relatives his story,' I say. 'It's a mysterious, dark corner of the Russian soul which I will never understand.'

'People were ashamed. They didn't put you in prison for just nothing.'

'Yes they did! They locked you up for taking a bit of corn, a bottle of milk, or a handful of glue, or for being late for work. That's for nothing!'

'Well, come on!' Tamara interrupts us at this awkward moment. 'Let's drink to the fact that we've survived!'

'One in the eye for our enemies!' Vanya chimes in.

So we drink. We're snacking on the smoked pork I was given this morning on the Highway in Yagodnoye. For the moment we can't speak.

'My father told me some more,' says Vladimir Mikhailovich, finally breaking the silence. 'He said that here in Burkhala there was a custom that whenever a particularly brutal criminal zek died, the paramedic responsible for dead bodies would tie him to a post in the parade ground, and then anyone who wanted could come along and whack him with an iron bar as much as they liked. A very large number of them did, but not my father.'

'Did he live for much longer?'

'He outlived my mother. Probably because she smoked, and he didn't.'

'He didn't smoke?' I say in amazement. 'Almost everyone smoked in the camps. They traded bread for cigarettes.'

'And did you know that in those days there was already *anasha* [marijuana] in Kolyma? A Gypsy woman came after one of the Gypsy men and brought a whole bundle of it. My father said it was awful, because it made you feel hungrier than ever. He'd smoked it, and felt ready to bite off and devour his own hand raw. He'd have eaten anything, any filth, he'd have boiled his own boots. And after all those dreadful experiences, can you imagine, Jacek, my father lived to the age of eighty-nine. He had an easy death. I was already in Kolyma myself by then. In Burkhala. He went to the outhouse, sat down, and it was all over.'

'In the crapper?'

'Yes. That was in 1994. He even outlived the Soviet Union.'

KING SERGEI — TWENTY-SEVEN GOALS

I met him several days earlier in Yagodnoye. Sergei Bazavlutsky is one of the most powerful gold oligarchs in Kolyma. He sluices gold to the north of Yagodnoye, in the neighbourhood of Serpentinka, the place Vladimir, the man who puts up crosses at camp graveyards, talked about.

Bazavlutsky employs 107 workers and extracts more than half a tonne of gold a year. He has made various deals for himself, including exclusive ownership rights to a gigantic hunting ground for forty-nine years, by arrangement with the late lamented governor Tsvetkov. It covers 7500 square kilometres of taiga, an area as big as a large Polish province. He advertises in the *Severnaya Pravda* newspaper to announce that he does not allow any hunting or fishing there at all, and will shoot at poachers without warning, just like animals.

'Fortunately people are afraid of me and don't trespass,' he says. 'Probably that's why the security service from Magadan came and tried to persuade me to take over as mayor of the city. I refused.'

'First of all you'd have to win an election, not just take over,' I reply. 'And secondly why were the secret police getting involved in that?'

'Ask them. This is Russia, after all.'

'Lots of your friends are in politics.'

'To protect their own businesses and money. They're not doing it in the interests of the public.'

Before Bazavlutsky arrived in Kolyma in 1974 he was a professional Soviet soccer player for the Krivoy Rog team Krivbass, and for the Rovno teams, Khimik and Horyn, in Ukraine. He did his military service in the forces subordinate to the Ministry of Internal Affairs, and in Burkhala they made him chief engineer at the Molodyozhny plot.

'And there the labour force consists mainly of former prisoners, *blatniye* and *izmenniki*, meaning those who betrayed the fatherland. Mostly fascist policemen. They'd all been released from the camps many years earlier, but they weren't allowed to go back to the mainland. The authorities gave them jobs and a minimal, basic salary, but those former prisoners didn't give a shit about our mining plan. At work they'd sit in the pit and do nothing, just play cards, and when that type gets his pay, he doesn't leave the barracks at all, he just plays cards and drinks till the money runs out.'

So Molodyozhny always failed to meet the extraction plan. All the workers suffered as a result, earning very little.

The foreman at this plot was Vladimir Mikhailovich Lyskavyets.

The two of them decided to force the scroungers to work, and proceeded to implement a masterful piece of psychological warfare. They built a soccer pitch in the middle of the settlement, founded a Komsomol soccer team and challenged the former zeks to a match.

'It was appalling,' says Sergei Bazavlutsky. 'They thrashed the zeks, twenty-seven nil! The flower of the Kolyma criminal class let themselves be trounced by twenty-seven goals! Of which I myself scored twenty-three. Then Mikhailovich handed me all his savings, and I started playing them at *ochko*. I'd learned that card game as a child from the best champions. Nobody has ever beaten me at it, so Mikhailovich stood in for me at work, and in three shifts I'd cleaned out the whole of Burkhala.'

'How on earth did you do that? Against criminal zeks? They'd done nothing but play cards for half their lives. You must have cheated.'

'Sure I did! On the last night I got up from the table when I'd won the lot, shoved the cash under my sweater and calmly headed for the door. And I was just waiting to get stabbed in the back, because for them losing at cards is a disgrace, an insult. But at the door I turned around, went back to the table and emptied out all the money. I gave it back to them. That's an even bigger insult. But they took it, and from that day on they started helping me with everything. I only wanted them to work normally. And they started to do it.'

KING VLADIMIR — A GOLD HARVEST

'They let those *blatniye* of ours go back to the mainland in 1976,' Vladimir Mikhailovich tells me. Our evening feast at Tamara's is still in full swing. 'They only let the fascist policemen go when perestroika came, at some point in the mid-1980s, but they were afraid to go back to Europe because they would have been executed in Belarus and Ukraine for their ancient crimes.'

'We've known each other for thirty years, Mikhailovich, and I didn't know half these stories,' says our hostess, raising her glass. 'We've never talked so openly.'

'You can live with a person, but you can't get inside his soul,' he replies. 'Come on, everyone. To friendship!'

In the late 1970s Vladimir Mikhailovich found the most magnificent seam of gold. It's a story that was talked about for years in the world of Soviet gold prospectors. All of a sudden, from the first day of June, the entire management team at the Burkhalinsky Mining Conglomerate took leave, including the general manager, the chief engineer, the geologist, the accountant, the head of the trade union and the company's Communist Party secretary. Bazavlutsky took time off too, and under the leadership of Vladimir Mikhailovich they formed an eight-man brigade. While their deputies took charge of the conglomerate, the bosses spent a full month working like ordinary labourers. There were days when they sluiced eighteen kilos of gold. It is an achievement which to this day has never been bettered.

The idea was for the management to show the labour force how they should be working. Vladimir Mikhailovich had had his eye on this spot for ages. He knew, or rather sensed, that this would be a gold harvest such as Kolyma had never seen before. Every member of the improvised brigade earned a vast sum of money. A month later each of them was able to buy a car.

Not all the houses in Burkhala were burned down by vandals. The residents still tell a story about the time Vladimir Mikhailovich went to have a cup of tea with the English teacher after a party at the local club.

'Were you studying English?' I ask.

'I wasn't, but my son was. We put on the kettle, drank a few shots each and tumbled into bed. We were woken up by the fire alarm. The kettle was on fire, so was the kitchen, and so was the entire house. The whole settlement laughed at my English lesson.'

'Were you a good student?'

'Not bad. But I've forgotten a lot by now.'

'How old were you?'

'Seventy-one. And she was married. Her husband was in the army. You know what life's like . . . It may taste bitter, but it's a pity not to take it if they're handing it out for free.'

Vladimir Mikhailovich has been a widower for thirty years. After the English teacher he took up with a cook from the local nursery school. They've been together for nine years, but they don't live together. The woman is thirty-five years old. Our hostess Tamara has no objections either, as the king of the *khishchniki* puts it.

'I've told you quite enough stories. Let's drink up.'

Day XX

Susuman. Kilometre 626 of the Kolyma Highway

We're in Vladimir Mikhailovich's kitchen, eating a solid breakfast consisting of yesterday's leftovers. Black bread, pork and garlic, with cold water and brandy to drink. My host has no kettle. On the table is a biography of Ivan the Terrible, a tractor maintenance manual and a magnifying glass. The floor is strewn with geological charts of 'recognized gold deposits'. I think this is the dowry with which Vladimir Mikhailovich left the state mining enterprise.

Today there are local council elections in Russia. We go to vote. Then we have a cup of coffee with the election committee and return to Vladimir Mikhailovich's for my backpack. He declares that I'm not going to hitch a ride by the roadside because he's arranged transport for me to Susuman, which is sixty-nine kilometres away. This is the next town I have to reach. My host refuses to talk about money and is offended when I insist. He's already covered all the costs himself.

A friend's fifteen-year-old Lada Niva drives up to my host's house, we put my backpack and new sheepskin coat in the car and drink a farewell glass of brandy, then Mikhailovich takes me in his arms, and I'm off.

My next *poputchik* is a retired welder called Vasily Alexandrovich Kaitash. He lives in Burkhala, though he isn't a *khishchnik*, but a *volnoprinositel*, a small-scale, manually operating, independent but legal gold prospector. These people are organized into something like a cooperative, a collective, because they don't have their own individual licences. Vasily's firm is called Ametyst. He's only allowed to sluice gold on its plots, the ones which have already been dug up by large machines. He has to sell the output back to his own collective. They pay the market price minus all the taxes.

This year hasn't been a success for Vasily. He sluiced on average twenty to thirty grams of gold sand per month, which after subtracting taxes is 17,000–25,000 roubles (£340–£500). It looks as though he's going to have to transport coal to the plot, heat up the earth and the water, and work all winter. The trouble is, the Kolyma gold seams are hard to get at. They range from fifty to a hundred centimetres thick and are hidden away ten or twelve metres below the ground surface. Vasily has worked in the past at a seam in Yakutia which was seven metres thick and lay on the surface.

I ask if he has ever found a nugget. Never. We are just driving through the settlement of Polevoy, near which in 2005 the biggest Russian nugget since the collapse of the USSR was found. It's called the Adamovich, after the owner of the cartel that sluiced it out. It weighs 2.976 kilos and is the size of a child's fist.

A few dozen kilometres further on we reach Susuman, which is known for a major palaeontological find. In its suburbs in 1977 a mummified mammoth calf was carved out of the permafrost, almost untouched by time. It's a seventy-kilo, one-metre-tall baby from forty thousand years ago. Its name is Dima.

The town of Susuman has five thousand inhabitants (in the entire region there are only nine thousand left of the forty-seven thousand who were living here twenty years ago). A few days ago, thanks to a daring robbery, the town briefly featured in the media all over Russia.

The robbers stole seven kilos of gold sand from the strongroom at the Susuman Zoloto conglomerate. Earlier they had broken into a power station and switched off the electricity supply for the whole town. The lighting, alarm system and video surveillance all stopped working. The police caught the thieves at an airport in Moscow. They were boys of eighteen or nineteen, gold prospectors, not professional criminals. Until recently they had been working at the conglomerate, but their bosses had cheated them and hadn't paid them for an entire season's labour. They had sold the gold instantly for seven million roubles to dealers in Susuman (its market value was eight and a half million).

At the hotel I get what's called a 'half-lux' room – in a normal state at last (I'm not disgusted by going to the toilet or getting into the bed), though there's no shower, but compared with what I've had until now, and what is sure to be lying ahead of me, it feels like being on holiday. I spend a few hours doing nothing, just watching television and the changing light outside. Only in northern Siberia, and only in winter, is it like that, especially towards evening, just before darkness falls. A sort of inland transparent murkiness. The air takes on an unbelievable transparency, but of a sinister, even a terrifying kind. It's hard to describe. As if the air and open space had a colour, ever so slightly blue, an icy azure, although the ice, snow and frost are white.

I take a photo, but I can see that it doesn't really convey the climate outside.

Susuman. Outside the bakery.

Oxana Kaproska is an inspector for Rosselkhoznadzor. The Russians are past-masters at combining and compressing words. This is a peculiar assembly of four: its official name in English is the Federal Service for Veterinary and Phytosanitary Surveillance.

Oxana is a vet, and also a *metis*, a 'half-breed'. She is thirty-one, and she was born in a yurt, a Siberian native tent. She spent her childhood at the village of Topolovka in the east of Kolyma, at the top end of the Kamchatka peninsula. Her father is a Chukchi and her mother a Koryak. The Koryaks are a tiny people native to Kamchatka. They are reindeer herders, and there are about eight thousand of them.

Her parents met at a professional training school. Her mother usually spoke in Koryak and her father in Chukchi, they could only communicate with each other in Russian, so their four children only speak Russian.

Oxana left Topolovka when she was twelve to go to school.

'I thought it would be like at home, but in my class apart from me there were three Chukchi and ten Slav children. And I was a half-breed, "neither dog nor otter". Fourteen kids in the class, and I wasn't one thing or the other. I was all on my own. A foreigner. I felt like the away team. Not even the Chukchi accepted me as one of theirs. Then came school in Magadan. There the children used to run after me throwing snowballs and abusing me by calling me "Chukchi". It's a disgrace to be a Chukchi. The Chukchi is a dimwit, an idiot, a slob. That was why I didn't want to be a Chukchi girl.'

Oxana went back to Topolovka for her student practical training.

Earlier they'd announced in the village that a new vet was arriving, and what's more, 'one of us'. 'Who is it?' asked the reindeer herders. 'Oxana Kaproska.' 'Oh, she's not one of us.'

'It turns out I was a foreigner to them too,' says the young vet. 'Just as they were to me. They complained to my mother that I was badly brought up, I didn't know the language or the traditions, but I absolutely loathed all those old-fashioned superstitions and customs of theirs. I'm a normal girl educated in Russia, accustomed to treating people equally, but to them a woman matters less than a draught reindeer. She can't even eat with the men. So when the hell was I supposed to eat? I'd be working, but when I got back, first they'd eat, then the second group, then the first lot would want a cup of tea and I still couldn't eat. The men do none of the housework in the yurt at all. A man doesn't even pour out his own tea! He won't even say he'd like some, he'll just put down his mug so it can be seen and heard. And then he waits.'

Oxana went to college in Omsk in central Siberia, on the border with Kazakhstan, where slightly slanting eyes are perfectly ordinary. Everyone took her for a Kazakh, or thought she was a Tatar or Uzbek. The main thing was that they didn't ask.

'Who did you say you were?' I now ask her.

'A Koryak.'

'Why not a Chukchi?'

'Because that's a disgrace! Chukchi is a rude name, not a people. Do you know any jokes about the Chukchi?'

'Not by heart,' I say, 'but from Kolyma I'm going to Chukotka, so I downloaded some from the Internet. A few thousand.'

'Dad is annoyed with me and my sisters for not admitting that we belong to his ethnicity. It feels stupid. But being a Koryak is all right. Here in Susuman I'm the only one. And I'm on my own. Single. With just a dog. There is one Komi, an Aleut and an Itelmen, but what do

I care about them? I'm probably more of a Russian. I come out as a marginal. Foreign among my own people, and not accepted among foreigners. I've been living here for seven years now, and nothing has changed. I want to get out of here. First to Magadan. Then further, because I don't want to live in Russia. But I don't know where. Maybe Denmark? As I have no motherland, why not there?'

Oxana has two first names, her Russian one, and a Koryak one, 'Kaproska', which is the name of a bird native to Chukotka. Only the Russian name is for everyday, public use; the other one, given by the grandparents, is a private name, usually known only to the nearest relatives. It is the name of one of her ancestors, which can only be uttered in particular situations, for instance when she needs his help because she's sick or in danger.

'If I ever have children,' she says sadly, 'and my parents live to see them, they'll have two first names too. And if they don't live that long, I'll be the last generation in the family to have a private name. The last real Koryak.'

Day XXI

Susuman. Kilometre 626 of the Kolyma Highway

Yesterday evening I wrote about the weather, more specifically that the light here is strange and unsettling, and that there's something hanging in the air, a sort of threat, a murky fog, the omen of something.

And now I've got it. Winter has finally come to Kolyma. As usual it has arrived with its typical underhand urgency. It has raced in with a *purga*, meaning a blizzard, a snowstorm, but not a hurricane – that sort of blizzard would be called a *buran*. A *buran* is an ice-cold killer, quite simply death by freezing. The season for it starts in November, but today there's just a strong wind and it has been snowing all day. And it's calming down. Once again it's pretty, frosty and sunny, except that it has chucked down another half-metre of snow.

The Kolyma winter was the greatest ally of the men in charge of the Gulag, the deadly enemy of all zeks. Especially those who dreamed of doing a runner. It would catch them by surprise in the middle of their escape, and kill them or march them back to the camp gates in a frost-bitten state.

The Maldyak camp is nearby, where Sergei Pavlovich Korolyov, the father of Soviet space exploration, was imprisoned. Sentenced to ten years in the Gulag during the Stalinist purges of the late 1930s, the brilliant designer of rockets and space ships was already a *dokhodyaga* (a goner) when he was rescued by his mother. By some miracle she managed to get through to the legendary Soviet test pilot and polar explorer Mikhail

Gromov, who was decorated with the Hero of the Soviet Union medal by Stalin himself. The woman persuaded Gromov that the country needed her son, because he was the most outstanding aeronautical engineer in the USSR. Gromov had Korolyov brought out of Kolyma. He spent several more years in prison, but when the war ended he was released and included in a team researching V-1 and V-2 missiles captured in Germany.

But getting back to the winter, how am I so sure it has finally come? There's been snow on the ground for ages, ever since Yagodnoye, even from the first pass on the Highway, and it was already minus twenty at night in Debin. So how come I know for sure?

I'm going to play at being David Attenborough, and say something about nature, about a clever plant. It's a large coniferous bush, similar to the mountain pine (*Pinus mugo*), which also grows on Kolyma's mountain slopes. It is a close, dwarf, arctic cousin of the Swiss pine (*Pinus cembra*), and its Russian name translates literally as the 'Siberian cedar', but it is actually a pine (*Pinus sibirica*). It is the only plant in the Far North to stay green all year round. It has very tasty pine nuts and is the wisest plant in the world.

On the very last night before the definitive arrival of winter (and not just some mild frost bordering on minus twenty degrees), this smart shrub measuring about 1.5–2 metres in height lies down on the ground. The entire bush spreads itself out, and with all its might it huddles close to the earth. It does everything it can to get covered in as thick an eider-down of snow as possible, and it does it at the very last moment – after all, winter lasts for eight months round here. Thus it pulls the last blanket of snow over itself before the big freeze. And it NEVER gets it wrong.

Here they call it *stlannik* – the 'spreader', from the verb *stelitsya*, meaning to spread, or lay (for example, bedding or a tablecloth).

Last night in Upper Kolyma (my present location) the Siberian pines laid themselves flat, and now they won't get up until spring. And once again, thanks to these plants, people will know when it's coming. It will look as if it's still the middle of winter, but then the pines force their way out from under the snow – winter is over. By Kolyma's standards, the spring has arrived.

Since this morning I've been trying to get rid of my beard, because I look like Father Christmas, or some sort of hermit, an eccentric recluse from the taiga. My stubbly face makes me feel old. I haven't shaved since leaving Magadan. I never take a razor on the road, because I use an electric one and it's heavy. I usually go to the barber's and tell him to cut it as short as possible. But there's no men's barber in Susuman, and at the ladies' hair salon they refuse to serve me. There used to be a barber at the local baths, but out of fear of AIDS he was banned from practising his profession.

So, ugly as I am, I pay a visit to the local television studio, and give them an interview. Every regional town in Kolyma has its own TV studio. The woman in charge, who says she is 'the director' (the entire team consists of four people), is called Makka. This is a name given to Muslim girls in honour of the site sacred to all followers of Mohammed. Makka is an Ingush, she is thirty-one, and like all her compatriots in Kolyma, her dream is to return to her homeland. She is a very liberated young lady. She gladdens the eye with an immense, luscious cleavage, and is wearing a G-string, and shoes with such high heels that she can hardly walk, but she keeps telling me that a man should not offer his hand to a woman. It's not acceptable in Russia, nor is it appropriate towards a Muslim woman. Makka recently split up with her husband and has gone to live with her parents again, because a young woman cannot live on her own. Her mother and father are away for a few days, so I can only drop in at her place for tea once her twelve-year-old brother comes home from school.

That evening on Magadan television they announce the results of the local elections. Alexander Basansky, the gold oligarch whom I met in the regional capital, has won seventy-five per cent of the votes on his list in the election to the oblast parliament. It is the best result in the oblast. And of course the United Russia Party has won the most votes.

The Palace of Youth, with a modelling workshop protruding into the street.

The only people to have kept their human face in the Gulag, wrote Varlam Shalamov, were the religious ones: clerics, churchgoers, and 'sectarians', as all non-Orthodox believers were called. As moral decay engulfed everyone and everything, somehow they alone held out.

It's a weekday, Wednesday, so there are just eight people at the evening liturgy. But only three are members of the congregation. The rest are church people — the two-woman choir, the old biddy from the little shop that sells candles, Father Igor, and the elder from the church community, who has to be here every day, to clear the snow from the entrance.

It's a symbolic place, not just because it's the house of the Lord. In the 1940s the head of the North-Eastern Gulag Administration, the man who provided the slave labour force for the whole of Kolyma, lived here with his family. Then it housed the Komsomol regional committee, and after that the regional dental clinic. At the end of perestroika the people went to the authorities and demanded a place of worship, and so since 1990 the clinic has been an Orthodox church, dedicated to St Nicholas the Wonderworker.

Father Igor Yaroslavovich Terentyev is forty-one. After the service he invites me for tea and biscuits with honey. Honey from the taiga, but it wasn't made by bees, because there aren't any here — it's too cold. Kolyma honey is made by people, from Siberian pine. The young, green cones are boiled for a very long time, then strained; sugar is added to the stock, which is boiled again, and the honey's ready. It's thick and sweet, and tastes like cough syrup.

This is not the only use of Siberian pine. Varlam Shalamov claims that fires made with pine are warmer than others. And in the Gulag hospitals the mattresses were stuffed with chopped-up sprigs of it. In the barracks the zeks slept on bare boards.

The ultimate torment there was the 'medicine', or 'prophylactic preparation', for scurvy, with which all prisoners were compulsorily poisoned from 1942 to 1952. This substance was made by boiling pine needles to a pulp. A vitamin conglomerate was set up in Yagodnoye to produce it for the needs of all Kolyma.

The 'medicine' had a very nasty taste, so the prisoners did everything they could to avoid their daily ration of this gunk. They quickly realized that it was harmful to the kidneys, and that especially after such lengthy boiling, there wasn't a trace of vitamin C left in the pine needles.

Father Igor was in Susuman in 2007 for his one-year practical training. He fell in love, got married and went back to the mainland with his bride to finish his studies at the seminary. Once he had taken holy orders he was sent to Kolyma for good. It is he who blesses the crosses erected by Vladimir Naiman at the camp graveyards, because he is the only priest on the 800-plus-kilometre stretch of the Kolyma Highway from Omsukchan to Ust-Nera.

'Are you here for long, Father?' It feels silly to call someone ten years my junior 'father'.

'On the referral they wrote "for a long time",' says Father Igor, strangely morose. 'That means no one knows how long I'm here for. Someone has to work here. Last year my daughter was born, but I've sent her and my wife to the mainland. It's terribly cold here, there's no fruit, and the only vegetables are Chinese.'

'Maybe they'll send someone to deputize for you,' I try to console him.

'For God nothing is impossible. And here the impossible happens every single day. Last November two pagans came to see me at the church in a town called Seymchan. They were on their way home from a hunting expedition.'

They were Yukaghir hunters, representatives of a tiny people numbering barely twelve hundred, eighty of whom live in the village of Gukhariny in Kolyma.

In the Far North in winter there is a very frequent occurrence known as *pustolod*, literally 'empty ice', or sometimes *pustota* – a vacuum. After a freeze, the water in the rivers and streams can abruptly drop, so that a complete but not very thick slab of ice is left hanging in the air. It's a lethally dangerous trap, often impossible to spot, even by natives of the taiga – unless they have a sixth sense.

Weighed down by backpacks, the Yukaghir hunters from Gukhariny had set off hunting. Out in the taiga they had made their way across a stream. The ice had broken and both men had fallen into the water. As they battled with the current to stop it from dragging them under the ice, they had thrown off their backpacks, and then one after the other they had crawled out onto the surface. However, the ice had cracked again, and every few steps it kept breaking. Struggling along for a good quarter of an hour, by some miracle they had managed to reach the riverbank. Dead tired and completely wet, they had no camping gear or change of clothes, no guns, food or matches. Night was coming on, and the temperature was dropping to almost forty degrees below.

They were freezing to death. They hadn't the strength to walk, so they just sat huddling by the stream and waited for the inevitable.

'If I come out of this alive,' groaned one of them, 'I think I'll bloody well get baptized.'

They were on the point of freezing to death when suddenly they both felt all right, warm, then hot, as a shower of snow and stones came down from the high bank above them. They saw an oldish, bearded man come sliding down the slope, wearing hunting clothes, but with no gun. He wasn't a Yukaghir. He was a Russki. He changed the hunters into dry clothes, skilfully made a bonfire, gave them vodka and hot tea to drink, fed and dried them. The next morning the stranger shared his food rations with the hunters. Then he said farewell, and as a parting remark he told them not to forget their promise; finally he set off in the direction from which he had come.

'Who was he?' I ask Father Igor.

'That's just it! The hunters began to wonder too. After all, they were two hundred kilometres from the nearest human settlement. It's their own hunting ground, so they are the only hunters there. They got up from the bonfire and followed the stranger onto the high bank of the stream. But there were no footprints in the snow.'

A few days later they reached Seymchan, where they went to the church and asked Father Igor to baptize them. And just before the ritual, when the lights were lit, they saw the old icon and said it was him. St Nicholas the Wonderworker.

Day XXII

Bolshevik. Kilometre 663 of the Kolyma Highway

I follow the Kolyma Highway out of Susuman. The display screen at the head office of the Susuman Zoloto gold-mining company shows minus twenty-six degrees, so to avoid freezing to death I'm not standing by the road as I did in Yagodnoye, but keeping moving. I have even dressed very lightly on purpose, because it might be a while before I catch a ride, and I may get too hot as I hike. There's very little traffic, about one car every five or six minutes.

My first *poputchik* only takes me as far as Kholodny at Kilometre 641 of the Route. Tolik drives the fire engine for this settlement, and he advises me not to hike, and not to get too far away from people, because if I don't catch a lift I'll still need somewhere to shelter for the night. He's an experienced driver, so he also advises me not to stand just before or on an uphill stretch. No trucker will stop his lorry at a spot like that, because he won't be able to move off uphill afterwards. The road is as slick as glass. No lorry will stop on a downward slope either, because the driver won't want to lose speed before the next uphill bit. It's not easy to fulfil these requirements in the mountains. There aren't any flat stretches, and I want to keep moving, not stand on hilltops with my teeth chattering.

But I only wait a minute for the next car. It stops facing uphill, because it's a light UAZ jeep with four-wheel drive. Vitaly is thirty-four and he has several gold teeth. This is another detail which distinguishes the people of Kolyma from all other Russians – the fashion for gold teeth has survived here, even among the young.

Vitaly works for a large gold prospectors' cartel. He is taking spare parts for machines into the taiga. He drops me only a few kilometres further on, and I catch a Kamaz tanker truck with forty-seven-year-old Uzbek Mustafa at the wheel. All this man's teeth are made of gold. The cab of the truck is his only home for ten months of the year from February to December. For the two coldest months he goes back home to Bukhara.

Mustafa spends six days a week on the road. He only spends one night in a bed. To tell the truth, he is no longer capable of sleeping in a workers' hotel, so when he can't get to sleep he goes to his cab.

He very rarely picks up a hitchhiker. He's afraid of bandits, who are extremely keen to hijack tankers, because they carry very valuable, easy-to-sell cargo.

And so in three short hops I reach Neksikan at Kilometre 651. I'm extremely sorry I haven't got the chance to get better acquainted with the people driving me. There's such decency in them, such kindness and authenticity.

There are fifty settlements in Kolyma – cities, towns, and villages where at least one person lives, as in the hamlet of Neksikan.

Vladimir Kuklin is a modern-day hermit, an eccentric recluse, except that he didn't choose to hide away in the taiga. He never fled from people, from the world, or from civilization. Unlike the former zek who is famous in these parts, and who lived a few kilometres away. His surname was Prokhorov, on top of which he had the old-fashioned first name Prokhor, just like his father, and so, including his patronymic, his full name was Prokhor Prokhorovich Prokhorov. He died last year at the age of eighty-four.

In Vladimir's case, other people ran away from him, or to be precise very gradually moved away until finally, twelve years ago, Vladimir was left on his own.

He hasn't even got a dog, as other hermits have.

Visitors turn up at his place every two months, when they bring him drinking water. Once a week Vladimir walks or hitchhikes to a shop, either ten kilometres east to Kholodny, or eleven kilometres west to Bolshevik. And that is it. He sees fewer people than Robinson Crusoe, because he had his Man Friday every day of the week.

Bolshevik is not a person, but the name of a hamlet. Five families live there, but there is a shop.

Vladimir has to have his drinking water brought in, because the gold prospectors have polluted all the local streams so badly that the water in them isn't even fit for washing or laundry. To do the laundry he collects rainwater, and in winter he melts snow. Vladimir lives and works at an electricity transmission station. He tends and maintains the equipment, and the only thing he has in abundance is electricity. And it's free too, so he uses it to heat his two-room cottage and to cook his meals.

Any day now, the fate that has befallen Neksikan will undoubtedly befall Burkhala, where I was a few days ago. Both settlements have the bad luck to be sitting on seams of gold, but all the precious metal in the area has been removed. Gradually the inhabitants have been relocated, the houses demolished, the streets ripped up, and then a fire broke out and consumed all that was left of it.

The electricity station and Vladimir's cottage are on the only scraps of land in Neksikan that haven't been churned up and sluiced through.

Vladimir hasn't left his settlement for a very long time, although every two years the state pays the cost of a free plane ride to the mainland for everyone on its budget. In 1989 he went to Magadan, but these days he no longer has the confidence to go. He has a poor grasp of money and prices, he doesn't know how to travel by train or bus, how to pay with a card or use an ATM, and mobile phones fill him with horror. He has no family, woman, gun or phone, and fifteen years ago his entire life history burned up in the fire that destroyed the settlement. His entire past, all his memories, all his photos, books, school certificates, Komsomol diplomas and military awards, his entire biography, went up in flames. There was nothing left.

Vladimir the hermit at his solitary retreat.

VLADIMIR THE HERMIT — THE PARTRIDGES
HAVE DISAPPEARED

'So do you ever look for gold, Vladimir?' I ask. 'You've got so much of it underneath your house.'

'It's too deep down. Twelve metres. When we were little, after school we used to go and get a sieve and do some panning. We could always pile up a few grams for pocket money. No one ever stopped us, in fact they encouraged us, then in the 1970s the Ingush came flooding in, wanting to buy gold, they built up a black market, the gold disappeared in Turkey and the authorities banned prospecting for yourself.'

'Aren't you sad on your own?'

'Yes, I am,' says the hermit. 'But I don't need any comforts. It's peaceful, quiet, and beautiful here, there are no neighbours making a noise, and luckily there's the television. I've got a video recorder and I watch tapes. I don't read books. I used to have a great deal of them, but they were destroyed in the fire.'

'Vodka?'

'I don't drink heavily. In winter I go into the taiga to hunt hares. I set snares. But the partridges seem to have disappeared.'

'Women?'

'Badly needed! But no decent woman's going to come out here to live. I was married, but a very long time ago. We were together for two years, we had a son, I was conscripted into the army, and she let herself go wild. One man, then a second, then a third . . . By the time I got back she'd gone.'

'Are you in touch with your son?' I ask.

'We haven't seen each other for twenty-two years.'

'What does he do?'

'I don't know.'

'Where does he live?'

'I have no idea! Apparently I've got some grandchildren. I often wonder where I'll go in my old age. I'm fifty-nine already. It'd be better to grow old somewhere else, among people.'

Vladimir earns 27,000 roubles a month plus 10,000 for his pension (a total equal to £740). I've been with him for about two hours, and I can tell he's extremely relieved to be saying goodbye to me.

Now I'm hiking towards Bolshevik, and for the past quarter of an hour a mongrel has been tagging along behind me. I thought it was a fox, but it's getting closer by the minute, and I can see it's a young dog. Very young, battered, scabby, skinny and hungry. Where did he come from in this remote spot? He doesn't look as if he can survive the approaching night. It was minus twenty-six last night. I try to chase him away.

The more I try, the closer he keeps to my heels. I tell him no car will stop for me because of him. They'll think we're together.

Then Foxlet nudges my calf with his nose.

I spend the night in Bolshevik at Kilometre 663, where I'm put up by Vera Konstantinovna, owner of the little shop, who took pity on me and let me stay at her place. At her house, not in the shop.

Day XXIII

Myaunja. Kilometre 705 of the Kolyma Highway

In the language of the Evenks, nomadic reindeer herders, Myaunja means 'heart'.

In the morning when I set off on the road from Bolshevik, it is twenty-four degrees below. An hour later I'm starting to think my reporter's luck has abandoned me. On and on I walk ... A second hour goes by, and I'm still walking, to avoid freezing to death. Freezing to death! Let's just keep walking. I've got my pack on my back, I'm deep in the taiga, the sun is hiding behind the clouds and it's getting colder and colder – it's not very nice. I should have stopped where I was, then at least I'd have been among people.

The traffic on the road is minimal. Seven vehicles have gone by in my direction. I've been counting them. Two passenger cars and five trucks – *ugolshchiki*, in other words coalmen, from Magadan. They're off to fetch coal from the Arkagalinsk open-cast mine. I was counting on them the most. After all, they're colleagues of mine, fellow Highway-travellers, but like all Russians they're suffering from indifference.

After three hours I'm pretty fed up. Luckily it's only the middle of the day, but my spine is telling me I'm not as young as I was in the past when I could run about all day with a backpack. I eat on the move, take occasional photos, and think about rogue bears. And I thank God there's no men's barber in Susuman and that I had nowhere to shave off my beard. A beard is very handy in sub-zero temperatures, although your breath makes your moustache freeze to it, and you can't open your mouth without using your fingers.

The worst thing is that I haven't got anything to drink. That was a big mistake.

At two p.m. I cross the Frolich river. I'm at Kilometre 675 of the Kolyma Highway. That's one third of my route, like the fourteenth kilometre of a marathon. But I'm still on foot.

After walking fifteen kilometres in three hours and ten minutes, I get my first ride. Then a second one. Suddenly there's one car after another, each of which takes me a few kilometres. They're local people, villagers (rather than through-traffic townies from Magadan). Very often they are the sons or grandsons of former zeks, or people who put down roots here decades ago. These are people who follow the old principles. For them a man on the Route is sacred. They cannot fail to stop. The ones in the trucks are city types, from Magadan. They arrived in recent years, since the collapse of the USSR. They came to earn money in the 'golden heart of Russia'. They have the 'red disease' – that's what these old folks say about them, because the Soviet ten-rouble note was red. They're not real Kolyma people. The real ones call them *vremyenshchiki* – 'temporaries' (from the word *vremya* meaning 'time'), or even 'invaders'.

I reach Myaunja, the site of one of Kolyma's two power plants. This older, coal-powered one was put into operation in 1954. It was built by Gulag prisoners.

Before nightfall the manager of the power plant lends me his car and driver, with whom I travel to nearby Kadikchan. This was once a large settlement with three thousand inhabitants. Most of them worked at an underground coal mine, but it was unprofitable and closed down, and the settlement died. It froze in the middle of the dreadful winter of 2001, when a boiler at the local furnace exploded and the then governor, Valentin Tsvetkov, decided that as the mine had been closed down it wasn't worth spending money on a new one. Most of the residents were relocated to Myaunja.

I spend a few hours trailing about the settlement without encountering a single living soul apart from a few partridges. There aren't even any tracks in the snow. It's a gloomy place – a modern-day, Kolyma version of Pompeii.

Why does a deserted town turn into a ruin? How do five-storey blocks split in half and collapse? Is it the same as with cars? If you lock a car in the garage and never drive it, it falls to bits. Is it the same with shoes? And musical instruments?

There's still enough scrap metal in Kadikchan for years and years of pillaging, but there's not a single window left to be smashed.

In the central square, on a high plinth, there's a smashed head with no face. There's no doubt it was Lenin. Or rather, I should say: a horrid concrete cranium full of holes, with reinforcing wire sticking out of it, and a cap of snow on its bald patch. It's completely hollow inside, but very well reinforced. With size number-five wire.

People say that before Lenin's face was smashed in somebody painted a pair of specs on him.

I've been having an educated conversation with Vitali Borisovich Garushov, manager of the power plant, on the topic of boiler productivity, transmission lines and energy surpluses in Kolyma. They're so great that in summer his plant suspends operations, and the surplus energy which it produces in winter is sold to Yakutia. Our conversation turns to the assassinated governor Valentin Tsvetkov, also known as 'the Bulldozer'.

I tell Garushov that while I was still in Magadan I heard three theories about his death from the local journalists.

The first theory is that Tsvetkov was trying to push the middlemen out of the energy trade in Kolyma. There's nothing for them here, because the region is too remote to be connected to the national grid, but they stick around, jacking up the prices.

In Kolyma heating is almost as important as food. Coal for the Magadan thermal power station is brought in from Sakhalin across the sea, or else travels thousands of kilometres by rail and ship from the Kuzbass region in central Siberia. It's cheaper than transporting coal from Kolyma's own deposits, which would have to come almost 800 kilometres by road along the Kolyma Highway. The wonderful hard bituminous coal which can be bought at the mine beyond Myaunja for 1000 roubles a tonne (£20) costs as much as 4200 roubles in Magadan.

There are two power stations in the oblast, and there is vast overproduction of electricity. Gurashov's power plant only operates in the winter, and the huge hydroelectric power station in Sinyegorye works at half-power. But Russia has not entirely given up its planned economy.

Any day now a second huge hydropower station will go into operation at Ust-Srednekan. Its construction was planned in the days of the USSR, and if they plan it, they build it.

The second theory: apparently Tsvetkov was planning to switch the Magadan thermal power station to electricity. It sounds fantastical, ridiculous even – no one on earth would do that, but that was just why the idea gave Tsvetkov such a buzz. In any case, it was suggested to him by his neighbours' ten-year-old son.

So Tsvetkov was killed because he fell foul of the coal lobby. Or the electricity lobby. Or the Norilsk gang.

For the third hypothesis is to do with the mountain by the port in Magadan. It has always been thought that there's a lot of iron there, because the compasses go crazy, but it's molybdenum – a very rare precious metal, and there's a whole mountain full of it sitting right there. And Tsvetkov set about taking it. And he was killed. This time he'd have disturbed Norilsk Nickel, the mining and smelting giant that belongs to some of Russia's most powerful oligarchs.

'That's ridiculous gossip and old wives' tales!' the manager erupts. 'What absurd fantasies! There's no way you would ever heat a city with electricity.'

'Because you never build a power plant where there's a surplus of electricity.'

'I talked to the investigators from Moscow who were conducting that case. They never took that sort of theory into consideration.'

'Maybe that's why they never solved it. They never found out who commissioned the hit.'

Two years ago the Spanish police caught Tsvetkov's killer. He is from the Caucasus. He was deported to Russia, but he wouldn't betray who had commissioned the assassination, or the motive for it. Or how much he was paid, either.

And to think that already in the 1930s, 1940s and 1950s you could become a rich man in Kolyma. Varlam Shalamov described it beautifully in one of his stories. The most profitable businesses were trading in tobacco and tea, and pig breeding. Everyone in Kolyma kept piglets, even the residents of housing blocks in Magadan, where manure would leak through the ceilings onto the neighbours' plates.

Naturally, pig farming was only accessible to free people. But even prisoners could earn something selling tobacco and tea, because no form of oppression has ever stopped enterprising people from making money.

Day XXIV

Myaunja. Kilometre 705 of the Kolyma Highway

Once again I'm in the ghost town, Kadikchan. In the days of the Gulag there was an enormous camp here, and the prisoners worked in the coal mine. In the 1940s Varlam Shalamov was imprisoned here. At that point there weren't any barracks yet – the zeks slept in army tents, with cells lined with tar paper built inside them. The prisoners had to survive several winters in temporary shacks of this kind.

In his story 'The Unconverted' Shalamov describes the fortunes of Doctor Miller, head of the camp clinic, who like many free people bred a fine pig for his own needs. However, the animal drowned in a huge cesspit, but was then fished out, upon which one of the most heated arguments in local history flared up, involving every social group. Special meetings to discuss the matter were convoked by the Party cell, the veterans' organization and the union. Everything else was ignored, while for several days on end the entire population of the settlement and the camp concerned themselves with the fate of the dead pig. The issue in question was who would eat it, because Doctor Miller certainly couldn't consume the whole thing on his own, and everyone was keen to have a share in it. So there was an ardent debate about whether the pig should go to the free men's canteen or the prisoners'.

Doctor Miller, a former zek, decided the matter in favour of the camp, the prisoners. The next day he was accused of cosmopolitanism. He was a Jew, and at the time there was an anti-Semitic war raging against cosmopolitanism in the USSR. Following a preliminary conversation with the investigator, the doctor went to the clinic and injected himself with a lethal dose of morphine.

Nobody in Myaunja, including the manager of the power plant (who has lived here for twenty-four years) and his driver, can tell me where this camp was. But I find it. Despite a great deal of snow. Without any trouble at all, because the camp is right by the entrance to the ghost town.

Only the remains of it are left. The barracks were burned down, and there are no guard towers left, but tangles of rusty wire are still hanging on poles in a double line. A floodlight cover has survived too, and the huge mouthpiece of a loudspeaker. Stalin's death must have been announced through it.

I snap off a bit of wire. It's rusty, as fragile as a twig. I rip a timber anchor off a charred beam, and put a ceramic insulator in my backpack. The wires must have been live. I feel awkward, as if I were rummaging in a grave.

How can the locals not know where the camp was? Why are they so utterly unconcerned? Why don't they preserve it?

And why am I carping at these Russkies again? Because they've got it right here next to them. The power plant where they work was built by zeks from this camp. They walked at least a dozen kilometres from the camp to work and back again on foot. In winter too. They ought to teach the children about this at the local schools, because every school in Kolyma is near a former camp. Innocent people were incarcerated and died there – their grandparents, and just beyond the site of the burned-down camp are the allotment gardens of the Pompeians who now live in Myaunja.

I spend the night in a service flat belonging to the local power plant. The plant is supplied with coal from the open-cast mine fifty kilometres further down the Route. Lorries come there from Yakutia too – I'm hoping to get a lift with one of them for my onward journey.

235

Lieutenant-Colonel Valery Yerokhin, who has battlefield syndrome.

YEROKHIN THE POWERLIFTER — HEAVYWEIGHT

We're looking for a socket I can use to charge up my phone.

'This one's for the fridge,' I say.

'It's all right,' he replies. 'There's nothing in it anyway.'

This man is not in the least bit domesticated. He doesn't even know how to make a cup of tea properly. He pours enough water into the kettle for twelve people, not two – the typical mistake of an old bachelor.

The flat looks as if he only moved in a week ago. It's not lived-in, but lifeless, as if it has just been decorated or is ready to be vacated. But he's been living here for five years.

And the only music he has is French songs, best of all Joe Dassin.

After fifteen minutes in the company of retired Lieutenant-Colonel Valery Yerokhin, who is a military preparation instructor at the local school, I sink into a deep depression.

'I'm past the watershed in my life,' he says. 'I had to get as far away from my dear Astrakhan as possible, because what the eye doesn't see, the heart doesn't grieve over.'

Valery is fifty-one. He looks like an overgrown, 135-kilo, cuddly teddy bear. Kind, gentle and sad. He used to be a professional weightlifter in the heavyweight category (with a record of 390 kilos for bench press and deadlift), but his health was ruined by taking anabolic steroids, so he went to work for the militia. He completed officers' training school and, like all giants, was taken into OMON, the Special Purpose Mobile Units.

But that was in the 1990s, the USSR was collapsing, and armed conflicts were gradually breaking out on the frontiers.

'Operational tours began,' Vallery tells me. 'I served twelve tours of duty in various wars. Ossetia, Chechnya, first for a month, then two, three, and finally half a year in combat. From 1993 to 2001 I spent five years at war and was promoted to the post of deputy commander of the Astrakhan OMON.'

Somehow I can't imagine him as a grim Caucasus veteran in camouflage, a black bandana and fingerless gloves, a menacing butcher of Chechen women and children.

'Did you have to do a lot of fighting?' I ask.

'Oh yes,' he groans. 'In 1995 I was in Grozny twice, then in Khasavyurt, Pervomaysk and Urus-Martan. And for the whole of 1996 we were based in Shali and made sorties into the mountain villages. One time we raced into the hills, but were surprised to find so few men in the villages, so we asked the women about it, and they said they'd all gone away for work. But that was the moment when the Chechens retook Grozny. They'd dragged us into those mountains on purpose.'

'What a fabulous trick!'

'Before we got back it was very tough in the city. The boys from Krasnodar were fighting there. Encircled for three days without any water supply. And it was as hot as hell! Because it was summer, August. They preserved their dead comrades in salt, like meat. Luckily there was a huge supply of salt.'

'Bloody hell, they had plenty of salt but hadn't thought about water?'

'That's Russia for you,' mumbles Valery, as if he's surprised that I'm surprised. 'But we recaptured the city, and straight after that General Lebed flew in and finished off the war. The result was that we'd lost.'

'But three years later the second war broke out.'

'And I was there again. First at a base in Mozdok, then they smuggled us into the mountains by helicopter. We got a huge Mi-24 transport helicopter, into which, apart from our fifty-man shift, we packed our field kitchen on wheels. New equipment, the pride of the Astrakhan OMON. And after six months they were supposed to relieve us, so we called out the helicopter but they sent a tiny little Mi-8. What about our kitchen? Management had spent three million roubles on it only a few months ago!'

'So did you go everywhere with your own equipment?' I wonder.

'What else would we do? There was an order to take weapons, three-day supplies of food and ammunition, all the equipment and fittings. Everyone travelled like that, and they still do. The guys from Murmansk, Magadan, Vladivostok—'

'Wouldn't it be better to have shared equipment and just change the personnel? Not carry all those tents, mattresses, portable toilets, field kitchens and boilers to and fro the length and breadth of mighty Russia—'

'Shared means nobody's,' says Valery. 'It'd soon get lost, vanish, but everyone takes care of his own stuff. But I'll tell you what happened next. They sent the small helicopters. You can't imagine what a fuss we made about that kitchen! We dismantled it into the smallest parts, but it wouldn't fit, so we stood the pilot a crate of Dagestani brandy to attach it underneath the belly. He agreed, though he'd never carried a cargo like that before, but on take-off the wind set the kitchen swinging, and it dragged down the helicopter, which caught its blades on the trees, and then it crashed. We lost a helicopter worth sixty million.'

'And the blasted kitchen.'

'Exactly. I went back to Astrakhan. I made a report to our commander. "Comrade General, mission accomplished with honour and without any losses." "Well done, Valery," he replied, "but where's our kitchen?" "There's no loss of human life, so it has to be equipment, Comrade Commander." That's how I replied, and I didn't get a promotion to full colonel or a discretionary bonus for exemplary performance of a mission.'

'I wonder how the pilot who lost the helicopter explained himself?' I ask.

'Not long afterwards I lost my job. The kitchen was the pretext. There was a change of commander, and he wanted to have his own deputy, and as at war one day counts as three, I had already worked long enough to reach retirement age. In Chechnya alone, in five years I'd totted up fifteen of the requirement for retirement from the militia.'

COLONEL YEROKHIN — BATTLEFIELD SYNDROME

'Did you enjoy your tours of duty?' I ask Colonel Yerokhin.

'Oh, and how! It really gets you going! The emotions . . . The most incredible thing was when we took Grozny in 1995. The city was blown to bits like Stalingrad. In the daytime it was calm, but each night they'd creep out of their holes and the pounding would start until dawn. We held our positions by the presidential palace. We lost six people. Then the commander sent me to Rostov, where they had the central storage for those killed in action, to supervise the shipment of our fallen comrades to Astrakhan. Back home. If you didn't see to it yourself, they'd lie in a corner somewhere and they'd get lost in all the military mess. Or a couple of weeks would go by and they'd be unrecognizable, because it was summer, blazing hot, and they were in a hangar under a tin roof. So I sorted out some coffins, got the lads out of storage, called in a helicopter from Astrakhan, and we flew home. I delivered each one in person into the hands of his wife or parents, but one of our boys was a Tatar, a Muslim . . .'

Colonel Valery is looking for something to wipe his nose, but he can't find anything, so he goes into the bathroom and blows it into the basin. He comes back a little calmer.

'Muslims are buried wrapped in white cloth, but I'd brought them all back in galvanized coffins that were welded shut, and I also had to make sure they weren't opened, because it wasn't allowed. There was a terrible fuss about it. The father hacked open the metal coffin with an axe. There was the most appalling scene. I had to give way – I wasn't going to fire at a man because he wanted to look at his son. And in 1996 we had dead and wounded again. I was hit twice myself, when a remotely detonated mine exploded under my jeep on road patrol. I got shrapnel in my elbow, although we had the vehicle lined with bullet-proof vests.'

'Wouldn't it be better to have armoured cars?'

'We had those. Even the helicopter pilots line their vehicles with bullet-proof vests.'

'And now you're an instructor, and you train kids from the Caucasus too.'

'I had a problem with that for a long time,' says Valery. 'There are lots of Caucasians in Astrakhan too. But for me they're like a red rag to a bull, every single one is a Chechen guerrilla. As soon as I see one of those boys I start feeling my pockets for a weapon, I start looking around to see where to hide if anything happens.'

'That's called post-traumatic stress syndrome, or battlefield syndrome.'

'Not all of us could cope with it. We had tons of money, because when we got back they paid us for half a year in the trenches. So what does the average Russki do? He sods off to the boozer. Then there's a free-for-all, a right punch-up. They call out the militia, and they come along to fight their own mates from the Front, their comrades from the trenches, because they're throwing their fists about, or chairs, or knives—'

'Were you called out to deal with them, or were they called out to deal with you?' I ask.

'Sometimes the one, sometimes the other. In those days there was no psychological help. I couldn't live at home, with the family. I didn't care about the children. I only knew how to give orders. Chechnya was the only place where it was possible to live, to function somehow, so you just vegetated from one tour to the next. Seventy per cent of each shift took every tour, as many as they could. And that's what I did. And like that my children's entire childhood passed me by. I missed it. I still had a bit of feeling for my daughter.'

'What about your son?'

'A cry-baby. A loafer and an idler!' Valery gets worked up, but immediately wilts. 'I lost him. And he lost me. Because I was always away at war, so his mother made him into a mummy's boy. But I helped his sister to get into police training school. It got harder and harder for me to switch every few months from home life to the trenches. So everything got smashed to bits. And in 2001 I had to retire and things got tough financially. They paid us extremely well, mainly because of the countless extras for night service and risk-taking, and at war everything was double, plus a trench bonus for taking part in combat, but the pension money was tiny, because it was calculated from the basic salary. I get nine thousand roubles a month [£180].'

'You could die of hunger on that.'

'Yes. And my wife was always complaining that I wasn't doing anything, but the worst thing was that suddenly everything in my life stopped happening. There was absolutely nothing going on! A total vacuum. Utter boredom and inactivity. And I was the man who had built the Astrakhan OMON – all one hundred and fifty men had been through my hands. Do you know how much work that was? How much there was going on? Even at our base in the city. A day when there wasn't any shooting was a great rarity. And suddenly, at the age of forty-two, I was a pensioner. I had to do something. So I got a job in security. It was dreadful. So boring. I stuck it for a year. And gave it up. And started to drink heavily. It got worse and worse with my wife. We divorced in 2004. Then it got through to me that I was going to drink myself to death in Astrakhan. I had to get away. I got a map and looked for the furthest place I could possibly run away to. And that's how I ended up here.'

'And you're coping without a battle.'

'I did have a battle against vodka. And it worked. Now I'm battling my blood pressure, because it's soaring badly. At night that piece of shrapnel makes me lose the sensation in my arm, on top of which I can't lose weight, and my hormones are going crazy. I've tried to do a bit of exercise, pump some iron, but it's tough on my knees.'

Day XXV

Ust-Nera. Kilometre 1007 of the Kolyma Highway

So in terms of kilometres I've got almost half the journey behind me now. This is no longer Magadan oblast, it's Yakutia, as the Russians call this region, and in the Yakut language it's the Sakha Republic. And the people are the Sakha. Thus the official name of this largest federal subject of the Russian Federation is the Sakha-Yakutia Republic, or written slightly differently, the Sakha (Yakutia) Republic.

The word *yakut* comes from the language of the Evens, who have lived here with the Dolgans and the Evenks since time began, and means 'newcomer', because in actual fact the Turkic-language-speaking Sakha travelled to this land much later, occupying a territory more than thirteen times the size of France. Now almost half Russia's gold, and all its diamonds, are mined here, and the income covers seventy per cent of Yakutia's budget.

In the morning, at the crack of dawn, I leave Myaunja on a company bus going to the Arkagalinsk open-cast hard coal mine at Kilometre 750 of the Highway.

What I shall remember best of my visit to the mine is the story told me by Sveta, who works in the canteen. A year ago she fed a union delegation of Japanese miners. She noticed that throughout the dinner the guests watched her work as if spellbound, then finally one of them couldn't restrain himself, came up with the interpreter and asked why

Sveta kept interrupting what she was doing to play with that old children's toy? But it's simply that to this day she still uses an abacus.

The first Japanese appeared in Kolyma in 1945. They were prisoners of war. They were released four years later. The first group of two thousand prisoners were loaded onto a ship and sent back to Tokyo. On disembarking, six hundred of them spontaneously formed a prison column, and in their padded zek rags with numbers on their backs they marched through the city to the Japanese Communist Party headquarters. On the spot they sang 'The Internationale' and declared their wish to become members of the Party ranks.

And which is the more striking phenomenon? The Japanese mentality with its tendency to submit to any authority, or the power of Soviet propaganda, the Bolshevik art of brainwashing?

At the mine I board a lorry which has come from Yakutia to fetch coal. I travel in a convoy of two vehicles. My Kamaz truck is driven by Volodya. Twenty-three years old. The same age as my son! Not Volodya – the Kamaz truck. Volodya is ten years older than that. The other vehicle is driven by Dimka. They're fantastic, really nice guys. Not only do they give me a lift, but they feed me all day and refuse to hear a word about money for it all.

At Kilometre 810 of the Route, twenty-eight kilometres before the border with Yakutia, we eat lunch, for which a fourth mate from Dimka and Volodya's base joins us, who's driving in the opposite direction. In my cab we light a gas stove to cook pelmeni (stuffed dumplings), which Volodya carries frozen under the bonnet, behind the cold-air intake. We devour them straight from the pot along with the 'stock', meaning the water they were boiled in. With it we have some sausage that's like mortadella and bread with ketchup on it. Then the obligatory cup of tea using water boiled in a great big shiny kettle. And all in the middle of the remote taiga, in the depths of dismal, frozen Kolyma.

Once we're already in Yakutia, at a damaged bridge which has to be bypassed by driving through the taiga and fording the Kara-Yuriakh river because it's a very old wooden structure built by zeks, we find two people next to a broken-down lorry. They've been waiting for help for twenty-four hours. They've burned all their tyres to keep warm, but they can't withstand the cold any more, so one of them is coming along to the city with us to organize help for his companion.

They shouldn't have crossed that ford. Something in their undercarriage packed up, and while they were fixing it, the diesel oil in their lorry froze because they're using summer diesel (which freezes much more easily). So they warmed it by lighting a bonfire underneath the vehicle, and the frame cracked.

We drive across the damaged bridge very slowly indeed, although the road sign only permits vehicles weighing up to five tonnes, and each of our trucks weighs forty-two (they're overloaded by fifteen tonnes). For several years Volodya has held the record for the size of a cargo in Kolyma. He loaded 47.6 tonnes of metal ore onto his Kamaz.

We cover the 290 kilometres to Ust-Nera in eight hours.

This is the northernmost point in my journey. Ust-Nera, which has a population of seven thousand (two-thirds of whom are Russians), is situated at an altitude of only 800 metres above sea level, but there's only as much oxygen here as at 3500 metres. It's the coldest inhabited place on earth. Some years ago the lowest temperature on record in an inhabited place was registered nearby – minus 71.2 degrees. This is also the only place in the world where the annual temperature fluctuation exceeds one hundred degrees – from thirty-three degrees plus to minus seventy-one.

And in Ust-Nera itself what must have been the lowest temperature in the history of the Orthodox faith was recorded during a traditional ritual bath. On 19 January 2009, the Day of the Lord's Baptism, also known as the Feast of Jordan, a temperature of minus fifty-six was recorded. As custom dictates, the festivities included a mass bath for the entire congregation in the nearest natural body of water, and thus in ice-holes cut in the frozen waters of the Indigirka river.

The weather is murderous in summer too. In mid-July 1980, in the taiga near the town, a party of schoolchildren and their guide got lost in a snowstorm. In a period of two hours the temperature dropped by thirty degrees. Before nightfall, not a single one of the twenty teenagers was still alive.

At my latest fellow travellers' vehicle base I meet their boss, Sergei Gennadyevich Romanov. Together we work out how to send me on my onward journey. I have little time left. In four days navigation on the Aldan river will come to an end when the ferry will stop running, because of the ice floes. To reach the crossing I must travel the tough-est six hundred kilometres of all, because this stretch runs across huge mountains, and west into the depths of Yakutia. This journey is expected to take two days in good weather. It isn't bad – there's sunshine, and during the day it's only about fifteen degrees below. If we don't get there in time, we'll have to wait a month to cross the river, over the ice.

In two days Sergei is sending a truck to Khandyga, the city at the crossing point. This is the last chance for my onward journey. If we make it, and I get across, I'll have to be quick to find my next ride along the road to Yakutsk. This is the worst moment and the worst place, because once I have crossed the Aldan I'll be in between two immense rivers. Behind me I'll have the Aldan, and ahead of me the even bigger Lena. Nobody in Ust-Nera knows when navigation on it comes to a stop. We only know that it's bound to end any day now.

So I might get stuck between the two rivers for a good month or longer. It depends how quickly the ice forms, and when the so-called *zimoviki*, or ice crossings, start.

Lunch at Kilometre 810 of the Highway. Volodya, Dimka and their pal from the base.

The man whom we pick up from the Route at the ruined bridge is called Dmitri, Dima, or Dimka for short. He is thirty-five and he comes from Khanty-Mansiysk in western Siberia. He reeks of booze and a hangover. Before coming along with us, he had hitched a ride down the Highway to a settlement called Artyk, where he bought his travelling companion a loaf of bread and several bottles of vodka, but in the few hours they spent waiting for a lift to Ust-Nera, the two of them drank the lot.

Dima is a security guard for a gold prospectors' cartel from Ust-Nera. The season has ended, so they're on their way back to base with the mining equipment. In town he is to settle up with his boss for half a year's work and then return along the Highway to Myaunja, where his pregnant wife is waiting for him.

'The boss will go mad when he sees you in such a state,' I say.

'What could we do?' mumbles Dima. 'We were starting to freeze, and I've got a family, a child, so it'd be a crying shame to die. If we hadn't drunk it all, we wouldn't be alive now. The boss will understand that. He's all right. He took me on because he wanted someone like me, with a permit and my own gun.'

'You've got a gun?'

'A pistol. I was given it by the Russian Ministry of Defence with thanks and a message engraved on the butt.'

'What for?'

'For Beslan. 2004. But what exactly did they give those awards for? I have no idea. So many people were killed there, hundreds . . . About

249

a hundred and fifty kids. So what were those awards and medals for? I think mine was just for the fact that I lost my unit to the last man.'

'How on earth did that happen? The police didn't have those sort of losses!'

'There were only three of us. And we weren't police, we were army. Squad 145 of the Spetsnaz [special forces] three-minute-reaction brigade. The last two lads in my unit were killed. I was their commander and friend, the senior officer. For a commander it's terrible when all your men get killed, and you're still alive. And you know ... I had to take them home, deliver their bodies to their mothers, and they said: "You're bringing me my dead son, Captain, and you're alive?" What can you say? So I said: "Take him, this is your son, he's a hero, he died in my arms, and on the point of death he called out to his mother."'

'Did you bring both of them back?' I ask.

'Yes. As the group commander should. A terrible duty. That last one was from here, Roman Golubovich, from Myaunja. That's how I got here, and then I met a girl, married her and stayed. Before I brought him home Golubovich had told me a lot about Kolyma, all the romantic stuff, the Far North. My wife and I got the furniture for our flat in the frozen town, Kadikchan. People were moving out of there to go to the mainland and leaving everything behind. You only had to look inside the houses.'

Dima was conscripted straight after school when he was eighteen. First some basic training and then the Georgian–Abkhaz conflict of 1993, in which the Russians 'intervened'. Two years later the army gave him a permanent contract, and the first Chechen war broke out. There were six soldiers in his squad – Vladimir, Roman, two Dmitris (both Dima for short) and two Maxims – part of a three-minute-reaction brigade, so called because of the time in which one of these units is ready to fight, or goes into combat. They are usually dropped by parachute or from on board a helicopter.

When he joined the army Dima had just got married. Three months later he became a father.

'And three months after that my wife came to see me in Abkhazia to show me our daughter,' says Dima. 'And that was that. They drove and drove, and never got there. Their bus got shot up.'

'Who did that?'

'Fuck knows! Guerrillas, partisans, rebels . . . Fuck knows! Terrorists, that's all. They shot everyone on the bus. My wife was killed but my daughter survived. That was my first wife – I've got another one now. And my daughter's a real brainbox. She's eighteen. My mother raised her. My girl finished school with a gold medal and has just gone to college at the State Institute for International Relations in Moscow. It's a very prestigious academy.'

The first of the six men in Dima's squad was killed in Abkhazia. During the operation to recapture Grozny towards the end of the first Chechen war the two Maxims were killed. This was the campaign Colonel Yerokhin talked about, the military preparation instructor from Myaunja. Before the second conflict broke out, the three who were still alive completed officers' training school. Dima took command of the squad, now reduced by half.

'We managed to survive the whole of that bloody war without casualties,' says Dima, 'not one of us was even wounded, until Beslan. And so I was the only one left in the unit. I toiled away for a few more years, and took retirement. It was bad enough that my daughter had no mother. I was thirty-three, and I'd done thirty-nine years' service, because in our army each year counts as three. Now I'm going to get the money for the season and hurry back to Myaunja, to my wife, and then we're off to see my daughter in Moscow. My daughter's only nine years younger than my wife. They're very fond of each other. And when my son's born, he'll be called Maxim, like my two pals from the squad.'

251

We're driving down an extremely beautiful valley, along the Nera river, the right tributary of the Indigirka. It is exactly how I imagined Alaska when I read Jack London's books as a child. And it would be very romantic, if my two companions weren't chain-smoking fags and turning the cab into a gas chamber.

'How much is your pension?' I ask Dima through my tears.

'Trade secret. But I've got enough cash to buy make-up for two women. And for my daughter's studies, a flat in Moscow for her . . . I won't go short of a living.'

From this it would appear that he's having a fabulous retirement, but he keeps shamelessly helping himself to Volodya's cigarettes, which in Russia is considered bad form.

'I started smoking in Grozny,' says Dima. 'We were lying behind a pile of bricks, under fire. Maxim too, though he already had a hole in his head. I saw Roman take the cigarettes out of his pocket, light one and toss the packet to the other Dima, who was lying a few paces away. He lit up too, took a drag and tossed them back again. I saw those cigarettes fly through the air, and Roman caught them, but his hair had gone completely white. It had changed colour in a matter of seconds. While those fags were in mid-air. So I shouted to him: "Toss them over here too."'

'Did you have a light?'

'Everyone had to have matches. Anyway, the house we were lying in front of was on fire.'

DIMA THE ROMANTICIST —
TRAVELLING-COMPANION SYNDROME

To me, Captain Dima is the typical *poputchik* – someone I'm never going to meet again. Until that night when we bump into each other in the hotel corridor, and he drags me into his room for a brandy.

He has seen to all his business. He has sent a rescue team to fetch the broken-down truck, and settled up with his employer; now he's been shopping, got himself a room at the hotel and very nicely, in his usual colourful way, God knows why, is telling me about *poputchik* syndrome – travelling-companion syndrome.

He says there are two kinds. More often you get the sort of *poputchik* who very frankly tells you all about his life, everything that's bothering him, every heartache, all his misfortunes, hidden secrets, sufferings and shameful episodes, all the dirty tricks he has played, all his wicked deeds. You can't reveal those things to anyone who's close to you, or who knows you, but you can tell a stranger whom you're never going to see again – why not? So you talk, you open your heart, and at once you feel better. And you do it without fear, because the stranger can't betray you or inform on you.

Then there's the second kind. Only on the road can you get away with telling any old story you wish, whether it's true, or something you overheard, someone else's story, or something made up, and the listener has no chance of catching you lying. You can fantasize and daydream to your heart's content. You've got a shitty life because your wife's left you, your son's shooting smack and your daughter's a whore, but for a few minutes, hours or days, when you're on the road, you can be whoever you wish – an astronaut, the first tenor at the Bolshoi Theatre, or even an officer in a three-minute-reaction brigade.

Dima finishes his lecture, and into his room comes a stranger. It's Talik from Uzbekistan, whom the captain stopped in the street to ask about a hotel. The three of us drink brandy together, and after a while some other guys turn up too. It's starting to get crowded and dynamic, like in an underpass, as if all the dregs of Ust-Nera had suddenly found out there's a sucker in town, at whose expense they can get pissed out of their skulls.

And they're all in the race, trying to show him respect, fraternizing

253

with him, praising his generous Russian soul, and now I can see Dimka hasn't wasted his life at war. I can see he's from the world of the *blatniye*, covered in tattoos, which weren't visible until he stripped down to his undershirt. He's roaring drunk. He hands out money and sends for snacks and vodka, he's acting the *blatnik*, the old lag, the prison vagabond, but I think it's all lies again. But nor is Dima just a small-time prison creep with a tendency to confabulate, a labour-camp pathological liar. He's a master of the living word, the king of fantasists, a romanticist and storyteller – a representative of one of the most unusual, still highly regarded camp professions or arts. They can see through you at first glance and tell you the story that will appeal the most.

Dimka starts to tell one, but as listeners he's got the local scum, so the story is seemingly banal, about card games, and prison power plays. It's a real eruption of fantasy, an orgy of big-headedness, a geyser of total and utter lies. It's impossible to convey it in words, because not only is the story told in *fenka*, the prison jargon, but half the performance is acted out in gestures, grimaces and noises. You'd have to see it to understand, because almost the only words are nouns. Dima draws the verbs and adjectives in the air with his hands, he acts them out, making menacing faces, puffing out his cheeks and rolling back his eyes – it's sheer pantomime, a symphonic orchestra of strange hisses, pants, whistles, growls and sighs that act as words. It's as if an animal or an infuriated deaf-mute were trying to say something important.

Day XXVI

Ust-Nera. Kilometre 1007 of the Kolyma Highway

Last night my Russki mobile phone went completely crazy. It has sent 146 text messages telling me I've jabbered away all my money and need to top it up. I'm switching it off, because it keeps clucking away like mad and won't let me sleep.

And that's when I get the idea, that as I'm writing this diary anyway, perhaps I can put in a personal note? I've got half the journey behind me, so it's a good opportunity. I'm finally going to come clean, let the cat out of the bag, give the game away, and then it'll be off my plate. There'll be no going back.

I'm going to write about a big wad of banknotes. A bundle of them, in a paper wrapper from a major Siberian state bank – a hundred notes, each with a value of 1000 roubles, in other words 100,000 altogether (worth £2000). For the past week the money has been in my right inside breast pocket, burning a hole in me. And tempting me like the devil. It won't let me forget about it, because I'm in the habit of walking along with my hands in my pockets, so I keep feeling that wretched wad in the recesses of my jacket. So how did it get there?

It came from Alexander Basansky, the oligarch and Kolyma gold king whom I described in my account of Day XI. He gave me the whole bundle ... On the other hand, apart from me nobody knows how he pulled a fast one on me. Maybe I should just accept the money with open arms? Such a big bundle of dosh!

But he knows too. And that's the worst thing.

It was like this. That morning, we started off with a chat in his office. He must have taken a fancy to me, because he changed his plans for the entire day and decided we were going to his restaurant for a party. He got up from behind his desk, took a photo album out of the cupboard and also the bundle of money, and gave it to me. I got palpitations, I protested, I screamed, I pushed him away and explained that this was unacceptable, against the rules, unthinkable in my country. He told me to stop being stupid, that in their country they all did it to everyone, and to every journalist. He couldn't remember any journalist having such hysterics or putting on such a performance, and he stuffed the wad into my pocket by force. I took it out and put it on the table in between us. We talked for a while, and then the oligarch invited me to the car.

I walked out, and the bundle remained on the table. He saw that, and with an offended look on his face, he said it was very wrong, after all, the whole thing had already been decided, and shoved the money into my pocket again. I said that if my employers learned about this, I'd be out on my ear, and that I'd go to a church and give it all away to the poor, and he said that was my affair.

It was important to him that I should take it from him, or rather that I should get a payment from him. I can feel the shivers running down my spine as I write that sentence.

I should have flung the money in his face and stormed off, but as a reporter I found him exciting, and now he attracted me even more. I'm incapable of refusing the chance to examine a monster of this kind under a magnifying glass. I decided that somehow I would force the money back on him once it was all over.

The drinking lasted the entire day, and it was a major booze-up. That evening, when he drove me to the hotel, I furtively left the 100,000 on the seat and got out of the car. He got out too, we said goodbye, and he drove off.

But once I was in my room I discovered the blasted wad was in my pocket again. The same one, or maybe another one by now. Maybe he'd tried to bung me a second bundle of cash.

I felt like throwing up. The guy had shafted me, had his way with me, screwed me as a reporter, put me on a level with the Russki journalists, all for sale.

This cash is still in my pocket, but now that I've let the cat out of the bag, I'm feeling better. I'm poor again!

And now I know what I'm going to do with it. I'm going to buy some dollars or Euros, then through the Association of Siberian Deportees in Poland I'll find an old Home Army (Polish wartime resistance) soldier who was forced to dig up gold in Kolyma, and give it to him. As a sort of microscopic compensation for his forced labour. After all, Russia has never paid compensation, and has no intention of doing so.

They deserve Kolyma's gold more than anyone.

One hundred thousand roubles and a gold nugget from Basansky.

NOLIK THE ARMENIAN — BLACK, WHITE, GREY

There are very few stories by Varlam Shalamov in which you won't find a mention of bread. He goes on about it to the point of obsession. He associates everything with bread, just as Vladimir Mayakovsky associates everything with Lenin in his famous poem.

> We say — Lenin, but that's to say the Party,
> We say — the Party, but that's to say Lenin.

One of Shalamov's stories is devoted to the dozens of ways in which a prisoner can eat bread. For instance, he can lick it up in its entirety. Not just the surface, but its entire volume, just as you lick an ice lolly, or animals lick a block of salt in the forest.

In another story he writes about how many different kinds of excrement are produced by various sorts of bread and what it's like. After the kind baked with American flour from Lend-Lease wartime aid you only went to the latrine once in several days. After the black, Kolyma filth, you shat out almost as much as you'd eaten.

Nowadays in Ust-Nera they have black, white and grey bread, which isn't white or black, as well as rolls and Armenian lavash flatbread, because there are forty Armenians living in the city now. They all belong to the family of Nolik Meliksetyan, the only local construction entrepreneur, and owner of the restaurant and bakery, who turned up twenty years ago with a shipment of ladies' carpet slippers, made in Armenia. That was the last year of Soviet life, when there was nothing to eat, drink, smoke or wear in the country.

259

'I sold a thousand pairs in ten days here,' says Nolik in delight. 'It was my first big deal. After all that, Vasily Alexandrovich Mestnikov, head of the regional administration, called me in and asked if I could carry out the renovation of a heating plant in a village called Tomtor, because they didn't have any experts. I was only involved in trade, but I said it would be done, and since that time I have built a stadium in Ust-Nera, the local administration building, a hospital, and the house in which I live. My older son runs the construction business, his wife runs the restaurant, my daughter runs the bakery, and my younger son is my personal chauffeur. And I keep an eye on everything.'

'Let's talk about the bakery.'

'I didn't want it,' says Nolik. 'It used to be a state enterprise, so there was a constant bread shortage in this town. Vasily Alexandrovich called me in and asked if I could deal with organizing it. I said I could, but only if the bakery were mine. And so for the past four years there hasn't been a shortage of bread. They come to me with everything that's running badly round here. I even had to put up a monument. In honour of those who built the Kolyma Highway, which President Putin was going to unveil, but at the last moment he went to Arkhangelsk to open a new bridge.'

'What a shame,' I mumble.

'It is, because afterwards he was supposed to be dining at my restaurant. I bought new plates, cutlery and glasses . . . I even had it painted. But nothing was wasted, because two sheikhs came from the Emirates just after that to hunt elk and reindeer, and I had to feed them.'

'Where did they stay?'

'At your hotel.'

'Good grief! How did they survive that? It's such a shitty dump.'

'I had two rooms redecorated for them.'

And now on the high bank of the Indigirka river, Nolik has organized an icy picnic for me, with Armenian brandy, Russian vodka, a bonfire and shashlik roasted on skewers, beef lights and pork sausages. It's bloody cold, a black night, and the river is scary to look at – there are such a lot of ice floes coming down it. It's rattling along like the Trans-Siberian Express, because the Indigirka is a hellishly dangerous river with the fastest current of all the world's major rivers. It races along at twenty-five kilometres an hour. A beautiful, terrifying sight.

Day XXVII

Ust-Nera. Kilometre 1007 of the Kolyma Highway

I love the last few days before an expedition. It's exciting to be drawing back the bowstring, feeling the anticipation, and making the preparations ... I've been on the road for a month, so in fact I've been on standby the whole time, but today I have an especially strong sensation of that pleasant ripple of excitement before the next leap forward. I buy provisions for three days, though if the weather's good we can make it in one. But it looks as if it's snowing in the mountains. And we have to cross the Verkhoyansk Range to Khandyga, where the ferries cross the Aldan river.

Today at the transport base I'm going to meet the man with whom I'll be setting off on the Route tomorrow morning. His name is Yura. We'll be travelling in a Kamaz tanker truck, but it'll be empty. Yura is going to fill it up in Khandyga and return to Ust-Nera, while I hurry across the river and try to find a lift to take me to Yakutsk.

I've got some spare time, so I wander the town aimlessly. I reach the city limits, an area where there are allotments. In Russia almost every family has a tiny patch of land for a vegetable garden, which in tough Soviet times, in the 1990s and even the 2000s, saved millions of people from starvation. Growing potatoes and cucumbers is a major Russian passion, and for millions of old people a necessity to this day. In many Russian cities the pensioners form self-defence committees each autumn to guard their potatoes and other crops from thieves.

In the coldest inhabited place on earth the vegetables are grown above ground in wooden plant pots and under plastic tents. But for sport and pleasure the amateur gardeners sometimes cultivate small amounts of potatoes in the ground as well. In the spring they go to the Yakutian villages to buy cow manure, which is collected and frozen by the herders in basins. In June, when the earth is defrosted, they dig a hole, toss in the shit-cake, cover it with a bit of earth, lay the seed potatoes on it, and bury it. The manure starts to ferment, warming the tuber from below, which makes it grow, and protects it from being frozen by the permafrost.

I admire the fences the allotment owners have put up to enclose their plots, because the Russians, like the Poles, have the absurd habit of fencing every little scrap of earth. The fences are wooden, made of planks of the worst quality. You bash them in like posts, and then you even off the top with a saw. But here I can see that nobody makes their fences even. None of it is in a straight line, and it looks awful with every board a different height.

Around noon I bump into 'Captain' Dima and Talik the Uzbek in the hotel corridor. They're partying for the third day now, boozing till they drop. They're drinking their way through Dima's season, and now they want to drag me off for a drink too. Naturally Dima is our host, but I've got work to do. So Talik gets nasty, pushy in a drunken way. He wants me to give him my jacket. But what am I supposed to wear? Then he wants the beads off my wrist, which my son gave me for the journey. I say I can't give them away because they were a gift, and they bring me luck. He gets even more intrusive, though a short time ago he was hugging me and kissing me. Dima disappears into his room; Talik hurls insults at me, so I disappear too.

Why does he think I should be giving him presents? Is it because according to criminal law the man from a higher caste, higher up in the prison hierarchy (in the past, and probably nowadays too), takes what he wants? Especially from suckers, people from outside the camp world. In Russian prisons this sort of refusal is unthinkable. A few decades ago it meant death.

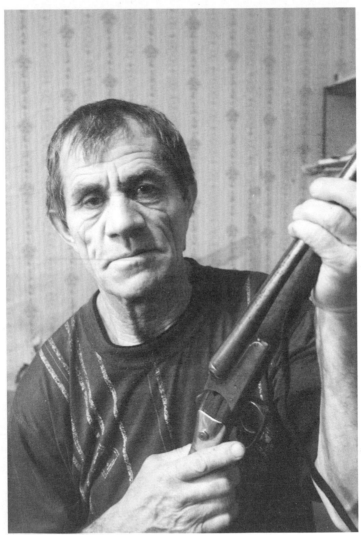

Andrei the adventurer and his rifle.

In a housing block known in Ust-Nera as 'the Great Wall of China' because it is the longest one in the world, I visit Andrei Ogarkov. He is sixty-two and has the soul of an adventurer. Four years ago his wife went to the mainland to visit their son, and somehow she still hasn't come back, so two years ago Andrei went on a trip into the taiga. He set off totally unprepared, with no map or compass (he claims he has one in his head), tent, mattress, sleeping bag or raincoat. He slept in shelters or on beds made of pine, keeping a camp fire going all night to scare off the bears. He had a large sheet of plastic (but it burned up on the bonfire), an axe (except that he soon lost it), a big home-made knife, a Chinese fishing net and an ancient 12-gauge shotgun. He hiked for seven hundred kilometres, across the mountains, taiga and swamps, with big rubber boots on his feet. I ask him if he knows how to find his way according to the stars, but he replies that it was summer, during the white nights, when there are no stars.

Andrei is a welder. He works at a mine deep in the taiga on the Elginsky Plateau, seven hundred kilometres north-west of Ust-Nera. They mine a valuable ore there containing antimony, which is heavier than pure iron, as well as almost all the other metals from the periodic table, predominantly gold, silver, platinum, uranium, nickel, wolfram and copper. You can only get there in winter, by lorry along the frozen rivers, and the mined ore is carried out the same way. In summer the mine ceases to operate, and at the end of April all the workers are brought out along the ice-bound routes with the ore.

Andrei's plan was not to return to the city with all the others when the season ended, but to wait until June for the spring, and then to set off on foot. First up the Aldan river, all the way to its source in a high pass in the Borong Range, and down the other side, along the Utachan river, then the Elgi, which is a left tributary of the Indigirka. From there he'd only have another hundred kilometres to go, the easiest ones, along this great river – because Andrei was planning to float down the rivers in a tiny two-man fishing dinghy. I am afraid even to look at them, so wild, rapid and dangerous are they. Andrei had never done it before and can't swim, nor had he ever hiked in the mountains. He had three hundred kilometres to walk, and four hundred to float.

He had hidden the dinghy and some food supplies in the pass six months earlier, when he went to work in the autumn.

'I set off up the Adycha river on the twelfth of June 2009,' he tells me. 'And three weeks later when I reached the pass, it turned out I'd come the wrong way. The river flowed from two streams, and I'd gone up the wrong one. And my food had just run out.'

'What had you taken for the journey?'

'A loaf of bread, a bag of rusks, some sugar, six tins of Spam and some salt. I had enough food for the uphill journey. I had plenty of buckwheat hidden at the pass with the dinghy. But I wasn't at the right pass. On the other side there was an enormous, terrifying abyss. When I started going back I had two handfuls of sugar. The weather had turned bad, there was a cold snap, and it was snowing. It can be like that here in summer.'

So for the return journey he had to survive on berries, mushrooms, grubs, fish and carrion. One time he managed to hunt down a reindeer. The more time and energy he devoted to obtaining food, the more slowly he travelled, and the weaker he became.

'I stewed berries with no sugar, and made fish soup without salt, but that wasn't enough for me,' recalls Andrei. 'I was dying of hunger. I lay in a shack and hadn't the strength to get up. I told myself that

267

tomorrow somehow I'd drag myself out of bed, but the next day I didn't have the strength either. I sank into a deep sleep for several days. The worst bit was at an abandoned gold prospectors' camp, about a hundred kilometres before the end of the journey. I wrote in my diary that I was dying, and that I'd never get out of the taiga, I'd never reach home. I was giving up. But three days later, somehow I did crawl out of the shack, found a mushroom, a caterpillar, and a big spider. I got down among the blueberry bushes and ate lying on my back.'

Constantly wet and chilled in the icy streams, his feet swelled up and refused to obey him. His life was saved by a wild reindeer, which wandered into his sights. He finally ate his fill and went on his way again. But when he chanced upon some clumps of Aaron's rod, he couldn't resist stopping to dig its valuable roots out of the ground with his long knife. The people of the taiga call it 'golden root'; it's a sort of local ginseng, which they use to make a healing vodka-based liqueur.

And that was when a huge female bear with two cubs suddenly came charging towards him. At the very last moment he leaped clear of a blow from her mighty paw.

'I was saved by the fact that I was downhill from her. Bears have much shorter front legs than back, so they can't run down steep slopes.'

Andrei goes into the kitchen to fetch an old Maxim coffee tin containing a liquid with a luxurious aroma, the colour of brandy. And it has a similar effect too, except that it's a hundred times stronger. This is golden-root liqueur. The recommended dose is a teaspoonful, but never before bed. We drink a shot glassful each at noon, and I have a sleepless night ahead of me.

In Ust-Nera everyone had already grieved for Andrei. But then he ran into a gold prospector and got back to town. He had spent forty-four days battling through the taiga. Then he was in hospital for two months while his feet were healing. He made the most extraordinary discovery a few months later, in November, when he went back to work at the mine.

Someone had stolen all the things he had left at the pass. The dinghy wasn't there, nor were the supplies of food. That's against all the rules in force in the taiga, where you're never allowed to take or use up all the provisions from a hunting cabin. You always have to leave a little salt, buckwheat, tea, sugar and matches, and you always have to leave a supply of firewood.

After all, even if Andrei hadn't lost his way, without those supplies he wouldn't have had a chance of getting home anyway.

From today Andrei has a small kitten. He saved its life when a pack of stray dogs attacked it at a graveyard. Andrei's other eccentricities include a small workshop for making shotgun cartridges, distilling golden-root liqueur, and the production on an almost industrial scale of wine out of watermelons. An Armenian shopkeeper had thrown the melons onto the rubbish heap, but Andrei discovered they were only rotten on the outside. Watermelons were so expensive in Ust-Nera that nobody had been buying them except the wife of the shop owner and his cousin Nolik.

Day XXVIII

Shaman's Brook. Kilometre 1459 of the Kolyma Highway

In the morning, as I'm leaving the hotel, the receptionist stops me to ask if that friend of mine is still there, because he hasn't paid for last night. I say he's not my friend, and go back upstairs. His room is not locked, and he's lying in the rumpled bedclothes. It hurts him to open his eyes. Even the pale light of the arctic dawn causes him pain. I warn him they'll be after him, because he hasn't paid for the room, and he says he hasn't a kopeck.

In less than three days, with the help of Talik and his pals he has drunk through the money for the entire season, blown the whole 180,000 roubles he was paid for six months' work. They have sucked him dry and done a bunk.

I ask Dima where he got the story about the captain from the three-minute-reaction brigade. He says, or rather groans, that he heard it at a prison hospital for drug addicts in Krasnoyarsk, where the officer was dying of AIDS. He hadn't retired at all. That was just Dima's adaptation of the original. A court martial had sentenced the captain to six years in prison for so-called marauding. With a gun in his hand he had robbed a jeweller's shop in Nalchik in northern Caucasus.

I have made an arrangement with Yuri Yermolov, the driver from the transport base with whom I am to travel, that we'll be setting off from Ust-Nera at ten o'clock. However, Yura displays a typically Russian casual, not to say irreverent, attitude to time. He arrives at the base at eleven. He starts up our eighteen-wheel Kamaz tanker and moves off. He drives out into the middle of the square. Then goes into reverse. There's no food for the journey. So maybe he'll nip home. Or get some on the way . . . We finally get going at half past one. Meanwhile the engine has been idling away for two and a half hours.

A few kilometres outside Ust-Nera, over the bridge across the Indigirka, Yura stops the lorry at kilometre marker post 1012. He goes into a small shop to get some tea for the journey, but comes back with a large bottle of vodka, because it's cold, and we're on the road, and out in the taiga you mustn't run short of it. For me that post is the halfway marker.

It's clear by now we won't get to Khandyga in one day. And I'm in a hurry, because they're just about to close the ferry crossing over the Aldan.

Two or three hours later our truck stops. Although the air compressor is working, we're losing compressed air, without which the brakes will stop working. We spend a good hour trying to find which way the air is escaping. And we find the leak – between the air compressor and the compressed-air storage tank, from the coupling between a metal and a rubber pipe. A small tube has broken off. This has happened to Yura before, two years ago, and he almost paid for it with his life, because he was a long way north, in the middle of winter, in a temperature of minus sixty-four degrees.

Our Kamaz is a nineteen-year-old crate lined on the inside (like all the vehicles at Yura's base) with patterned Chinese carpet. The windows are cracked, in low gears the accelerator has to be pressed down with a screwdriver, and the passenger door only opens from the outside. Yura doesn't know what mileage his Kamaz has because the milometer hasn't worked for years. It stinks like hell of exhaust fumes in our truck, and at this sort of temperature (about minus twenty) the engine has to run through the night. I'm worried we won't wake up in the morning.

I really like Yura. Once we're on our way, he tells me we've only set off because of me, so I'll be in time for the crossing – otherwise he'd have gone two or three days later, once the road gangs have dealt with the fresh snow . . .

We're driving north. After ten hours' drive we stop at a place called Shaman's Brook. Steam stinking of sulphur comes seething out of a great sinkhole. It was here several years ago that Yura met the mighty rogue bear with the metal noose around its neck, which trapped him on the roof of his truck all night. At last we can have a quiet bite to eat, make tea on a Chinese camp stove, and Yura opens the bottle. It's vile gut-rot, but I drink in tandem with my driver to be sure there'll be as little as possible for him. After all, we'll be setting off early in the morning.

That's Yura – an uncomplicated guy, forty years old, son, grandson and brother of truck drivers, he knew from the age of six that he didn't want to be an astronaut or a sportsman like the other Soviet boys, or even a militiaman, but a trucker. On the Highway. Like all the men in his family.

A magical supper and night in the cab of a Kamaz truck at Shaman's Brook.

The vehicle we're travelling in is Yura's own property. The boss at the base commissions him for haulage jobs. Yura would love to get a new Kamaz, but they cost two million roubles. As he has no official place of employment, the only bank that's willing to give him a loan is demanding a commission of eighteen per cent.

Furious with the world in general, Yura tells me a joke about a Jewish banker who is asked how come he's got so much money if he doesn't steal. 'Money is like lard,' replies the banker, 'you pick it up, hold it in your hands for a while, and then you put it down again.'

'And?' I ask.

'Your hands always remain a bit greasy,' says Yura.

'That's true for other banks too, not just the Jewish ones.'

'In this country there's no other kind. Russia is the world's third-biggest extractor of crude oil, but I don't get a fucking penny of it! I buy diesel for thirty-four bloody roubles!'

Yura has had this lorry for a year, and he has already driven fifty thousand kilometres in it. That's the same as driving a thousand kilo-metres each week from Ust-Nera to Magadan. A trip to Khandyga for fuel earns him a clear 33,000 roubles (£660). It takes him three days.

But there were times when he spent a whole week driving in one direction. He can remember making stops of this kind at Shaman's Brook when he would drink five or six bottles of vodka in three days. He'd get moving once they were empty and he'd made a very slight recovery. These problems are now behind him. Matters are worse where the forces of law and order are concerned, who are interested in him in connection with the theft of some roofing materials from a builder's warehouse. He is not allowed to leave the territory of Yakutia, but he has to be in Magadan in a week from now at any price. He has promised his younger son he'll come for the boxing tournament in which the boy will be fighting for the title of oblast champion.

The unfortunate thing is that, like any trucker, Yura is always on the road. He's always somewhere between Ust–Nera and Magadan. It's the only road in Kolyma. In Magadan he's been married for seventeen years to Vera, with whom he has three children, while in Ust–Nera five years ago he fell for Svetlana, a mature woman who had been through two divorces when they met, and had no children, but with Yuri she unexpectedly fell pregnant and his life suddenly grew complicated. Someone has now told Vera, the Magadan wife, a thousand kilometres away, about her husband's double life. She wants a divorce, but Yura is heartbroken at the idea of having to leave her and the children. He says he loves them very much. And he loves Svetlana and their daughter Sofia too.

Day XXIX

Khandyga. Kilometre 1605 of the Kolyma Highway

Oh shit. That's how things are looking – I am in the shit.

But to start at the beginning, first there was this morning. We managed to avoid being suffocated in the cab of our Kamaz, although there were clouds of exhaust fumes pouring into it. But my head is throbbing. The vodka may be partly to blame, because it wasn't exactly fit for a king. We're having breakfast, it's sunny and cold, and we're dozens of kilometres away from the nearest human habitation, when two Yakuts suddenly materialize out of nowhere, completely sloshed, and say 'Give us some booze!' We haven't got any. 'So give us some "Highway liqueur".' Yura says we haven't got any of that either, and they say we should buy some of their reindeer meat. They've got two whole legs and haunches, in other words just about half the animal. Yura asks how much they want for it. A thousand roubles (£20). Yura only has three hundred. That's fine! They take the cash and they're off to get vodka. Thirty kilometres to Vostochnaya – on foot, at a temperature of twenty below! There's a weather station in Vostochnaya, but the employees deal in vodka when they get the chance.

'Highway liqueur' is radiator coolant. And in the Gulag era meths was known as 'Blue Night liqueur'. Some people still call it that to this day.

For the whole of our ten-hour stop at Shaman's Brook not a single vehicle has driven past us.

We set off, and after a few dozen kilometres we stop at the Tomporuksky Pass, the final pass before the drive down into the plain. Like many of his fellow Kamaz truckers, Yura stops in this spot to pay tribute to a long-distance lorry driver from Khandyga who shot himself here. The guy had come home early from the road and caught his wife with another man.

Yura, who has two families and four children, aims a few coarse words at the scarlet woman, we stand under the cross for a while, and then we chop down two small fir trees. For Yura's two families. For the holidays! For New Year's Day and then Christmas, which in the Orthodox calendar falls in January. It is roughly mid-October, but in the Kolyma-Yakutian cold the trees will stay as they are. There are spruce trees growing here too, and even pines, because to the west of Ust-Nera it gets a touch warmer. Up till Ust-Nera the only trees were larches.

Well, so why am I in the shit? Because the ferries across the Aldan stopped running four days ago. There are ice floes thundering down it, and it's a mighty, rapid, terrifying river. Only the day before yesterday a big riverboat came across and took the last people off the jetty. But it couldn't go back. The old women at the fuel base that I reach with Yura promise to make some inquiries and call me, because there may still be something going to the other side, but they can't guarantee it. For the time being they send me to the local hotel, the Prezydentsky.

It's a small wooden building which looks like a hunting cabin. It's called the Prezydentsky because it was built for Vyacheslav Shtyrov, former president of Yakutia, who comes from Khandyga and often visits. I am the only guest, so I get the presidential suite. I ask for the key. They say the door's open, and there's no need to lock it, because no one has stolen anything here for the past seven years. I ask why exactly the past seven. Because that's when the hotel was built, replies my Yakut interlocutor.

Now I'm looking out of my presidential window at a mind-blowing view of the vast Siberian river. And there are tremendous ice floes rushing down it.

I'm looking forward to tomorrow. In the morning I'll get news about the ferry crossing.

Nina as she was in the days when she learned to drink rectified spirit.

In the part of Russia called Yakutia, a Buryat woman hands a Polish man with a German surname a cup of Chinese tea called Cleopatra's Night. We both burst out laughing when it occurs to us. On top of that she's not a pure Buryat but a mixture — Nina Khanarova is half Russian — a half-blood as they say here.

Straight after that Nina (or Ninochka) offers me the Emperor's Concubine. That's a kind of tea too. She has just come back from a trip to China, and now she's treating her guests to teas with strange names. But the tea comes at the end. To start with there's a wonderful pilaf made with reindeer meat, which she whips up in forty minutes.

She talks even faster than she cooks. She says a lot, quickly, intelligently and beautifully. By profession she's a TV director, and for twelve years she has headed the local branch of Yakutian public television.

'I've lived for fifty-six years and I don't regret a single one of them. My years are my riches,' she says. 'I've been through so much . . . Shall I tell you about the first time I ever drank rectified spirit?'

'Why not? We've known each other for a whole hour.'

'Then pour us a glass each,' she commands. 'A pity it's not better chilled . . . I came to Khandyga from Ulan Ude in my homeland of Buryatia. That was the work assignment I got. I was straight out of college . . . Bottoms up! Any man who leaves something in the glass is not sincere. Only women don't have to down the lot.'

'So what happened with the rectified spirit?'

'I'm coming to that. It was 1978. They gave me a job at the Komsomol district committee.'

It wasn't a good year. It was dry, and there were no blueberries or rowanberries, but there was a large number of hungry rogue bears. They were roaming the area of Khandyga in packs, and in a village called Topolino one of them had killed an entire family of reindeer herders. That wasn't unusual; the problem was that the herder's older son was meant to be going to Moscow as a delegate to the All-Union Komsomol congress.

'The authorities were shitting themselves,' Ninochka tells me. 'They gathered the entire staff of the Komsomol office and sent us out into the taiga. We were supposed to establish what had happened out there, and send a report to Moscow to say why Comrade Asenin, the boy who had been selected, wasn't coming to the congress. They gave us a car – as old as the Aldan river. It hurt just to look at that heap of junk. And we had three hundred kilometres across the mountains ahead of us, in December, in the snow – in Khandyga it was minus fifty-eight. That was how my very first business trip began.'

The men arrived at the assembly point. They loaded up the car. Nina couldn't believe her eyes.

'What on earth is that?' she asked.

'Rectified spirit.'

'A whole crate? What's it for?'

'Don't be a smart-arse. Get in.'

Nine people squeezed into the old jeep. They took it in turns to sit on each other's laps. The road was narrow, with hairpin bends. The first secretary of the district committee was driving.

'That creep shouldn't have been allowed to ride an old mare, let alone drive a car,' says Nina. 'The southern Verkhoyansk Range is treeless. There's nothing for the cars to crash into, and nothing for your eyes to fix on either. There's just the road ahead, and the precipice below. And it was night, with fog as thick as milk. And suddenly a stag sprang in front of the bonnet. It was the size of a mountain, over six hundred kilos of live meat, with antlers spanning at least two metres. It leaped up and crashed them through the windscreen. Then it fell and screamed like a child! Can you believe it? I can still hear that scream now. Oh, look how the hair on my arms is standing on end. In seconds we all went stiff with cold. Minus sixty-two degrees! And the car was smashed to bits.'

'Didn't you say it was minus fifty-eight?'

'That was down below. Up in the mountains it's always four degrees colder. At that sort of temperature first your face freezes, and your lips stop moving, so you start gibbering as if you're drunk, and then you stop talking at all. It all freezes in a flash. Our men got out the crate of rectified spirit, poured it into mugs and said "Drink!" I'd never drunk rectified spirit in my life before. "Do you want to live?" Of course I did! "So drink it! Inhale. Drink! Don't sip it, just pour it down your throat. Exhale."'

'Hemingway knew how to do that.'

'I managed it too, but the mug froze to my lips. I tore it free, taking a bit of flesh with it. Pour us another, Jacek.'

'To women who've seen too much,' I say, beaming with chivalry.

'A hussar's toast. The men stand up, and this time the women drink to the bottom. But up there in the mountains I can only remember the first three mugs of that spirit. And then I lost consciousness. I woke up in a sort of tent. I opened my eyes and saw a little girl in a summer dress come running in. I couldn't tell if I was in this world or the next. Even blinking caused me pain. I could feel that I was completely naked, but inside a bag, a sleeping bag made of fur.'

The little girl saw Nina open her eyes, so she called someone. Her mother came. From her looks she was clearly an Evenk.

'Hello, Nina,' said the stranger. 'You told me so much about yourself yesterday.'

'Really? There were two other girls with me – Yelena Prekrasna and Yana Shchepanska, secretary of the oblast committee. Where are they?'

'In the tents next door. They're both alive.'

'Why am I naked?'

'I rubbed you with alcohol. You were dying, you were frozen stiff as a block of wood.'

The men had given the girls rectified spirit to drink, and then sent them off to the nearest herders' encampment in the first vehicle that had chanced to come by. But those are wild mountains, and they had waited a very long time for a lift.

'If you pour rectified spirit into your body,' says Nina, 'it's like having fire run through you, but it soon stops heating you. And then you have to drink more of it. But in that awful cold we couldn't open our mouths any more, so the men had prised them open for us with knifes. The way they do for bulldogs that clamp their jaws shut. And they'd injured us in the process. They'd been drunk too. When I saw Yelena, I was shocked. Her face was slashed and frostbitten, and her fingers were black. I think the alcohol and the bear fat the Evenks rubbed on us saved our lives.'

'Did you ever get to the delegate who'd been eaten by the bear?'

'A week later the girls were airlifted out by helicopter and the boys continued the journey. The bear had scalped the delegate and pulled off his entire face. They never come at you eye to eye. They always attack from behind, swiping with their paws to rip all the skin off the head. It hadn't eaten our Komsomol friend, just buried him for later. It had buried his entire family. Bears very often do that, so the meat will acquire their favourite smell and taste of carrion. And that's what my first business trip was like. There were hundreds more after that. Pour us another, please.'

COMRADE NINA — POUR US ANOTHER

Nina is well known in Khandyga, not just from the television screens. She saved the town's statue of Lenin when the local authorities were considering taking it down. Nina mobilized public opinion and raised an outcry, saying it was harmless, nothing more than a pterodactyl, a fossil, a memento of a bygone era. And the revolutionary leader is still standing here to this day.

'The Yakuts call the Russkies invaders, but they came here from the outside too,' says Nina, on a completely different tack. 'They lived in the Baikal area, until my Buryat ancestors, Genghis Khan's warriors, drove them north. The Yakut are a very quiet, gentle people, they probably yielded to the Mongols without a fight, but here they had to conquer the local aborigines, meaning the Evens and Evenks, by force of arms. They're invaders just as much as we are.'

'Apparently that theory isn't at all certain.'

'Then why are there so many Yakut names on Lake Baikal? Because those places were named before the Mongol people, the Buryats, got there. Such as Mount Khamar-Daban. In the Buryat language that doesn't mean anything, but in Yakut it means "Walking Mountain". I've read a great deal about the indigenous peoples of Siberia. After a few years at the Komsomol I was transferred to a permanent job working for the Soviet Communist Party, and they made me manager of the Party library.'

'In a small town like this you had a library for commie party members?'

'Yes. And what a fabulous collection! The whole of world literature, something you couldn't dream of finding in a public library. Of course it was only available to Party people, and then only members of the district committee!'

'They created a whole library for six or seven people? And you just sat and waited for someone to turn up once a month?'

'I didn't just sit and wait,' protests Nina. 'I read. My duties included reading the Party newspapers and making summaries of every single article. The first secretary didn't have time to read, so I read for him.

To hell with the lot of them! Pour us another! I had to read each article and summarize it in three sentences. Once a week, on Friday at two p.m., I came to see the first secretary, and in the presence of the second and third secretaries, as well as the chairman of the executive committee and his deputies, I reported what they'd said in the Party journals that week in the Soviet Union. So in fact I was working for those six guys. And meanwhile I read all the best books published in the world.'

'Was everything translated into Russian? And published?'

'Of course,' says Nina. 'Just for the needs of the Soviet Communist Party. I also read all our dissidents. Solzhenitsyn's work was published here in samizdat and people wrote it out by hand, but I read the whole lot in Party publications for internal use. And in foreign editions I read all of Shalamov, who was imprisoned not far from here too.'

'I take it you were in the Party, Ninochka?'

'Screw that,' says my hostess, scowling.

'I'll pour us another.'

'Do,' she agrees. 'After five years working at the Party library the regional committee secretary for ideological affairs summoned me. Such a slimy little bastard, a real fox – and he asked why I hadn't joined the ranks. "Because I'm not yet ideologically mature, Kliment Kirillovich." Another two years went by. He summoned me again and asked if I was with them or against them. And he fixed that foxy stare on me, like an X-ray. I was afraid to fib again, because that man could feel everything through his skin. A Party X-ray, plain and simple. I loathed him like a dog.'

'You were scared of him,' I suggest.

'And I respected him for being dedicated to his cause. That creep also knew how to drink and pay the girls smooth compliments. He and our first secretary made a fine pair – that man, Ivan Dmitrievich, didn't actually know how to drink, but he liked a drop. Typical Yakut.

They really were a fine pair. Even to look at. Like Laurel and Hardy. And that cunning little fox worked on that big, strong, simple chump to get him to give me a Party recommendation. Then I no longer had any choice. The first secretary himself giving a Party recommendation to a librarian! They'd have stretched my guts from here to there if I'd refused.'

'In the first place they'd have thrown you out of the library.'

'And those books were like air to me. I always was a firebrand, a crazy Buryat girl, and as a Party member I could no longer allow myself any antics. It was hard for me to live with it. Now I know that slogging over Party literature wasn't a waste of time. I developed in the process, but when they made me manager of the cultural centre, the local artists regarded me as a Party bitch. Pour us another.'

'There's none left.'

Day XXX

Cherkyokh. Kilometre 1781 of the Kolyma Highway

Now I can make a confession – I originally wanted to make this journey by motorbike. I even got my motorcycle licence specially for this purpose, but everything went wrong. The man I'd arranged to meet in Magadan who was supposed to sell me a motorbike screwed up, and the winter came earlier than usual. There was already snow on the ground in the first pass outside Magadan, so I had to drop it. Once the snow has fallen it's impossible to ride a motorbike, but even if I had managed to put this plan into action, the whole exploit would have fallen completely flat in comparison with the seven minutes I had to endure this morning.

I'm talking about my journey across the Aldan river. But to go back to yesterday evening: when I finally managed to arrange the crossing, the people who helped me to do it said it's a bloody dangerous enterprise. That's all too obvious – I can see the river from my hotel room. And we're going to cross it in a small boat, not an icebreaker!

Once I'm lying in bed I start to feel scared.

In the morning a car collects me from the hotel and takes me and four other men a long way downstream, beyond the city. I'm still on the Kolyma Highway, but here it is often called the Magadan Route.

Two of our group are almost too drunk to stand up. None of them has ever crossed the river this way before, but they all have far more important reasons for doing this than I do. Vasyl, a Yakut by origin, is a gold prospector, on his way home to Yakutsk for the winter after six months working in the taiga. Ivan Ivanovich is going to Novosibirsk for a heart operation, and his twenty-three-year-old shaven-headed son Seryozha refuses to let his father go on his own. Valera the geologist is going to Moscow for his mother's funeral. I'm the only one who could give up.

Of our group, only Ivan Ivanovich keeps his cool. He says he's not afraid, because he's going to die soon anyway. The doctors have already established his life expectancy. The operation will provide a small chance of postponing his imminent death. But he is worried about his son, all the more because in spite of the early hour the boy has done some serious drinking and keeps glugging cheap wine out of a carton every now and then.

The jeep carries us right up to the water's edge. The driver takes 500 roubles (£10) from each of us. We can see vehicles on the other side, and then a tiny metal cockleshell, which is battling its way over to our side through the ice and water.

It's a battered old motorboat with a Yamaha engine. We help a terrified woman, white as a sheet, to scramble onto the shore, and then we take our own places. It turns out our ferryman wants to take us all across in a single trip. Including him, that's six hefty blokes with luggage. The sides of the boat are barely sticking out above the water.

Naturally, there are no life jackets on board. We dodge between the huge plates of ice, and ram into the smaller ones. Ice floes thump against the metal sides – a terrifying sound.

The crossing takes seven minutes. In this time our Yakut ferryman, whose name is Nikolai, tells us that for six years he has been the only man in all Khandyga to take people across illegally in the period when navigation is closed. He does it to earn a living and because he has a score to settle with this river. He enjoys subjugating it. A few years ago his brother drowned in the Aldan. He needed to get to the other side, but nobody had the courage to take him across, so he tried to get over the river by jumping from one ice floe to the next.

Nikolai takes another 500 roubles from each of us and we transfer our luggage to a car that's waiting on the shore.

Those two 500-rouble notes for today's crossing (worth £20 in total) are the only money I have spent on transport along the entire, 2025-kilometre Highway.

After crossing the Aldan I'm leaving Kolyma. Its border used to be this river, but the Kolyma Highway runs on, so I'm not ending my journey yet.

Crossing the Aldan river.

IVAN IVANOVICH — JOHN SMITH

Ivan Ivanovich, in other words John son of John. A sort of Russian Everyman. Like calling someone John Smith in Britain, Jan Kowalski in Poland, or Hans Schmidt in Germany. Even the dummy which flew into outer space before Gagarin in the Vostok spacecraft was called Ivan Ivanovich.

And in the Stalinist camps it was a term of abuse. That's what they called all the professors, writers, artists, engineers, Party activists and teachers — all the intellectuals. Their fate in that era was the worst of all.

Wave after wave of purges swept away at least half the Russian intelligentsia, shot dead or packed off to the camps. That was how 'the monstrous selection of the Stalinist period was achieved', writes the former prisoner Vera Schulz in her memoirs, 'which seemed to have created a new species of human beings: meek, torpid, reticent people, lacking any initiative'. Soviet man had been born, *Homo sovieticus*, a character without the slightest tendency to rebel, but with a vast talent for thieving. To this very day they say a thief doesn't steal, but just takes things left lying in the wrong place. The new Soviet man is passive, timorous and lazy, suffering from the syndrome of silence as well as travelling-companion syndrome. He's a man who doesn't scream the pain out of his soul, but whispers it to a stranger on a journey. Or anaesthetizes it with vodka.

On the road, following our successful river crossing, my tipsy *poputchiki* are becoming noisy. They're relieving the tension by drinking cheap wine out of cartons and by telling jokes.

'"Granny," asks the grandson, "is it true there wasn't any bread during the blockade of Leningrad?" "Yes, grandson, it is." "So did you have to spread your butter on sausages instead?"'

After Seryozha the strongman's joke, nobody's lip even faintly quivers, and Valera the geologist, who is in the least jolly mood because he's going to his mother's funeral, reckons it's a pretty moronic joke.

'A million people died there,' he grunts, and falls asleep.

There are three rows of seats in our van and it's as hot as an oven. In the front row sit the driver, stripped to his undershirt, and Vasily, the only non-Slav in our company, wearing winter boots, a sheepskin coat and a woolly hat. Ivan Ivanovich and I are occupying the middle row, and Valera and Seryozha are in the third, both in big fur hats, both asleep now with their mouths open.

'How did you end up in Kolyma, Ivan Ivanovich?' I ask the sad man sitting next to me.

'I came from Kalinin near Moscow, from a factory making weaving machines,' he says, taking off his Gore-Tex camouflage jacket. Fifty-eight-year-old Ivan Ivanovich Igoshin is a lifesaver – *spasatel* – for a voluntary service that specializes in mountain and water rescue.

'Eleven thousand people worked at my factory,' he tells me. 'The fight to fulfil the plan was a life-and-death battle. Literally. A month in which none of the engineers had a heart attack was an anomaly. My friends were drinking heavily, and dying, and I was slaving away like an ox, then I used to march in procession at the head of the workers' collective, carrying the red flag. It was bound to end badly. So now I'm going for my third heart operation. The only place they do them in Siberia is Novosibirsk. If it works, I might live a little longer, but if it doesn't, I've got ...'

Ivan Ivanovich sinks into thought for a few minutes, and I don't break the silence.

'I've waited six months for this operation,' he says when he comes back to earth. 'There's a huge queue, but they've brought me forward, because my condition has suddenly deteriorated. Now I've really got to hurry.'

'Why did you wait so long before crossing the river? You could have been killed getting over it, without ever reaching Novosibirsk. After all, you knew they'd be closing the ferries on the fifteenth of October.'

'Right. But I didn't have all my test results. They did them for me here. They only admit you to hospital with all your results.'

'Were you afraid on the river?' I ask.

'No. I'm dying anyway.'

'On the river you said only fools aren't afraid.'

'Of course. I said it out of respect for the river. With no life jackets, at that temperature, amid those ice floes we didn't stand a chance. It would have been enough for that stupid little engine to break down, it would have been enough to hit a bigger plate of ice, or perform the wrong manoeuvre . . . Last year a man from our town was swept away on an ice floe. It carried him sixty kilometres before he was taken off it by helicopter five hours later. They amputated his frostbitten hands and feet, but his mind never recovered.'

Ivan Ivanovich escaped from his weaving-machine factory in 1987. He wrote fourteen letters to fourteen different places in the Far North asking for a job. But nobody needed a weaving-machinery engineer in Novaya Zemlya, or Kolyma, Chukotka or Franz Josef Land. The only answer he got was from Khandyga.

'I came here with my wife and two backpacks. We founded a small sports and touring club for young people at social risk. We've devoted our lives to street children, but what I care about most is living in a vast, immense, boundless place. But what about you? Why did you get in that motorboat? Do you really have to get to Yakutsk? At any price?'

'No. This journey matters, but not its destination.'

293

PART THREE

Travelling-companion Syndrome

Don't be scared of ash, don't be scared of blame,
Fear not hell's fiery furnace,
There's only one thing that you need to fear –
The man who says 'I have the answers.'

Alexander Galich, from 'Stalin',
translated by Gerald Stanton Smith

A day in a Kamaz truck, an ancient, twenty-year-old Russki lorry of unknown mileage, on the Kolyma Highway, hacked out of the permafrost with pickaxes – full of potholes, stones, subsidence, cracks and landslides. In the evening, after some fifteen hours of furious vibrations and shudders through your entire body, you don't know if you've spent the day in a car or a meat grinder. You feel as if all your discs have slipped, as well as your kneecaps and the fillings in your teeth, as if inside you everything that wasn't tightly fixed has snapped off.

In Kolyma, the only way to escape was along this Highway, heading west, towards the world and the mainland. The prisoners called escape 'being freed by the green prosecutor' – into the taiga, into the mountains or the forest. Always in summer. The winter was on the side of the administration. Only a suicide escaped in winter.

These were desperate, hopeless actions. Nobody ever escaped for more than a short while, a few days, at most a fortnight, to rest, lie about in the sunshine, do nothing, eat berries, and get a break from the beatings and the hard labour. They also spoke of 'recuperative escape'. Everybody knew they would get caught, yet they still tried to escape, because in a pit at a gold-bearing plot they could die after five weeks on the job.

It was almost only political prisoners who escaped. The common criminals had short sentences, and the *blatniki* devoted all their energy to ensuring themselves a cushy life at the camp, where they had a privileged position.

A small handful of convicts managed to get away from Kolyma

during the Great Patriotic War. About a million prisoners were drafted into the ranks of the Red Army, but from the cruellest extremity on earth only six thousand common hooligans, pilferers and speculators ended up at the Front – not a single 'enemy of the people' tried under Article 58 of the Soviet penal code.

All those who were drafted ended up in *stroibataliony* (worker battalions which were not issued with weapons) or *shtrafbataliony* (penal battalions), sent out to almost certain death. However, several hundred of the latter survived, and two men distinguished themselves so greatly in action that they were both awarded the top combat medal – the Gold Star of the Hero of the Soviet Union. One had been sent to Kolyma for stealing a collective-farm horse (which he had slaughtered to feed his family), and the other was serving four years for stealing three bottles of paraffin.

Varlam Shalamov maintains that in the entire history of Kolyma there was only one successful escape, carried out, in fact, by a criminal convict, who went all the way to Yakutsk along the Highway, and then got back to his native Ukraine. Two years later, he reckoned the authorities had forgotten about him, and stopped being cautious. He was given another ten-year sentence, but a few years later was released for good conduct, but with no right to return to the mainland. He made an excellent life for himself in Magadan.

Escapees were charged under Article 58, paragraph 14 of the penal code, in other words for economic counter-revolution, because escape was a form of shirking work, or sabotage.

The most famous escape in the history of Kolyma was attempted by a Major Pugachov, a veteran of the Great Patriotic War, who had been captured by the Germans but had escaped in 1944 and made his way back to his own side. They gave him twenty-five years in a prison camp for espionage. In the camp he organized a twelve-man group of former soldiers, who killed several guards and got hold of weapons, army uniforms and a lorry. They set off east, the opposite direction to all other escapees. They were planning to reach Seymchan, take control of the airport (there was a pilot in the group), kidnap a plane and escape abroad.

Their dream was to get to Alaska. But the lorry broke down and they were caught on the Highway. There was a great fight in the taiga, in which twenty-eight security soldiers and ten of the escapees were killed. Major Pugachov was the only one who didn't fall into the hands of the pursuers, and he was never found. He probably committed suicide somewhere in hiding, or drowned in a swamp. Only a seriously wounded officer named Soldatov was captured alive. He was restored to health and then shot. Sixty people who were in the know and had helped the conspirators were given additional sentences. And the head of the camp got a ten-year sentence himself.

The events described by Shalamov must have occurred not much more than a year after the three-day visit to Kolyma of US Vice President Henry Wallace. Lenin used to call such people 'useful idiots'.

For thirty years the Soviet Union had already been the main supplier of gold to the United States, where they were perfectly well aware of how the precious metal was acquired. By hosting the vice president in Kolyma in 1944, the Russians wanted to convince their wartime allies that rumours about the cruel camps were anti-communist propaganda. They dismantled all the guard towers along the route of his trip, and the only gold prospectors he saw were Komsomol activists dressed up in work clothes. The female prisoners working at a collective farm near Magadan were replaced for the duration of Wallace's visit by female office staff from the prison-camp administration in the city.

The Americans needed Soviet gold as badly as the Russians needed their military equipment to fight against the Third Reich. But why did the American vice president say that 'the Russian and American peoples instinctively like each other'? How could he seriously pass on greetings to American union members from the Soviet president of the gold prospectors' trade union?

My first Yakut poputchiki – Ulana and her family.

Day XXXI

Cherkyokh. Kilometre 1781 of the Kolyma Highway

After crossing the Aldan, the van takes me to the large village of Cherkyokh. Only here do I start to feel that I'm in Yakutia. It's as if suddenly I'm no longer in Russia. There isn't a single European living in Cherkyokh, just Yakuts, about twelve hundred of them, including nine pregnant women – as I find out at the local maternity clinic.

I'm given accommodation for the night at the historical and ethnographic museum. The building is only thirty years old. It employs three academic and several technical staff members, but nothing in the place works – not one of the seven toilets (you have to nip outside), and not a single one of several television sets; there are mice crawling about on the table, there's no heating, no running water, and the water in the buckets is not fit to drink because it comes from a nearby stream.

But for the time being the warmth radiating from the eighteenth-century icon hanging above my bed is quite enough for me. I can't believe my eyes. The Son of God has prominent folds above his slanting eyes and a long, sparse beard – a typical Mongol in a crown of thorns.

The Yakuts, like the Evenks who also live here, adopted Christianity in the eighteenth century. In 1997 they celebrated the two-hundredth anniversary of Yakutia's baptism. To mark the event some Orthodox priests came to the village and christened two hundred new members of the congregation.

There are several small historic wooden churches standing within the grounds of the museum. There's also a wooden yurt, in which Polish exile Edward Piekarski spent thirteen years of his banishment. He was a great linguist and ethnographer, and an honorary member of the Soviet Academy of Sciences. Piekarski's life's work was the *Yakut–Russian Dictionary*, in which he collected twenty-five thousand words. To this day many people regard it as the best dictionary of the Yakut language.

Piekarski established a sizeable farm – he had forty cows and horses, and thus by local standards he was a sort of lord of the manor. He married a local girl, with whom he had a child, and when in 1905 Tsar Nicholas II released him from captivity for his services to Russian scholarship, he left Yakutia, taking his daughter with him. He did not go back to Poland but spent the rest of his life in St Petersburg, soon to be known as Leningrad.

Another Polish exile who also spent about fifteen years in Yakutia was Wacław Sieroszewski. In his great ethnographic work entitled *The Yakuts*, he wrote that the local dogs are half wild: '[the Yakuts] hardly feed them at all, so they obtain their own food, and are closer to wolves than to dogs'. Cows and horses lived – and still live – semi-wild, small herds of them wandering about the village and the surrounding area in single file, looking for dry stalks of grass protruding from under the snow.

Draped on fences, in cold weather and in sunshine, the skins of young cows and horses are left to dry. The Yakuts are the northernmost tribe to farm these animals – all their neighbours are reindeer herders.

With the first hard frosts comes the season for slaughter. Maybe that's why almost all the men I encounter in the village street are reeling a bit. They're slightly tanked up. The indigenous peoples who live alongside the Yakuts kill animals when they need food. The Yakuts are settled, and it's hard for them to feed their animals in winter, so when the cold weather sets in they kill and freeze the cattle and horses that are going to be eaten by the spring in any case.

303

At the village administration I come across a policeman. It's a very unpleasant encounter indeed, because he's an extremely stupid fellow, who speaks far worse Russian than I do, and feels the need to demonstrate his power to an outsider. He asks a lot of idiotic questions: how much money do I have, what have I photographed, what's this village called? And to pronounce the name with a correct Yakut accent is not easy. Then he scrupulously scours my backpack. He even opens my lip salve to look inside. He asks what it is, orders me to demonstrate how it is used, and scowls with disdain.

Several office staff witness this thorough frisking, but none of them takes any notice.

The policeman is clearly disappointed that I'm putting up with it so patiently. As a parting shot he advises me not to go near the shop where they sell alcohol (one of about a dozen shops), because I might get a punch in the gob before I've had time to say I'm not Russian, and not to go outside after dark.

According to the last Soviet general census conducted in 1986, the Yakuts constituted only thirty-six per cent of the population of their own region. Slavs were the dominant people. Once the empire collapsed, the Russians left the republic in droves, and are still leaving, while by the standards of the Russian Federation the Yakuts have a high birth rate. Only the Caucasians have a higher birth rate, whereas the number of Russians is decreasing steadily: the population of the Federation is shrinking at a daily rate of fifteen hundred citizens.

Dmitri Chagaan, acrobatics trainer, and his wife.
The pot contains yogurt which is whipped with a wooden stirrer.

Dmitri puts on a video of a sports display, in which he shows off his unusual skills. Somebody stacks a pile of bricks on his head, and then a man the size of a bridge support whacks them with an enormous hammer. The bricks crumble, but Dmitri just brushes down his shirt and shows the audience that he hasn't so much as a scratch on his shaven head. He explains to me that it's yoga.

Then he shows me a film of breaking the record for the biggest human pyramid. The Chinese had built a nineteen-man pyramid, but the Yakut one consists of twenty-eight acrobats. One of the building blocks is Dmitri Ivanovich Chagaan himself, the fifty-one-year-old acrobatics coach at the local sports school.

Acrobatics is Dmitri's last great passion. As a young man he went in for wrestling and boxing, which is plain to see. He has a broken nose, and the ripped ears of a wrestler. In 1978 he won the title of wrestling champion of Yakutia (flyweight, forty-eight kilos) and left for school in Odessa.

'That was where I first felt and understood what nationalism is, Russian chauvinism,' he tells me. 'At every step of the way they made it clear to me that the Russians are the cleverest, the smartest, the strongest, and the best educated, and that without them all the other Soviet nations would have starved to death. That was where I discovered that the Russkies tell jokes about us. To them, everyone who comes from the north is a Chukchi, and that's a term of abuse. A Chukchi is a fool. They also call all slant-eyed people *kitaytsy* [Chinese]. O-o-oh! That's a dreadful insult! The Chinese are devious, wily and treacherous. Ukrainians are conmen, cheats, thieves and mediocrities, while all Central Asians are *churki*, meaning blockheads. If someone is nasty, venal, cunning or mean, they say he's a Jew. "Jew" is another hideous insult.'

Dmitri started having problems with his identity; he had never actually regarded himself as a Yakut, just a Soviet citizen. He was prepared to fight and give up his life for the USSR, even in that miserable runt of a place called Poland, where counter-revolution was rearing its ugly head. So when he finished school in 1983 and was accepted into the army, he volunteered for the war in Afghanistan.

'But they told me they didn't need any Yakut morons there,' says Dmitri sadly. 'In fact you do have to be an idiot to want to go to war, but I wanted to earn admiration, and the respect of my Soviet motherland, which was more of a stepmother than a mother to me. I longed to make myself a martyr, a Yakut boy sacrificing himself on the altar of the great Land of Soviets. Let them all see that Yakut boys are the best, and the Sakha people are the most devoted, the most faithful of the faithful.'

The army was the toughest and worst period in Dmitri's life. He was always getting into fights. He learned to swear, to torture and to steal, but whenever he could, he helped his compatriots. He taught them how to fight. The army variety of Russian nationalism was intolerable. Dmitri couldn't understand why the Russians felt so much hatred towards everybody else. How could they feed boys from Central Asia on processed pork and at the same time tease and torment them for being bad Muslims?

'I served as a *smertnik*,' says Dmitri.

That word isn't easy to translate. It's a bit like a kamikaze, but not entirely, because among the Japanese pilots, at any rate to begin with, they were volunteers. A *smertnik* is a soldier who is sent on a hopeless mission, to face certain death, but is definitely not a volunteer.

The diminutive Dmitri (weighing only forty-eight kilos) served in an ONTOT – short for *niedvizhimaya tankovaya ognevaya tochka*, meaning literally a 'fixed armoured firing point', which is a sort of pillbox. By some strange quirk, there were a lot of Yakuts at these suicidal fortification points. They were made out of old tanks withdrawn from the armoured divisions, with no caterpillar tracks or engines, and then stuck into the ground with only the turrets protruding. They couldn't turn more than 130 degrees, so that if one of the ONTOTs happened to be captured by the enemy it couldn't be fired at its neighbours. They were positioned along the Chinese border.

At each point there were four men – a commander, a gunner, a loader and a telegraph operator. They had enough food for three days, 3000 rounds of ammunition for the tank's heavy machine gun and 160 shells, mainly shrapnel and anti-tank shells, and a few fragmentation bombs. Those were their supplies for a single day. The crew could not withdraw or surrender, but could only sit there, fight and be killed. The upper hatch of the tank was welded shut, and the lower one was filled in with cement, while in front of it, behind it and to either side of it there were minefields and entanglements.

CHAGAAN THE ACROBAT – LENIN IS WITH US

On leaving the army Dmitri entered the State University of Yakutia in the capital. They had just opened the Faculty of Physical Education. But there was no time to study. He trained and danced the *osuokhay*. The *osuokhay* is a Yakut ritual then banned by the authorities, a simple, trance-like dance with two steps and a terrifying tune. The *osuokhay* has always been an important element of shamanic ritual, a dance which served to unite the ancestral and tribal community.

'How can you ban a dance?' I naively ask Dmitri.

'They didn't ban it. Just as they didn't ban going to church. Nor did they ban the Sakha language. Yet the moment you tried talking in our language on the bus, they'd make a fuss and accuse us of hatching a plot against them. But once perestroika began, the Sakha would meet in squares and streets to dance the *osuokhay* on their days off. I used to organize it too. I'd agree to meet the students in some spot and we'd dance. Then we'd start discussing the fact that in the entire city there wasn't a single nursery school where Yakut was spoken, and that schools only taught it as a foreign language.'

In winter the young people would gather at the ice rinks formed by a stream flowing through the city near the university. Going skating was just for fun, but it was only Yakuts who did it. Almost all the students were Yakuts, because young Russians usually studied outside the republic.

The riots began on 30 March 1986, when a big gang of Russian hooligans came to the ice rink outside the college and beat up the students. The next day the same thing happened. On 1 April Dmitri mobilized the students to join forces and chase off the townies, as they called them. There was a distinct division among the young people into townies, in other words Russians, and Sakha students, most of whom were from small places in the countryside.

The Yakut-versus-Russian street battles went on all day. The students caught thugs all over the city. The lecturers tried to keep the warring sides apart with human chains, but things only quietened down at night. On 2 April there were no more punch-ups, just a demonstration and a march to Lenin Square in the city centre. Hundreds of citizens joined the students. They held a rally outside the Council of Ministers building.

'We had finally stopped being afraid. We could shout out all our woes and misfortunes, all the bitterness and injustice of seventy years of Bolshevik rule in our motherland. Yakutsk had never seen anything like it before. The government representatives came out to meet us, but they stood on the steps of the building, so it looked as if Lenin was on our side.'

'You mean his statue.'

'Right,' says Dmitri. 'We demanded equal rights, Yakut schools and nurseries, and for the militia to stop beating up or arresting us, because it was the Russians who had started the trouble. Most of the people serving in the militia were Russians.'

A week later they came for him. He got four years for assaulting a militiaman. Of course he hadn't assaulted anyone. He was tried with three other leaders of the protest and three Russian hooligans, but they were given shorter sentences.

Dmitri served his entire sentence to the very last day. He got out in 1990. Two years later, after the collapse of the Soviet Union, he finished his studies. He was never rehabilitated.

'We were the first,' he says proudly. 'The first rebels in the USSR. Long before the Lithuanians, the Latvians, the Estonians . . .'

Day XXXII

Churapcha. Kilometre 1831 of the Kolyma Highway

After my night at the museum and a morning spent at the local school (because it's the only place that has an Internet connection), I take to the road out of Cherkyokh. I'm walking west towards Yakutsk. It's only about fifteen degrees below zero, but it's unpleasant to stop.

After ten minutes the first car goes past, and after another five, the next one stops. It's a UAZ 'tablet', with a lovely Yakut family inside, siblings Ulana Plotnikova and Ivan Sleptsov. They have a Polish great-grandfather, who was exiled to Yakutia by a tsarist court. It is in his honour that Ulana has this old-fashioned Polish first name. She is very proud of it.

Ulana got her surname from a husband with whom she lived in Yakutsk after graduating from college. She spent ten years working as a history teacher, but then she ran away from her husband and went home to her parents and brother in the provinces. She used all her savings to open a tiny little shop with him, the eighth one in their village. They are on their way to Yakutsk for goods to sell.

Ulana doesn't look Slav in the least, but there is something playful and mischievous in her face and eyes that the Yakuts don't have. They are an introverted, reticent and morose people, with furrowed foreheads and no sense of humour. Unless it's nothing like ours, and I have no feeling for it. They very rarely laugh, even after a drink. They don't like foreigners, especially journalists, and they definitely hate talking to them.

Ulana and Ivan take me as far as Churapcha, which by Yakutian standards is a large town, with a population of ten thousand.

Now I'm going to write about the disrespectful – sorry, I mean scornful – attitude of the Yakuts to objects. I was amazed at the way they so blithely and carelessly reduce objects, appliances and buildings to ruin. It doesn't bother them in the slightest, they just live with it, and create some sort of makeshift alternative.

To illustrate, let's take my so-called hotel. Although 'hostel' would be a better word, a billet on the first floor of a small block on the edge of town. In the region as a whole, this hotel passes as luxury. There are seven of us guys staying here in three rooms. There are three in mine. But now I'm going to focus on water.

Our hostess Luisa proudly shows me the bathroom, in which there is a bathtub. Admittedly, there isn't any hot water, but if I need some, I can use a rubber hose to let it out of the radiator in my neighbours' room and then carry it to the bathroom in a bucket.

Under no circumstances can the tap water be drunk, not even after boiling. It is very dirty. It comes from the small local lake.

I ask what I am supposed to use to make tea, upon which Luisa brings water from a *lednik*, which is in fact a bucket of ice. A *lednik* is drinking water in the form of ice, something the Yakuts have been making for centuries. They make it at the beginning of winter, so that means now, for the entire year. Then they store the ice in pits, in other words in the permafrost, where it will never melt.

I ask my hostess where the ice comes from. She looks at me with large, astonished eyes. What do I mean, where does it come from? From the lake, in which the cows are watered and the horses are bathed, in which at the height of summer the animals stand to cool down, and into which they spend all day pooing.

One of several concrete monuments in town was erected by the townsfolk in honour of a local drainage engineer, thanks to whom they have this water in their taps. It was he who redirected the local stream towards Churapcha and formed the small lake out of it.

The season for replenishing stores of ice has just begun. Anyone who doesn't fancy hacking it out for himself can order it by phone. A small truck of ice costs 1000 roubles (£20). Public offices, workplaces and schools organize voluntary labour to hack out ice for their buffets and canteens.

I drink the water from the little bucket too. Everyone here assures me that after you freeze dirty water, it becomes clean.

Niurgun rejuvenates a plant.

NIURGUN THE DISCOVERER –
THE REJUVENATING DEVICE

Thirty-one-year-old Niurgun Filipov is a technician at the local television station. He graduated from a ten-grade primary school, where he was top of the class in physics. He barely scraped through in any other subject.

I can't think how he could be so good at physics, since he too assures me that water becomes clean once it's frozen. He gives me some sort of explanation involving tiny particles, atoms and water molecules. Molecules – his favourite word.

'Sometimes I make a discovery every day of the week. I immediately publish it on my website, where I've got my radio, all my inventions and discoveries, and a blog. Lately for example I discovered how to charge potatoes with positive energy, which delays the human ageing process.'

This is another of Niurgun's favourite topics – old age and ways to reverse its effects. This passion almost cost Niurgun's father his life when the son conducted an experiment on him. It was just after the son had come back from military service, and had set up his own business, a television repair shop.

'That's a great idea for a business!' I enthuse. 'Why did you give it up?'

'Because it turned out I didn't know much about televisions. That was a bad moment in my life. Even my own father refused to let me conduct any more experiments. He said it caused him pain, and that it made his heart jump. But the voltage wasn't very high.'

'You hooked him up to the electric current?'

'Yes. He's very interested in medicine. I constructed a device specially for him, which rejuvenates you and makes you wise. After only a month of daily treatments, his grey hair would have started to go black, and then he would have started to become more and more intelligent.'

'Even more intelligent than he was in his youth?' I ask, intrigued.

'Of course.'

'And who's this?' I ask, pointing at a photograph of an old man with unseeing eyes and white hair standing on end.

'That's my father just after the rejuvenating and intelligence-increasing experiment.'

We are having our conversation at the entirely empty television studio. Niurgun reaches into a cupboard and brings out a device packed into two empty plastic fizzy-drinks bottles which have been joined together lengthwise. Inside there is a small transformer, a high-frequency 8000-watt generator, some resistors and coils of electrical wire – all of which came out of some old Soviet television sets. He uses a bicycle pump to increase the pressure in the device and connects it to a third bottle full of powdered carbon. Then he snaps a small sprig off a plant standing in the corner and hooks it up to the device instead of to his father.

Soon a lovely plume of sparks appears around the little plant.

'This is an imitation, a miniature version of the energy of lightning,' he cries in excitement. 'The plant is getting younger and younger, and if it had a brain it would be getting more and more intelligent. What you are seeing is the shining of plants, discovered by me.'

'What do you mean, shining? It's simply that the electrical energy is jumping towards you because you're earthed, and the plant isn't.'

Niurgun switches off the light, and I see that he's shining. The palms of his hands and each of his fingers are producing a sort of luminous glow; he opens his mouth and it's like a fiery hole, full of flames.

'The dragon effect,' says the inventor, with childish joy. Then my heart stops for a couple of seconds when I go up to the radiator and a small flash of lightning from my body hits it. Legs like jelly, I carry my camera into the next room, so Niurgun won't rejuvenate my memory chip full of the week's photographs.

'What does your wife think of these experiments?' I ask, with a lump in my throat.

'She often drives me out of the house. For a month or two at a time. Last week she threw me out, but only for five days. I came and lived at the studio. I've got my own mattress here. My wife says I'm wasting my life, and hers too, spending all my time on stupid things that don't bring in a single kopeck.'

'You've got three children.'

'But I earn fourteen thousand roubles a month, which go into our account, and my wife has the bank card. As the wise man said, if his wife is good, a man is happy, but if his wife's a shrew he becomes a philosopher. My wife's good, but she's quarrelsome as hell. So I became an inventor. And people don't laugh at me much these days, because I have a large number of discoveries to my credit – I was featured on our television channel, and they wrote about me in the newspapers. I'm famous.'

We go out into the main street of town to find something to eat. On the way my Yakut friend tells me about the only one of his discoveries so far to have found a practical application: a new way of walking.

'I spent six months perfecting it,' he says. He stands on his toes, and then he's off like a shot, but his head and torso stay completely still. 'I had to develop my auxiliary muscles to walk like this. As you walk along, you wobble all over the place and waste a lot of energy. My method is highly energy-saving.'

'It's hard to keep up with you,' I say, shifting into a trot.

317

'I can move faster than cars.'

'That's not much of an art. Your streets are made of frozen mud. It's easier to walk than to drive.'

Breathless, we stumble into a little cafeteria.

'What's this Russki you've brought me?' cries the old bag serving hot dishes through a little hatch.

'Churapcha and the Churapcha region are famous throughout Yakutia for their nationalism,' Niurgun whispers to me. 'Perhaps deservedly. But when my rejuvenating device starts to make people wiser, I'll cure them of nationalism too. Because it's a stupid people's ail-ment. It'll be a great revolution, a miracle, salvation for all mankind. Have you ever heard of the Serbian prophet Mitar Tarabić? He lived in the late nineteenth century. He was an illiterate peasant. He prophesied the outbreak of both world wars, the birth and collapse of Yugoslavia, space flights, the invention of television, and of mobile phones . . . He also made a prophecy about me. About a little man from the Far North, who would educate people, but nobody would understand him.'

'How tall are you?'

'One metre sixty centimetres. That's how I can tell it's about me!'

Day XXXIII

Churapcha. Kilometre 1831 of the Kolyma Highway

Something has broken down, and now there's no water at all at my 'hotel'. But that's nothing. (Earlier on there was a power cut.) Luisa brings us water in a bucket, just as she brought us candles earlier on. Naturally one of my room-mates pours the whole lot out in one go, and we have to do without flushing the toilet.

My fellow guests, from Yakutsk, arrived with their own water in large five-litre cans. It isn't from a spring, nor is it mineral water, nor does it have healing properties. It's just pure.

Like all of Yakutia, Churapcha stands on permafrost. It is difficult to build sewage systems in such places. The pipes have to run above ground, or have very thick, carefully fitted thermal insulation. Septic tanks and cesspool-emptying trucks don't work well, because the faeces would freeze in the ground even in summer, and would have to be hacked out. Everyone uses so-called toilet buckets (a sort of large chamber pot with a lid, or a toilet without an outflow, but with a handle for carrying instead) and communal courtyard outhouses marked 'Ж' (Z) and 'У' (U) on the doors (*zhenshchina* – meaning 'woman' in Russian, and *uol* – meaning 'man' in Yakut), where, if the pit is deep enough, the excrement freezes in the permafrost for centuries. But there is a toilet in my Churapcha apartment.

Because, as I find out today, once again I'm lucky enough to be living in the Yakut president's house. And not a past president, but the

319

current one, Yegor Borisov, who comes from here. When he still lived here, he was head of the agricultural-machinery department, which by local standards is a powerful official position, so the next time a house was built, one of the apartments in it was prepared for him. Hence the toilet. Now Borisov lives in Yakutsk, and his apartment has been changed into a hotel.

Today I spent the afternoon at the *banya*, in other words the bath-house, of a former TB hospital, which has been converted into the base for a Workers' Commune, or *Trudovaya Komuna*, as it has been named by twenty-six ex-convicts gathered around the local entrepreneur Nikolai Vasilyev. These men served heavy sentences (from fifteen to twenty-five years, for murder); meanwhile their family lives fell apart, and when they were released they had nowhere to go, so they settled here and worked at the Commune. They get a roof over their heads, food and a symbolic wage. They specialize in tough, dirty jobs, such as forest clearance, 'ritual services' (in other words, grave-digging at the cemetery), hacking ice, and demolition. I have just interrupted them in the middle of demol-ishing the old hospital for consumptives. Nobody wanted to take on this job, because there were so many tuberculosis bacilli all over the fittings, floors and walls that the wallpaper was crawling with them, so the com-mune members simply set fire to the building, and now they're cleaning up the remains of pipes, radiators and nails. The hospital was made of wood. It was built by Gulag prisoners in 1938, and now ex-cons are dis-posing of it.

The burned-down building is still smoking. A stadium is going to be built nearby for the forthcoming Yakutian National Spartakiad. This event and this building are prestigious for Churapcha, but here's the old tubercular ruin next door, so the local authorities have made the decision to demolish it by fire.

Anyone can join the Commune. There's only one rule – no drinking on the job. Once a month Nikolai pays the guys from 3000 to 7000

Lena and Misha gave me supper and removed a spell which a bad woman had put on me.

roubles and lets them off the leash to *rasslabit* (that's another of my favourite Russian words) – literally, 'to weaken', but actually to get drunk, as sloshed as they like. These are the most dangerous times in the life of the local community. The communards indulge in insane, collective alcoholic binges. They become aggressive, terrifying, and evil. They fight each other non-stop and with no self-control, breaking each other's bones and wounding each other with knives.

The boozing continues until the money runs out. Then the men work for nothing but their food and a roof over their heads. Right now their accommodation is some communal wooden bunks in the TB hospital's bathhouse. They're not afraid of the disease, because many of them have already caught it in the nick.

I ask Nikolai if he served time too. He says he did, but only briefly – five years for assault.

There is one woman in the Commune, Larissa, who is their cook, but not long ago she won the favours of one of the men, and they're planning to get married and leave. That'll be the sixth family started by a female communard in the ten-year history of the community.

In the evening I have a meeting combined with supper. Lena and Misha Daczkowski (Polish surnames among the Yakuts are a memento of the exiles sent here in the tsarist era) are both fifty-five years old, and have been married for the past three. As head of the four-person team at the local television station, Lena is Niurgun Filipov's boss.

'When it was Soviet power,' Lena begins her account of Misha's life, 'this man work at Churapcha *sovkhoz* [state farm]. They said he is best welder, victor in competitions for best tractor driver.'

Lena speaks Russian using very simple, slightly comical language. A bit like a child, with a hilarious accent and weird syntax. And a logic that's not easy to follow.

'And then, when they dissolved Union in our country, our *sovkhoz* collapsed too. And big problem arose with the men. They had no work. Luckily they gave the former workers cows. One got one, another got two or three, it varied. And they gave this man, Misha, too. He took care of that for two or three years.'

'How many of those cows did he have?'

'Just one! But she die. She eat a nail and she die.'

'A nail?'

'In our place the cows are like that,' explains Lena. 'Stupid some-times. They consume everything. And Misha had enormous cat too. And one day he went out to the hay, and it was cold, so he light stove and asked neighbour to close chimney when it start to burn, so the neighbour closed it, but too soon, it make carbon monoxide and the cat died. So Misha was left with no cow and no cat. But he still had dog. Very good hunting dog. A laika. He was tied up, because it is spring, and the bitches are on heat. But Misha's brother came and he feel sorry for the dog, so he untie him. The dog raced after bitches and hasn't come back for fifteen years now. So Misha was left on his own. Without his faithful friends.'

'Didn't Misha have any people in his life?'

'He had wife called Marina, but she was not faithful. She went off to another man. And Misha got married a second time, but that woman drank terribly, and life with her was bad. Misha came home, and she was gone.'

'When I came home from a voyage,' says Misha, finally speaking for himself.

'Were you a sailor?' I ask in surprise.

'No, tractor driver' – it's Lena speaking again. 'They drove long way to fetch hay, about four hundred kilometres. By tractor, because here it is dry, the grass does not grow. One day Misha came back and she was not there. She had run away. So this man was left alone again. He was single for eight years. But the simple, rural people knew he had gift. They said "Misha is shaman." In Soviet times all Yakut shamans, four hundred eighty people, and that's half one thousand, were worked to death in prison camps. So the connection was only just there, and could have break off.'

'Between the spirit world and people?' I ask.

'Yes. Until Soviet times Yakut people were only treated by shamans. And they were strong and healthy.'

Misha became a private entrepreneur. The services he offered involved healing. He got himself the appropriate licence and a state certificate. He is one of 800,000 specialists in magic services operating legally in the Russian Federation (including healers, clairvoyants and fortune-tellers), consulted by one in five citizens. There are 640,000 doctors.

(I love to collect Russian stories apropos of nothing, and bizarre statistics about this country. For example, the fact that forty per cent of the population believe in miracles, or that every tenth medical facility in this country has no sewage system. And that a Moscow businessman, who is a fan of a particular Internet fantasy game bought himself a virtual 'super-sword' for 20,000 very real dollars. Every third lift in Russia has passed its use-by date, which means it is one hundred per cent clapped out. And the narrowest lift is in St Petersburg. It is forty-five centimetres wide, and forty-five centimetres deep. Finally, it is worth knowing that four and a half million Russians live in temporary, substitute accommodation, and that in 2010 six Moscow housing department officials were murdered.)

As a child, Misha was sure he had a sister. He would spend all day playing with her, and when he was due to go to school for the first time, he asked everyone if she was going too. So it became apparent that Misha was being visited by Chechurkke – a household spirit from the other world. Only the chosen few can see them. They are known to be very small, with long, fair hair.

'The spirits chose Misha and gave him power of healing,' says his wife.

'How do you do that?' I ask him.

'He looks at person like at television and sees everything,' replies Lena. 'He reads from patient's skin, because everything is written on it, and he can see all the organs.'

'I also look at the patient's aura, and wherever there's illness, I can see a concentration of energy or a dark hole in the biofield,' says Misha, uttering his longest sentence this week, wearing himself out so badly that he won't utter another word all evening.

After supper Lena tells me to undress, and Misha examines me. He whispers something to his wife in Yakut. He finds a gall-bladder infection (the first I've heard of it), a kidney which *burakhalit* (that word isn't in the dictionary, but there is *barakhlit*, which means 'is packing up'), stomach trouble (good shot!) and a *sglaz* – something like a spell cast by a woman who wishes me ill.

But Misha doesn't find the blasted problems I have with my lumbar vertebrae, or the haemorrhoids that are the bane of every journalist's life.

325

'Don't worry about anything,' Lena consoles me. 'Misha will get rid of that *sglaz* at once and will make your bile pure and thin.'

'How?'

'With his glance.'

'Oh, all right then,' I agree. Misha looks at me, but now and then, as if accidentally, he also gently touches me with his fingers, which gives me quite unearthly pleasure.

'There's special device for spine,' says Lena. 'I buy one for twenty-two thousand roubles from Yakutsk for my son. You introduce it through anus and it works in bum, massaging, tik tik tik. All problems go away. You'll be in Yakutsk, so buy yourself one. Eat porridge oats and do not buy tomatoes or apples here, because they inject them to stop from freezing and going bad. But your heart is good, you have the valves of a long-lived person. You have a very long lifeline on your palm. About ninety-six or -seven years.'

Finally Lena gives me a little rug woven out of the mane of a Yakut pony. These are tiny, but strong, brave and resilient creatures, spending the awful Yakutian winters outdoors. They feed on dry grass, which they dig out from under the snow. When a normal-sized man mounts one of them, he looks as if he's sitting on a dog. The rug is to massage all my aching spots, and is as rough and scratchy as wire.

Dead tired after my late night, I drag myself back to my lodgings. All I want is to collapse into bed and crash out. Tomorrow I have the last stretch of the Kolyma Highway ahead of me, to Yakutsk.

Day XXXIV

Yakutsk. Kilometre 2025 of the Kolyma Highway

I trudge back to my lodgings longing to SLEEP, SLEEP and SLEEP some more. But I have to drink a few shots of vodka with my two room-mates, who look a bit like a Yakut version of Laurel and Hardy. I've got to drink with them, like it or not. So we drink, and one of them, Laurel I guess (the thin one), is dropping. Like all peoples of the north, the Yakuts should keep away from alcohol. Their constitutions can't cope with it.

Hardy is dropping too, and I'm going to bed. But then some other men join my room-mates and the worst, most dreadful night I've had on this entire journey begins. A Pole or a Russian who has had a few drinks shouts a bit, falls over, throws up, and goes to bed – but not a drunken Yakut! He'll keep crashing about the place ad infinitum. They drive off to get more vodka, come back, drink, scream, quarrel, smash up the apartment, and mindlessly roar with feigned laughter.

Tonight there are seven or eight of them, including my pals, Laurel (head of the financial department) and Hardy (head of municipal construction). It's as if they're high on some drug. I can't bear to look at them. They seem to be suffering, as if they can't stand still or sit in one place. They lie down several times, but as soon as they fall asleep, they start to howl as if there were devils sitting on their chests, mercilessly trying to suffocate them.

Alcohol can give Europeans pleasure, satisfaction and delight. It always causes the Yakut anxiety and suffering.

327

I don't sleep a single minute all night (from Friday to Saturday), but my companions are going to be there until Monday. In the morning they're on their feet, so I complain that I haven't slept a wink; they give me a bit of fish and sausage lying about after their nocturnal rave. They're extremely sorry; Laurel takes some money out of his pocket, presses it into my hand, apologizes and explains that they're not alkies. He asks if I have ever seen a drunken Yakut lying about in the street. I have to admit that I never have. Because for them that's the greatest shame, a dishonour. So it's the norm for gangs of males to hole up somewhere, hide away from their homes and families, and then drink themselves stupid without restraint.

This morning I used the last of my strength to stagger onto the Route with a plan that if I didn't catch a lift by two p.m., I'd pay to travel to Yakutsk in a regular UAZ bus.

That's why I don't start walking. The first car I wave at stops – a passenger car with Tolik inside. He's going to Yakutsk too. He's my penultimate *poputchik*.

After three hours on the road we reach the banks of the Lena river. It's the longest river in Siberia, and the tenth-biggest in the world. The far side, where the city of Yakutsk is located and where the Kolyma Highway ends, is almost invisible.

There are two roads leading to the capital and both end at the river, because Yakutsk, with a population of twenty thousand, has no bridge, and no railway. The authorities have promised a bridge in 2015, which is to be built a few kilometres above Yakutsk, where at only four kilometres wide the Lena is at its narrowest.

You often have to wait hours and hours queuing for the ferry, though some years ago you had to wait for days on end. This led to regular shootings in the fight to board the boat. Cars that had driven on without queuing would be pushed into the river by desperate people.

Now there are three ferry services to the city, but no proper jetties.

The ferries open their doors onto the muddy riverbank, which is already frozen by now. The cars don't line up one behind the other, but wait in a compact, swirling throng.

The journey across is very expensive. Small passenger cars pay 800 roubles, and bigger ones pay 1100. For a Kamaz truck you have to pay 12,700, and if it has a trailer the price is 41,000 (more than £800). A heavy ferry for lorries runs until mid-November along a channel cleared by an ice-breaker, but the *zimovik* is already open in parallel to it, in other words a route across the ice for passenger cars. They allow lorries onto it in December, and it is in use until the end of April.

My final *poputchik* is Piotr Ivanovich Svechnikov, captain of the ferry across the Lena, who has been working on this river for forty years. He spends the winter half of the year at his cottage near Krasnoyarsk, and the other half on this ferry with his son and his spaniel Lassie, who are both members of his crew.

Andrei Savvich Borisov, Minister of Culture and Spiritual Development of the Sakha Republic (Yakutia).

Andrei Savvich Borisov, Minister of Culture and Spiritual Development of the Sakha Republic (Yakutia), was drafted in 1975, straight after graduating from the Moscow Theatre Institute. As a private, he too ended up at an ONTOT, a 'fixed armoured firing point', on the Chinese border.

'On my stretch there were some heavy Joseph Stalin tanks embedded in the ground, dating back to the Great Patriotic War,' Borisov tells me. 'That's forty-seven tonnes of deathly cold steel, with a 122-millimetre gun and armour plating sixteen centimetres thick. I was a gunner, operating a heavy machine gun, when they raised the alarm over the radio. The Chinese are on the move! A great horde of them. But there was such thick fog that you couldn't see a thing twenty metres ahead, and the safety catch on my gun had frozen. What could I do? I yanked at the machine gun, but they kept on and on marching towards us! I grabbed the lever in my teeth and set it to constant fire. That was how I lost my first tooth.'

'What happened to the Chinese?'

'They withdrew. But by then I'd bid my life farewell, because there was no escape from there. There were mines all around us. We were supposed to fire all our ammunition and then blow ourselves up. There was a sort of dial. Three turns to the right and ... We used to launch the same sort of fake attacks on the Chinese too.'

Borisov is the youngest creative artist to have received a USSR state prize, for his degree show. It was a play written in Russian based on a story entitled *Piebald Dog Running along the Shore*, by the Kyrgyz writer Chingiz Aitmatov, staged by the Yakutian theatre in the Georgian capital.

'It tells the story of the Nivkhi, a small ethnicity living on the Sea of Okhotsk,' says Borisov. 'It was the essence of internationalism – with sets by a Russian and music by a Jew. The prize was five thousand roubles in cash (I earn two hundred a month), but they divided it between five of the people who had put on the show. The envelopes were handed to us by Raisa Gorbachov, wife of the General Secretary of the Soviet Communist Party, who was also president of the Cultural Foundation, but I took the money from the guys because I thought that if I handed it back to Raisa, Mikhail would build me a theatre. In those days in Yakutsk we were performing in an old cathedral.'

'So did he build it?' I ask.

'Of course not . . . We built it ourselves fourteen years later.'

Andrei Borisov is literary manager and artistic director of the Sakha Theatre. He won a Russian Federation State Prize for his staging of *King Lear*, and has been Yakutia's Minister of Culture ever since the USSR collapsed. Three years ago, thanks to a joint effort by Russia and Mongolia, he made an epic moving picture called *The Youth of Genghis Khan*. The director's main consultant on meteorology, shamanism, traditional medicine, Mongolian traditions and customs was the shamaness Ediiy Dora.

'How does she know all that?' I ask.

'That's just the point!' says Borisov, shrugging his shoulders. 'God knows. She's not old, and she never studied it, but she knows. One time the whole crew had to spend the night out on the Mongol steppe. We were planning to move on the next day, but Dora said we wouldn't get across the stream ahead. Why not? It was only two metres wide. In the morning we got up, and it was two metres deep, rather than wide. The river was in flood and we had to get out of there.'

'They say she knows everything.'

'And she can do everything too. She created good weather for us. For a film crew, that's essential. She can actually stop the rain and bring out the sun. She blows into the sky and disperses the clouds.'

Day XXXV

Yakutsk. Kilometre 2025 of the Kolyma Highway

I never thought I'd make it! This morning I cut the hairs in my nose with my fingernail clippers. I've finally shaved off my beard, which has been growing since I left Magadan. I was starting to look like a Siberian hermit, a bearded Kolyma man, but I must admit it didn't particularly bother me.

Sometimes I'm surprised by my capacity to manage without basic items. You always find a substitute. For instance, I never take a spoon on the road. I eat my soup with a knife. Before leaving for Kolyma, I read in Shalamov that this way of eating soup has a name – it's called eating 'over the side', because the Gulag prisoners weren't issued spoons here. They drank straight from the bowl, gathering the soup to the edge in their fingers and then sucking it up with their lips.

I get an email from a friend which says: 'Please watch out for dogs in Yakutsk, and cheap vodka. If any drunken Yakuts accost you, just say "*min omukpun*", "I am a foreigner", because they might take you for a Russki.'

It's too late for that advice. I've been dealing with drunken Yakuts and dogs since before I got to Yakutsk.

Today I conduct an alcohol-related examination of conscience. While travelling across Kolyma from Magadan to Yakutsk I've been on the road for thirty-six days. In that time I have taken part in nineteen heavy booze-ups. I don't count the innocent beer drinking at roadside bars or outside the village shops at collective farms. I'm thinking of the serious vodka or brandy drinking.

In Siberia they say a hundred versts is not a journey, a hundred roubles isn't money, and a hundred grams isn't vodka. I can't entirely agree with this. A hundred versts is indeed not much by Russian standards, only 106.7 kilometres. If someone were to say they lived outside Irkutsk, they might actually mean 200 or 300 kilometres away from there. On the whole one can agree that 100 grams is not vodka, but 100 roubles can be changed into five times 100 grams, which is a pretty large amount for a normal Russian *muzhik* (bloke), and for an outsider like me it's an almost lethal dose.

It's important to know that Russian tradition doesn't let you walk away from a bottle that hasn't been emptied. In Russia people drink on command, with toasts, and to the last drop. As well as vodka, this principle also applies to brandy, wine and champagne. As Nina Khanarova reminded me, leaving something at the bottom of your glass means that you are insincere. The leftover liquid is an evil, creating animosity among the revellers.

There's also a rule that whoever pours the drinks all evening cannot change hands while doing it, or next day he'll have a splitting headache. And there are two simple rules concerning toasts. If it's to toast to the women, the men always drink standing up, and if it's to the dead you don't clink glasses – so the ringing won't disturb their rest.

I've been going to Russia for eighteen years, and every time there's drinking I always try to dodge it, leave out a round, or drink half-measures, but it never works. Out of the goodness of their hearts my drinking companions always make sure I drink as much as everyone else and to the last drop, even if I have to pay for it with my life.

In Russia there are five thousand registered types of vodka. That's how many names the producers have patented for themselves. There's a minimum official price in force – it can't be sold for less than 89 roubles per half-litre. But I have seen half-litre bottles costing 70, or even 60 roubles, and little plastic pots, like for yogurt, priced at 10 roubles (20p!), containing 'a token one hundred grams' of the world's most revolting liquid, forty-per-cent proof. 'A token one hundred grams' – yet another little phrase that Russian men love to use.

I look through my notes and discover that during my entire journey not once have I bought vodka. I'm not the one standing the drinks – quite the opposite. Even though I've been doing my best to avoid it as much as possible, it turns out I've been drinking the whole time. But then that's when you have the best conversations.

And sometimes I've had several boozy meetings in a single day. But what am I to say to a person I want to have a chat with, who opens his soul and stands me a bottle of vodka? That I won't drink with him, because I'm going on somewhere else? That I'm teetotal? A dried-out alcoholic? If I do that, there won't be any conversation at all.

In Poland we have a saying that he who doesn't drink, snitches. The Russians have exactly the same saying, except that for them a snitch, a nark, an informer or sneak is a *suka* – 'bitch', or a *stukach* – 'knocker', and *stukat* – 'to knock' – means 'to inform', and they don't repeat that saying for a laugh, as we do – among the Russians it's the most profound truth, a piece of practical wisdom repeated for generations since the days of Peter the Great, when they came to the fore among the world's alcohol-drinking nations.

I have finished my Kolyma journey, and now as I look back I can see, or rather feel, that after leaving Yakutia, in fact after crossing the Aldan river, I suddenly ended up in Narnia, or went to visit Alice in her Wonderland.

That's a poor comparison – it's too sweet. Yakutia is more like the land of one-eyed Sauron, Lord of the Rings and Mordor. It's a mysterious place, where there's twenty-two-per-cent unemployment, and a window into hell. That's what the local shamans say about the hundred-metre well dug in the capital two centuries ago, in which water has never appeared. (It couldn't, thanks to the permafrost!)

It is also the land of wandering holes in time. Anybody who falls into one is lost without trace, but there are also people who have got out of them at the last moment and tell incredible stories from hundreds and thousands of years ago. Holes in time appear in the vicinity of gigantic holes in the ground, in which people look for diamonds.

And finally, this is the land of Chuchun – the Yakut snow man, who kidnaps women and often sends them off pregnant. They always give birth to boys of enormous size, and a bit funny in the head. Those who have seen Chuchun never talk about it, and hunters who have shot at him don't go up to the carcass just in case. That's what they call it – the carcass.

There are spells, spirits, shamanic curses, freaks, healers and batty characters all over the place ...

The Yakuts have a logic no one could possibly follow. There were seven people staying at my favourite hotel in Churapcha, but only one key. The rule is that whoever goes out last in the morning locks the door. But the last to leave is rarely the first to come back. The first to return has to phone the landlady, who comes running from another house and opens up. I kept coming and going between the first and the last, so several times in the course of the day I dragged the woman with the key out into the cold. No one has ever thought of having some extra keys made.

Nobody has ever wondered how a Japanese tape recorder ended up in the river, either. The man who found it was pleased, so he went into the water where the music was coming from, and fished out a stone the size and shape of a human heart.

It weighs exactly five kilos – that was the first thing the stone said after being fished out. The finder went to the university and put the stone on an accurate scale, which showed a five followed by a string of zeros after the decimal point.

337

Two years have gone by since the talking stone – also known as 'the stone of fortune' – was found, in which time hundreds and thousands of believers have made a pilgrimage to visit it, each one with his own wish or request. They have locked it in a case, like the King of Yakutia's sceptre, worn it smooth with their grubby paws, made it greasy and slippery, but when I take it in my hands, I can feel I haven't touched anything quite like it since Mother Teresa dropped her medallion and I picked it up for her.

What message has this stone brought us? Straight after determining its own weight, it said: 'People! Don't be so hard. I am a stone, but I'm soft.'

The talking stone and its guardian.

ANDREI I THE TV PRESENTER —
THE SHAMAN'S NIGHT

'You're interested in shamanism,' he states, rather than asks. 'Be careful with it. Or better still, leave it alone. I'm giving you good advice . . .'

Andrei I is a Russian Manchurian, hence his short Chinese name. He's an A-list Russian television star, researcher, discoverer, conqueror and vanquisher of myths and mysteries, and producer of a programme called *The Searchers*. There's no legend capable of evading him, no riddle he can't reduce to rubble, no mystery he can't solve, no superstition he can't ridicule.

Andrei's third, young and beloved wife was from Yakutsk. But the couple lived in Moscow, because it was a pity to miss out on the high life, the bright lights of the big city, the clubs, pubs, and pals from stage and screen. She too was deeply involved in show business. Her name was Marina.

Their son was a year old when Marina set about writing the script for a documentary film about Yakut shamans. But she was killed in a strange car accident. For no apparent reason she drove off a railway viaduct, and her car went under the wheels of an express train.

'A shaman killed her,' says Andrei. 'He didn't want her to make the film.'

'How did he know she would?'

'They know everything. She died on the twenty-first of December, which is a shaman's day. The shortest one in the year. When the night is longest. Nowhere in the world are shamans, sorcerers, wonder-workers, charlatans and prophets as powerful as they are in Yakutia.

340

They derive their energy from the earth, and here it's tremendous, so thick you can cut it with a knife.'

Andrei buried his wife in Yakutsk, and came to live here permanently. It seems he hasn't yet recovered from her accident.

'And that shaman—'

'Died,' Andrei interrupts me. 'He was very famous, the chief shaman of Yakutia, a sort of official figure, so he had a state funeral, with lots of pomp, dignitaries and crowds . . . He's buried in the same graveyard as my Marina.'

'Why didn't he want her to make that film?'

'Let's not talk about it any more!' Andrei erupts. 'I don't want to talk about it!'

'Why not?'

'Absolutely not!'

'Because it hurts?' I ask. 'Or is it dangerous?'

'Of course it's dangerous! Extremely!'

'Are you serious? In the twenty-first century? An educated man, a producer, an astronautical engineer?'

'I'm not afraid for myself,' he replies. 'But I am for my son.'

'But the shaman's not alive any more.'

'That doesn't mean he isn't here,' says Andrei, looking around.

Day XXXVI

Yakutsk. Kilometre 2025 of the Kolyma Highway

Yakutia has gone mad, about a runner called Piotr Semyonovich Naumov. He is almost completely blind, because he can't see anything out of his right eye, and his left eye requires a correction of minus twenty-five dioptres. He's sixty-one and has just completed a 12,009-kilometre run from Kaliningrad to Vladivostok. It took him 206 days. He ran over fifty-eight kilometres per day.

He tells me that at school he was always let off PE because of his disability. He started to run after the age of forty, at the worst imaginable moment in life, when his wife had died, leaving him in a rented one-room flat with six children aged from two to eleven. They did have his disability pension equivalent to £160 a month, but he was a 'bed man', as he puts it – for months he hadn't got out of bed because of a spinal injury.

But he did get up, and thanks to the running he bounced back from the very bottom.

He has never had any luck with sponsors – they say that as he's blind he won't be able to find the way and will get lost – so he was given the money for the run from Kaliningrad to Vladivostok by his children, his siblings, neighbours and friends from his native village. He ran with a two-shaft rickshaw made out of a wheelchair. He had eight kilos of water, food and kit, including a wood-burning stove. He lived in a tent, and on the way he was lucky enough to encounter all sorts of kind people, who supported him, fed him and took him under their roofs.

To meet the runner I've come to the Yakut Council of Ministers building. The authorities are organizing a celebration for him, at which they're going to pin a medal onto his white jacket lapel, which probably has the longest name of any decoration: Jubilee Medal '65 Years of the Victory of the Soviet Nation over Nazi Germany in the Great Patriotic War 1941–1945'. Piotr Semyonovich ran to commemorate this anniversary.

The policeman at the reception desk greets me by my full name. But only an hour ago I didn't know I was coming here for this meeting.

For many days I've been feeling the red eyes of the security services fixed on me – ever since I called Viktoria Gabyshova, a journalist who writes for a paper called *Basha Prava* (Your Rights), and who fell foul of the Yakutian Minister for Internal Affairs, Stakhov, by writing an article about him. She is an unusual woman.

The minister came up with the idea of tormenting Viktoria through civil lawsuits in defence of his honour and good name, and he employed ten of his underlings for this purpose. In total they are demanding a million roubles in damages. So the journalist is involved in ten lawsuits, never leaves court, and cannot live or work normally.

The Yakuts elect their own president and government, but the Minister for Internal Affairs is appointed from Moscow.

When I go back to the hotel and fire up my laptop, it says it was shut down incorrectly. How did that happen? I think I know how to switch off my own computer! I'm familiar with all its moods. The battery is totally flat. SOMEONE'S BEEN POKING ABOUT IN IT! The knuckleheads! They didn't plug it into the socket. That's why it switched itself off.

Luckily I copy all my work, all the conversations I record and all the photos I take onto a pen-drive which I always carry with me. My book about Kolyma is the most valuable object I have. But now I'll have to take the laptop with me too. However, I change my mind, and leave it in my room. I'm going to pretend I'm not aware of their activities, because

343

otherwise they'll take corrective measures. After all, they could easily grab everything off me in the street by thuggery.

I come back a few hours later. They've been there again. I know, because I trapped a small piece of paper in the door. And they've been rifling through the laptop again. This time they didn't let it switch itself off. I check the files, and two are missing – 'Vika1' and 'Vika2'.

That evening Minister Borisov takes me to the premiere of the first Yakut-produced feature film. It's one of the worst films I've ever seen in my life, so as soon as the screening is over I leave the reception, because I can't face answering my host's questions about whether I liked it.

It's two steps to my hotel, but before going in I'm stopped by some plain-clothes policemen. They spend a long time checking my documents, rifling through my backpack and my file full of notes, and then apologizing for the mistake. They're giving their colleagues, who once again are busy scouring my laptop, more time.

I've had enough of Yakutsk. I've got to get out of here. Go home. I used to live in a country like this one too, but I'm not used to it any more. I can't do it. I don't want to do it.

On the way to my room, I buy a pair of underpants at the hotel shop, because I like to have two pairs on the road, and one of mine is torn right across the butt. The saleswoman proudly tells me that they are from Poland. So why did they have to travel all the way across two continents just to go back to their homeland on my bum?

Maybe I should fly off somewhere else abroad, since I've bought these pants, and I'm so far from home already? My visa's still valid, and thanks to Basansky I've got a spare 100,000 roubles. Chukotka perhaps? That's the furthest it's possible to go on the Eurasian continent.

The runner who raced from Kaliningrad to Vladivostok in only 206 days.

'Can stones talk?' I ask Ediiy Dora, the legendary Yakut healer and teacher, who doesn't like to call herself a shamaness. Nor does she look like one, because she dresses the same way as everybody else.

'Yes. There are stones that have tremendous strength, a power. I have lots of them, and they are not for decoration. They're working stones. They were sent from heaven. With each one a new strength comes to me, a power, an experience. They carry a vast amount of information gathered over centuries, thousands and millions of years. Stones are like books, except that not everyone is able to read them.'

I tell Dora the story of Marina, wife of the film-maker Andrei I, who was planning to make a film about Yakutian shamans, but their leader wouldn't give her permission for it. She ignored the ban and went on writing the script, so even though they were thousands of kilometres apart, the shaman caused her to have an accident.

'Can you kill a person long distance?' I ask.

'With no trouble at all!' replies Dora. 'I know that story. When the Yakuts care very greatly about something, they never talk about it. She broke that law. The spirits didn't like it, so the shaman acted correctly. He's not to blame. He did warn her, after all. Andrei and his wife are bold people, seeking sensations, comical curiosities, superstitions and supernatural phenomena. That's how Marina was writing the script — in spiritual matters those people are very primitive.'

'I don't think Andrei is any more,' I say. 'He was even afraid to talk to me about it. He said he fears for his son.'

'That means he still doesn't understand what happened. When he does, he'll calm down.'

'Why did the shaman forbid her to make the film?'

'Because she wasn't mature enough. Too young, too inexperienced. You wouldn't hand your child over to a school with nothing but young, inexperienced teachers, would you? You don't go to a medical student for an operation. The spirits refused, and that was that! After all, they allow wise, experienced, careful people to do these things. There are such films. Andrei and Marina didn't obey the spirits and they were punished. Each person has specific capabilities. You shouldn't take on something that's beyond you. If you're a poor swimmer, but try to swim across a great big river, you'll drown.'

'It's that simple.'

'Don't you want a picture of yourself with me?' says Ediiy Dora, suddenly changing the subject.

'I'd love one, but I didn't have the courage to ask.'

'Oo! Look at him! He's pretending to be shy.' The teacher is now in an excellent mood. 'But sitting down, so you can't see the height difference. You can't be taller than I am in the picture.'

The height difference isn't all that obvious, because Dora is a formidable woman – large and stout, with a big belly, which looks fit to burst as she quivers with giggles. Somehow she finds me and my Japanese camera comical. She teases me for coming so close to her, something she never lets anyone do.

'Am I supposed to be afraid of you?' I ask, as if joking. 'Because you know all about me.'

'I do. I can see everything. I can see two trees outside your house. On one side there's a birch, and on the other a spruce. I can see a "little mother" river, which you cross on your way to work. But you are rarely there. I can see your yellow bicycle, and your new book in a green cover with gold lettering, in which you're going to write

347

about me too. I can see your dog. And I can see who you were before you were born, and how and when you will die. But I never tell anyone about that. Not even people who have very little life left.'

'Do you know what will happen to every one of us?'

'Yes. I can see it, but those are inappropriate questions. You're not allowed to ask about death. It's a sin. You mustn't even think about it. Especially you, because you've got so much work ahead of you, a sea of ideas and tasks . . . Only then does the soul return to its place for a time. A man doesn't die. Only his body dies. I'm confirming something for you that you already know—'

'Careful, Ediiy. Those might be the last words in my book about terrible Kolyma.'

'There is no death.'

SIROTINSKAYA THE ARCHIVIST —
INSTEAD OF AN ENDING

I am to search in the Kuntsovsky cemetery. Not far from the gate, the third avenue. Or the fourth, on the right. No, no – on the left. I will recognize it. The inscription on the gravestone is clear. Varlam Tikhonovich Shalamov. I just have to read the words.

'But there's almost half a metre of snow in Moscow,' I complain.

'I put up a very fine monument,' says Irina Sirotinskaya. 'A head of bronze. But it was stolen. Look for a head on a plinth.'

'Stolen? So how will I find it?'

'I had another one made out of cast iron. When I was last there, it was in place. They buried Bobov next door – he was a famous soccer and hockey player. He has a football and a hockey stick on his grave. But made of bronze. Look for a football and a hockey stick.'

Scrap-metal thieves are savages, barbarians and pillagers. How could they fail to take a head like that, the football or the stick? What superb swag!

After seventeen years in Kolyma, Varlam Shalamov went back to Moscow in 1953. Although she had waited for him all those years, his wife did not dare to live with him. She tried to persuade him to forget about Kolyma, and to give his memoirs and his writing a rest. They didn't even spend the first night together. At the Yaroslavl train station she could tell that each of them had been waiting for somebody quite different. His daughter was a dedicated Komsomol activist, and for years she had been stating that her father was dead on all the forms she filled in. She did not come to the station with her mother.

In the 1960s Shalamov met Irina Pavlovna Sirotinskaya, an employee of the State Archive of Literature, his last great love.

'He said that the years when we were together were the best in his life. That as long as I was with him, he could live.'

'And did you love him?'

'Yes. But with a different sort of love. In his love there was a physical element, but I loved him spiritually. I adored him. He was my prophet.'

'Surely that wasn't what he was hoping for?'

'No. He wanted me to leave my children and husband and live with him alone. But I would have killed them. My husband loved me very much too. Varlam was only thinking about himself – he was such a difficult, fierce man. And at the same time such a wretched, pitiful cripple. By the time he died he was decrepit; blind and stone-deaf. He wanted me to take care of him. He desperately didn't want to go into a home, but I was working, I had the children, a family.'

In 1982, he died alone in a mental hospital. He was never cured of the camp trauma of compulsive eating, hoarding food and leftovers, and keeping dry bread crusts under his mattress. And he didn't live to see the publication of his *Kolyma Tales*, which had been his lifelong dream.

Shalamov's only companion as he died was a *suka* (literally, 'bitch'), as the Russians say – a female KGB undercover agent who kept an eye on him at the mental hospital.

His wife wasn't present at his funeral. When his daughter was told her father had died, she replied that she didn't know him.

He only gained great fame and recognition after his death. His stories were translated into dozens of languages. He bequeathed all his copyrights to Irina Sirotinskaya.

'I have published everything he wrote,' says Irina Pavlovna. 'To the very last line.'

'Including his correspondence with his wife?'

'It didn't survive. She destroyed his letters, and hers were stolen by criminal prisoners. Then they read them aloud and held group masturbation sessions.'

'Irina Pavlovna, I'm not going to let those be the final words in my account of Kolyma.'

'Shalamov always used to say that life without love is meaningless.'

Ediiy Dora. Finally I made her laugh a great deal.

'I've got a problem with the cash I brought back from Russia, from Kolyma, Mrs Durlik. It was given to me by a very rich man who mines gold there, and I'd like to give it to you.'

'But what's it got to do with me?' says Mrs Durlik, who was an officer in the Polish resistance during the war, and on whose lips even questions sound like orders. 'Haven't you got anyone to give it to?'

'I want to give it to you. There are only two Kolyma survivors left in Poland. It's your money.'

'Why don't you give it to Caritas, to the Church? They send sick children on summer holidays.'

'If I give you the money,' I try to negotiate, 'you can give it to Caritas.'

'I can't walk! Give it to Caritas yourself. And an orphanage — an ordinary, state one. Just make sure they give you a receipt.'

Janina Durlik from Radom was the leader of the scout unit at a high school in Lida, a city in the former eastern borderlands of the Second Polish Republic. Then she joined the resistance, and lived through the Russian invasion, denunciation, interrogation, and Article 58 of the Soviet penal code, paragraph 1 — betrayal of the USSR. She got '10-5-5', as this sentence was called: ten years in a prison camp, five in exile and five more years deprived of civil rights. They took her gold wedding ring — six months before her arrest she had married. A Soviet official had even drawn up the marriage licence, but the Soviet Union never returned her property.

★

352

Jan Stański from Zabrze was taken prisoner in 1945 in Lwów (then a Polish city, now Lviv in Ukraine). The Russians picked him up in the street by chance, but he had a gun on him, and the friend he was with had an application for promotion to corporal in the resistance. That was how the purge in Lwów began. The friend broke down under interrogation and betrayed a number of their associates.

'In the first letter I received from home at Kolyma, my father wrote that my brother had died. In my experience the Front came through my hometown twice, then I was in the resistance, after that I went through interrogation, prison and the camps, and there I was, still alive. My brother just sat there quietly through it all, and was killed on a motorbike after the war was over.'

Mr Stański and Mrs Durlik returned to Poland on the same train in December 1955. Before that, Mrs Durlik's friends from the resistance had sent a contact to Radom to find out if her husband had waited for her, or if he had started another family.

'Did you have a conversation with him about fidelity?' I ask.

'I had a clean conscience. There had been girls chasing after him, because he was handsome, he played bridge and danced superbly ... But he always told them he had a wife. And that she was sure to come back.'

'Where did you spend the first night?'

'On Malczewski Street,' she says. 'At my husband's family's flat.'

'Were you given your own room?'

'We shared the room with his father.'

'Good grief! You hadn't seen each other for eleven and a half years and his father was registered to live with you in the same room?'

'What was the alternative? Were we meant to put him out on the stairs? We got our first and only flat in 1961. Two rooms and a kitchen, as you can see, but very well laid out. There's a cupboard in the alcove where I keep pots, roasting tins, goose girls—'

'What's a goose girl?' I ask.

'A long platter. Bigger for turkey, smaller for duck.'

'So why is it called a goose girl?'

'O God! The middle-sized one is for goose! Let's have your wife make some tea.'

'Yes, of course,' says my wife, jumping up from the sofa.

'The red tap is hot water,' says Mrs Durlik, giving instructions, 'and the blue is cold. There are drawings by my daughter on the kitchen wall. She teaches interior design in Toronto. Hello! Can you see? What's your name?'

'Agata!'

'I'm coming over!' Mrs Durlik grabs her Zimmer frame and gets up. 'Oh Christ, oh my aching knees! Don't sit in that armchair – that's where I sit to drink my tea.'

The next day Mrs Durlik calls and asks me to send her the money from the Kolyma oligarch after all. They are collecting donations at her church for a family from near Sandomierz who lost their entire belongings in the spring floods.

'What happened to the man who shopped you to the Russians in Lwów?' I ask Mr Stański.

'He went to prison. And he was in Kolyma too. He survived and went back to Lwów – he was poor and lonely, with no family, so when I came back to Poland I got him to come and join me. I worked at a mill, and once I'd passed my high-school exams, they made me a catering inspector at the TSD.'

'What's that?'

'The Trading Standards Department. For ten years I was in charge of collective food supplies, and then I became manager of the Polonia restaurant in Pyskowice. After starving for Poland in Kolyma, at the Polonia restaurant I fed others.'

Also by Jacek Hugo-Bader from Portobello Books

White Fever